Mac OS X
Unwired™

Other Macintosh resources from O'Reilly

Related titles

Running Mac OS X Panther

Mac OS X Panther Pocket Guide

Learning Unix for Mac OS X Panther

Windows XP Unwired

Mac OS X: The Missing Manual, Panther Edition

Building Wireless Community Networks

Wireless Hacks

Linux Unwired

Macintosh Books Resource Center

mac.oreilly.com is a complete catalog of O'Reilly's books on the Apple Macintosh and related technologies, including sample chapters and code examples.

O'REILLY®
mac devcenter.com

A popular watering hole for Macintosh developers and power users, the Mac DevCenter focuses on pure Mac OS X and its related technologies including Cocoa, Java, AppleScript, and Apache, to name just a few. It's also keenly interested in all the spokes of the digital hub, with special attention paid to digital photography, digital video, MP3 music, and QuickTime.

Conferences

O'Reilly & Associates brings diverse innovators together to nurture the ideas that spark revolutionary industries. We specialize in documenting the latest tools and systems, translating the innovator's knowledge into useful skills for those in the trenches. Visit *conferences.oreilly.com* for our upcoming events.

O'REILLY NETWORK
Safari Bookshelf.

Safari Bookshelf (*safari.oreilly.com*) is the premier online reference library for programmers and IT professionals. Conduct searches across more than 1,000 books. Subscribers can zero in on answers to time-critical questions in a matter of seconds. Read the books on your Bookshelf from cover to cover or simply flip to the page you need. Try it today with a free trial.

Mac OS X
Unwired™

A Guide for Home, Office, and the Road

Tom Negrino and Dori Smith

O'REILLY®

Beijing · Cambridge · Farnham · Köln · Paris · Sebastopol · Taipei · Tokyo

Mac OS X Unwired™

by Tom Negrino and Dori Smith

Copyright © 2004 Tom Negrino and Dori Smith. All rights reserved.
Printed in the United States of America.

Published by O'Reilly Media, Inc., 1005 Gravenstein Highway North, Sebastopol, CA 95472.

O'Reilly Media, Inc. books may be purchased for educational, business, or sales promotional use. Online editions are also available for most titles (*safari.oreilly.com*). For more information, contact our corporate/institutional sales department: (800) 998-9938 or *corporate@oreilly.com*.

Editor:	Brian Jepson
Contributor:	Wei-Meng Lee
Production Editor:	Philip Dangler
Cover Designer:	Edie Freedman
Interior Designer:	David Futato

Printing History:

November 2003:   First Edition.

 This book uses RepKover™, a durable and flexible lay-flat binding.

ISBN: 0-596-00508-3

[C]   [6/04]

Table of Contents

Preface

People want to communicate, and history shows that they always gravitate to technologies that make it easier to reach out to one another. The printing press, universal mail service, the telegraph, telephone, motion pictures, radio, television, and the Internet have all served people's need to communicate. And the easier it is to communicate, the more communication occurs, as a quick glance at your email might tell you.

The general rise of communication technologies has made the world smaller, and the Internet in particular has made it practical for people who may never have otherwise met to work together. This book is a great example: two of the authors (Tom and Dori) live in northern California; Wei Meng lives in Singapore; and Brian, our editor, lives in Rhode Island.

The Internet is so useful, in fact, that many people think of Net access as a necessity, rather than a luxury. And when something is a necessity for your work or play, you want it available, well, *everywhere*, or at least everywhere you go with a laptop computer.

That's where wireless networking comes into the picture. Mac users can connect to the Net whenever their iBook or PowerBook is in range of a Wi-Fi network. That could be at home, at school, at conferences, or even in public hotspots such as an airport, a local Starbucks, or Borders Books and Music. Or, with a laptop and a Bluetooth phone, you don't even need the Wi-Fi network.

Wireless technologies in Mac OS X aren't just for Internet access, however. You can also use your Mac to communicate wirelessly with peripherals such as mice and keyboards, to connect to your cell phone or PDA, or to share files and use iChat with other computers.

What This Book Covers

This book explains the following wireless technologies and how to use them with a Macintosh computer running Mac OS X, Version 10.2 or later:

Wireless Fidelity (Wi-Fi)

Wi-Fi is the generic term for technologies that Apple brands as AirPort or AirPort Extreme. You can use Wi-Fi to connect with the Internet wirelessly at high speeds, and to replace Ethernet wires and hubs in a Local Area Network (LAN). Wi-Fi uses radio waves to transmit information. Chapters 1, 2, 3, 4, and 5 discuss Wi-Fi.

Bluetooth

Bluetooth is often touted as a "cable-replacement" technology. Like Wi-Fi, Bluetooth also uses radio waves, but operates within a shorter range. It is useful for replacing cables that connect two devices. For example, your keyboard and mouse can use Bluetooth technology to transmit signals to your computer, eliminating the need for USB cables. You can also synchronize your cellular telephone or PDA with your computer wirelessly via Bluetooth. Chapter 6 discusses Bluetooth.

Infrared

Infrared technology has been around for a number of years, but its cachet on the Mac is fading fast. Infrared requires "line-of-sight" (LOS) to transmit data. It shares the short-range capabilities of Bluetooth, but is hampered by its dependence on LOS. Infrared uses light waves that are just outside the spectrum of visible light. You'll find a discussion of Infrared in Appendix A.

Radio Frequency (RF)

RF devices are short-range units primarily used to control peripherals, such as wireless mice and remote controls. Appendix A covers RF, too.

Cellular Telephone Connections

While Wi-Fi allows you to connect to the network wirelessly, it has limited coverage. Physically moving out of range of a wireless network breaks the connection. For situations when you're really on the go, cellular telephone technologies such as General Packet Radio Services (GPRS) and Code Division Multiple Access (CDMA) may be the ideal solution (or a complement to Wi-Fi for network connectivity when you're away from a hotspot). CDMA and GPRS are two leading networking technologies used by high-speed (30 to 70 kbps, and sometimes higher) cellular networking called 3G (third-generation, but usually called 2.5G because the current technology didn't quite live up to the high speeds originally promised). As long as you are within reach of a compatible cell tower, either protocol will keep you connected to the network (and Internet).

The choice of CDMA or GPRS is generally dictated by your choice of wireless provider. For example, AT&T Wireless and T-Mobile use GPRS for their 2.5G cellular networking, while Sprint and Verizon Wireless use CDMA. At the time of this writing, unlimited data plans that support tethering a laptop to your phone were available for around $80 a month in the United States, with the notable exception of T-Mobile, which offers unlimited data for $30 a month ($20 if added to most of their voice plans) at slightly slower than typical (56k) dialup speeds. Chapter 7 discusses cellular networking.

Wireless Security

With the convenience of wireless technologies comes a new host of security problems. Unlike a wired network—where security involves limiting physical access to routers, hubs, and cables—a wireless network's most vulnerable point (the radio waves beaming through the air) has no physical substance. This makes security a challenging task.

In this book, we will take a look at the various ways to secure wireless networks, using standards such as Wired Equivalent Privacy (WEP), 802.1x, and 802.11i. We will also look at the security features found in the Bluetooth and Infrared technologies. Chapter 5 discusses how to communicate securely.

Conventions Used in This Book

The screenshots (and their accompanying descriptions) in this book are mainly from Mac OS X 10.3, also known as Panther. In most cases, you'll find that the descriptions will still work fine for Mac OS X 10.2 (Jaguar).

This book uses the following abbreviations:

Hz, kHz, MHz, and GHz
    Hertz (cycles per second), kilohertz (one thousand hertz), megahertz (one million hertz), and gigahertz (one billion, or 10^9 hertz)

bps, kbps, Mbps
    Bits per second, kilobits (1024 bits) per second, and megabits (1,048,576 bits) per second

KB/s, MB/s
    Kilobytes (1024 bytes) per second and megabytes (1,048.576 bytes) per second

This book uses the following typographic conventions:

Constant width

Constant width is used for listing the output of command-line utilities.

Italic

Italic is used for emphasis, for first use of a technical term, and for URLs.

...

Ellipses indicate text that has been omitted for clarity.

 This icon indicates a tip, suggestion, or general note.

 This icon indicates a warning or caution.

Comments and Questions

Please address any comments or questions concerning this book to the publisher:

O'Reilly & Associates
1005 Gravenstein Highway North
Sebastopol, CA 95472
800-998-9938 (in the U.S. or Canada)
707-829-0515 (international or local)
707-829-0104 (fax)

To ask technical questions or comment on the book, send email to:

bookquestions@oreilly.com

O'Reilly has a web site for this book where examples, errata, and any plans for future editions are listed. You can access this site at:

http://www.oreilly.com/catalog/macxunwire/

The authors also maintain a companion web site for the book, with news about the wireless world and information about the book, at:

http://www.macosxunwired.com/

For more information about other O'Reilly books, see the O'Reilly web site:

http://www.oreilly.com

Readers who would like to contact the authors with questions or comments are welcome to do so at:

book@macosxunwired.com

Acknowledgements

The authors (Tom and Dori) would like to thank the following people and organizations for their help with this book:

Our biggest thanks go to our co-author, Wei Meng Lee, author of *Windows XP Unwired*, also from O'Reilly. He helped us out by writing some of the knottier chapters, specifically Chapters 5, 7, and 8. We deeply appreciate his technical expertise, as well as his fast help on a difficult schedule.

Our editor, Brian Jepson, deserves much of the credit for the way this book turned out. His knowledge of all the technologies involved, plus the fact that he's a total cellphone geek, have made the book much better.

Our thanks to ORA's Chuck Toporek for bringing us into this project. Thanks also to our agent, Studio B's Neil J. Salkind, for putting us together with Chuck, and for seeing the contract negotiations through.

We would also like to thank our technical reviewer, R. Emory Lundberg, for making our work better.

Chris Stone and Pascal Honscher at ORA helped us out by shooting a picture for this book late in the production process. Many thanks to them, and also to Jessamyn Read, who prepared the photo for print under tight deadline.

Our love and thanks to our son, Sean Smith (who made more than one dinner for himself when his parents were working late), for his support and patience.

Dori would like to thank the W&S ladies for their loving kindness and virtual hugs, and the Wise-Women's Web community at *http://www.wise-women.org/* for their depth of knowledge and inspiration.

Thanks to our colleague Glenn Fleishman for pointers and connections.

This book covers various products from many vendors. There is no way that we could have purchased all of the software and hardware we reviewed, so we'd like to express our gratitude to the following people and companies who loaned us some:

- Nancy Koprowski of Maples Communication
- Jenice Sakai of Linksys

- Melody Chalaban of Belkin Corporation
- Apple Computer's WWPM Seeding Lab
- Joanne Hwang and Cori Locklin of JABRA Corporation
- Dr. Bott, LLC
- Rick Estes of QuickerTek, Inc
- Jonas Salling of Salling Software AB

The soundtrack for this book was graciously provided (in Tom's office, at least) by Liz Phair, Aaron Copland, Lucy Kaplansky, Warren Zevon (RIP), Evanescence, Patty Griffin, Michelle Branch, and Mary Chapin Carpenter.

Introduction to Wireless Computing

Welcome to *Mac OS X Unwired*! If you're reading this book, you've probably heard a lot about wireless networking, but want to know more about what it means and how it can make your life easier. Or maybe you've dipped your toe into the wireless world and are a bit confused by all the different terms you've heard: 802.11b, 802.11g, Wi-Fi, Bluetooth, IR, RF, etc. Or maybe you understand the buzzwords and want to go wireless, but need to make sure that you're buying the right hardware for your particular situation (and setting up that hardware and the accompanying software in the best way). If any of these descriptions apply to you, you've come to the right place.

One of the best things about Mac OS X is that it supports many different wireless technologies, each with its own unique advantages. From connecting to the Internet in airports and other public places, to working with a cell phone, to connecting to printers without wires, Mac OS X lets you do it all without the annoyance of a difficult and tweaky setup.

In this chapter, you'll get a bit of background on the technology behind wireless networks, see a few examples of how you can benefit from wireless networking, get an overview of the wireless alternatives for home and office, and look at some of the software that can help you get more out of your wireless experience.

Why Go Wireless?

Do you remember the first time you held a wireless phone and realized that you were no longer tied by a cord to the wall? Or the first time you used a cell phone and realized that you could get in the car, drive away, and continue to talk? Or the first time you used a laptop computer and could work on a document while sitting on your comfortable couch, instead of at a desk? In all of these cases, there's a sudden rush of freedom, of not being tied down to a chair and at the mercy of technological limitations. Instead, the technology is serving *you*.

If you've had any of these experiences, you should be able to imagine what being unwired feels like. But really, it's even better than that, because now you can do anything, almost anywhere. But there's more to the freedom that wireless brings than just not being tethered to the wall: once you live with and get used to working wirelessly, it changes your perception of where, how, and when you can get work (and play) done. Suddenly, you can be out of your office (perhaps at a coffee shop) when inspiration strikes you. You can dash off a note and send it to a friend or a colleague on the spot, or use Google to find supporting information for a report while sipping your java. And soon enough, you'll probably be griping when you visit places that don't have wireless connectivity. Or you'll start bringing your own.

Connecting Without Wires

There are many situations where wireless makes sense. Actually, there are only a few situations where it doesn't (when you need an extremely high-bandwidth connection, for instance), but here are a few examples of places where using wireless is clearly superior to being wired.

At Home

A home generally starts off with one computer, with the expectation that everyone will be able to share it. Then the kids want their own computer. Then someone needs a laptop. Eventually you end up like us, with 12 computers (distributed among 3 people) that all need Internet connectivity. Even if you're not in our over-the-top scenario, you still might not want to string wires everywhere, or pay for the cost of having a professional come in and run them through the walls and floors. Believe us: we've had two houses completely wired for Ethernet, and it was painfully expensive. About two months after we bought the second house, Apple introduced AirPort. Had we known that wireless networking was going to be available, it would have saved us a bunch of money. On the other hand, we do have those convenient Ethernet jacks in the kitchen and the bedroom.

We use the jack in the living room to hook a wireless access point up to our wired Ethernet network, which is connected to the Internet by our cable modem. This configuration allows us to sit on the front porch with a cool drink, enjoy the view, and surf the Net, picking up our email and convincing our editors that we're working. Seriously, the point here isn't our decadent geek lifestyle, but rather that wireless connectivity allows us more flexibility in our work life, without that leash we once required for our connection to the rest of the world. In most cases, you'll find that wireless is simply the most cost-effective and least obtrusive way to connect all of your computers.

In the Office

While a family might be surprised to realize how many computers they've come to own, a business usually has at least one computer per person. And if you're in charge of hooking up that company's computers and your business is expanding or moving, finding new places to arrange for connectivity can be a pain. After you've re-run more wiring (again), bought more hubs (again), and rearranged the spaghetti mess of cables for the nth time, going wireless looks like a great idea.

At a minimum, wireless is the best bet for certain groups of office users:

- Telecommuters
- Visitors who need Internet connectivity
- Temporary workers (when your staffing needs fluctuate)
- Laptop users
- Frequent travelers

Wireless connections in the office bring their own set of challenges for the person in charge of the network, not the least of which is security. Chapter 5 deals with wireless security in depth.

On the Road

While you may be able to arrange to have wires brought into your home or office, it's unlikely that you'll be able to bring connectivity everywhere you travel, such as conferences, hotel rooms, or coffeehouses. Thankfully, many of these places now have wireless connectivity, whether it's public and free, private and fee-based, or private but insecure.

We'll cover security and open networks in Chapter 4, but here are some travel situations we've run into that demonstrate the capabilities of wireless while on the road:

- One of us stayed with friends in Manhattan during the New York Macworld Expo in July 2002. These friends, unfortunately, made do with a dialup Internet connection. Using a PowerBook and MacStumbler (more about the latter in Chapter 4), Dori was able to show our friends just how easy it was to find open networks in a major city—without ever leaving her friend's apartment (Figure 1-1).

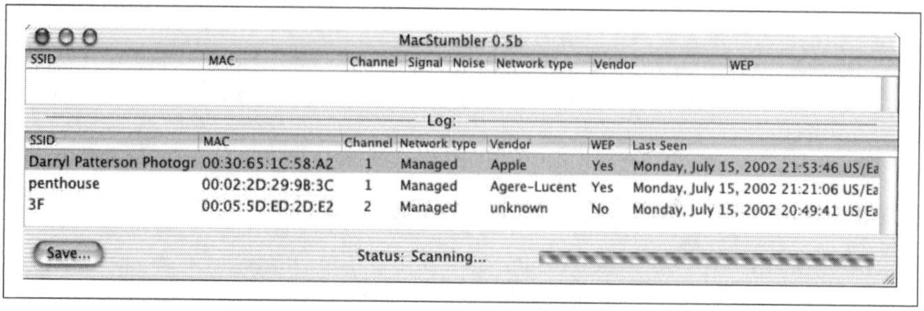

SSID	MAC	Channel	Signal	Noise	Network type	Vendor		WEP	

Log:

SSID	MAC	Channel	Network type	Vendor	WEP	Last Seen
Darryl Patterson Photogr	00:30:65:1C:58:A2	1	Managed	Apple	Yes	Monday, July 15, 2002 21:53:46 US/Ea
penthouse	00:02:2D:29:9B:3C	1	Managed	Agere-Lucent	Yes	Monday, July 15, 2002 21:21:06 US/Ea
3F	00:05:5D:ED:2D:E2	2	Managed	unknown	No	Monday, July 15, 2002 20:49:41 US/Ea

Save...   Status: Scanning...

Figure 1-1. Networks found within range of a single, moderately-sized Manhattan co-op

Keep in mind that this was with a stock Titanium PowerBook and its notoriously terrible wireless reception range. It's quite likely that either an iBook or an Aluminum PowerBook would have found considerably more wireless networks. If you have a TiBook, Chapter 2 offers some ways to improve your reception.

- In our pre-wireless days on the road together, we'd squabble over who got to use the hotel's high-speed network connection first, and for how long. Now, we simply hook up one laptop to the hotel's connection, activate Internet Sharing on that computer, and voilà! Both laptops are online.

- The last holiday season was a wireless extravaganza. For Thanksgiving, we stayed with one of our parents; since Mom didn't have broadband, and we needed to send in work, we lurked at a local Starbucks and used their Wi-Fi connection. Over Christmas, we visited a relative with broadband, but no wireless. We brought along a wireless router, and kept in touch with friends until the New Year.

- Sometimes we're not in range of a Wi-Fi network, but we still need to send an important piece of email from our laptops. No problem: we use Bluetooth to create a wireless connection between our PowerBook and our cell phone, then use the cell phone as a modem to hook up to the Internet. Chapter 7 covers how you can use cell phones for Internet access.

Wireless Hardware

To go wireless, the first thing that you'll need to get is the proper hardware. While this book is primarily about 802.11x, it also covers hooking up your peripherals (such as printers, PDAs, cell phones, and even keyboards and mice) without wires. While all of this will be discussed in much more depth in later chapters, here's a brief overview of the technology this book covers.

802.11x

802.11x is the generic term for the 802.11 family of standards for wireless radio network connections, which includes 802.11, 802.11a, 802.11b, and 802.11g. This book focuses primarily on the last two standards, as Apple has chosen to support them on the Mac. The original AirPort uses 802.11b, while the newer AirPort Extreme supports 802.11g (and still maintains 802.11b compatibility, as described below).

The 802.11 designation comes from the Institute of Electrical and Electronics Engineers (*http://standards.ieee.org/*, IEEE for short, and pronounced "Eye-Triple-E"), a nonprofit, worldwide technical organization that develops technical standards for many different areas in the electronics field. Representatives of wireless manufacturers are often members of the IEEE subcommittees that hammer out the standards. The IEEE 802 Committee is responsible for networking, and its 802.11 Working Group deals with standards for wireless local area networks (WLANs). Each flavor of wireless has its own Task Group, which begat the different wireless-related standards and proposed standards, such as the original 802.11 (a 1-2 Mbps wireless protocol that is obsolete), as well as a, b, d, g, h, i, j, and k. A wireless standard is proposed in a Task Group and hashed out through a consensus process until it is voted on and finally approved. This process often takes years—the 802.11b standard had its beginnings in 1997, but didn't become an approved standard until 1999.

While the IEEE creates the standards, the Wi-Fi Alliance (*http://www.wi-fi.org/*) is the group that certifies products to work correctly with each other. Wi-Fi is an abbreviation for "wireless fidelity," and came about because "Eight Oh Two Dot Eleven Bee" doesn't roll well off the tongue. The Wi-Fi Alliance is a nonprofit trade organization, made up of hardware manufacturers and service providers that tests 802.11x devices for interoperability. Hardware that bears the Wi-Fi logo is guaranteed to work with any other hardware that also bears the logo (Figures 1-2 and 1-3). So if you have an Apple AirPort (i.e., 802.11b) card inside your computer, you should be able to connect with any 802.11b or 802.11a+b (also called "dual-band") device.

Figure 1-2. This symbol declares that a device meets the Wi-Fi (802.11b) standard

Figure 1-3. The Wi-Fi Alliance certifies multiple standards; hardware with this label supports 802.11a, 802.11b, and 802.11g

In order to use 802.11b or 802.11g with your Mac, you'll need two pieces of equipment: a card (to go inside your computer) and an Access Point (AP) to hook up to the Internet. The good news is that if you have a recent Mac, you're likely to already have the former, or be able to add it easily.

Cards. Since 2000, Apple has shipped computers that are either "AirPort built-in" or "AirPort ready." The former means that you already have a card installed in your computer, so you're ready for wireless. If the latter describes your computer, you'll need to purchase an AirPort or equivalent third-party card. In our experience, your best bet is to stick with the Apple cards: you know they'll work, and they're reasonably priced. Apple offers two AirPort cards: the original AirPort card ($79), which is an 802.11b unit, and the AirPort Extreme card ($99), which uses the 802.11g standard.

Laptops that use AirPort Extreme are not compatible with the original Air-Port card, and laptops made for the original AirPort card cannot use the Apple AirPort Extreme card. If you have an older Mac that isn't AirPort-ready, Chapter 2 discusses some of the other options (such as PC and PCI cards) that may work for you.

Wireless Access Points. Practically speaking, Access Points, APs, gateways, wireless routers, and base stations are all different names for the same thing. Technically speaking, there are significant differences between some of these, but thanks to the slippery terminology used by wireless network manufacturers, the distinctions have tended to blur, causing network engineers to mutter darkly under their breath. In this book, we'll be using the term AP to describe most wireless units that give you access to networks, including the Internet. Sometimes it will be necessary to make a distinction between the different types of units, and we'll specify the differences when needed.

The Road Apple Built

Before IEEE could create wireless standards and the Wi-Fi Alliance could certify gear, the road to wireless networking first needed to be cleared. In this case, the road clearing needed was allocation of a band of the radio spectrum that would eventually be used by wireless data networking devices. In May 1995, Apple Computer filed a petition with the Federal Communications Commission (FCC) to set aside a radio band for future unlicensed use by wireless networks. The Apple petition envisioned using the band for high-speed (24 Mbps or more) devices that would allow schools, libraries, and communities to create networks at relatively low cost. The petition dovetailed with one of the Clinton Administration's (and former Vice President Al Gore's) pet projects, the "National Information Infrastructure," which began in 1993 and was the U.S. government's push to accelerate the growth of the Internet and expand the reach of information technologies to the general public. After a rulemaking process and comment period, the FCC approved Apple's petition in January 1997.

Interestingly, the original Apple petition asked for spectrum allocation in the 5 GHz band, a band that Apple eventually didn't use, preferring instead to use the 2.4 GHz band for AirPort and AirPort Extreme. Other manufactures have used that band, however; see the discussion of 802.11a later in this chapter. But the real point is that all wireless manufacturers and users owe Apple a debt of gratitude for having the vision to get the wireless networking ball rolling.

Apple's versions of the AP are the AirPort Base Stations, which have shipped in three flavors: Graphite, Snow, and Extreme. Of these, the Graphite and Snow models, which supported 802.11b, have been discontinued in favor of the AirPort Extreme Base Station, which supports both 802.11b and the faster 802.11g standard.

The not-so-good news is that although the AirPort Base Stations feature Apple's renowned ease of use, they range from somewhat overpriced to horribly overpriced, and do not always offer the best performance. The good news is that many off-the-shelf APs will work just fine with your Mac. You'll find more information about base stations from Apple and other manufacturers in Chapter 3, which shows how to choose and set up an AP for your network.

Differences Between 802.11a, b, and g

802.11 was the original wireless specification in this family of protocols. It operated in the 2.4 GHz spectrum and offered speeds between 1 and 2 Mbps. The a, b, and g specifications are extensions to the original 802.11.

802.11a. This was one of the first flavors of 802.11 to be worked on, but it wasn't the first to market because it took longer to develop than 802.11b. 802.11a devices run in the 5 GHz radio band, and can achieve a speedy theoretical throughput of 54 Mbps. The effective distance between radios for these speeds is approximately 50 meters; at longer distances, speeds degrade. Because 802.11a uses the 5 GHz band, these devices are not compatible with the far more common 802.11b devices. Workarounds exist; there are 802.11a units that are "dual-band," meaning that they contain both 802.11a and 802.11b radios. As you might guess, such dual-band units are more expensive and more complex in both hardware and software.

This lack of compatibility with 802.11b units led Steve Jobs to pronounce that 802.11a was "doomed to failure" during his keynote speech at Macworld 2003 in San Francisco. As a result, 802.11a support for the Macintosh by Apple is unlikely. Third parties may make Mac OS X drivers available for 802.11a equipment, because the standard does have some advantages: 12 channels can be used without interference in the same area, the 5 GHz band doesn't have the congestion that sometimes exists in the 2.4 GHz band, and there are some frequencies reserved for 802.11a outdoor use, which could make the standard useful for linking buildings in the same campus.

In addition, just as there are dual-band 802.11a and 802.11b devices, Linksys has announced a dual-band 802.11a and 802.11g PC card notebook adapter. It's reasonable to assume that there will soon be a variety of a+g products available, though probably not from Apple. Of course, because 802.11g units are backward compatible with 802.11b, dual-band units will effectively incorporate all three standards.

802.11b. 802.11b was the standard behind the first consumer wireless hardware to ship, and is by far the most popular. You'll find 802.11b networks in a wide variety of places, including airports, convention centers, the Starbucks down the street, and many other public buildings. Over the past few years, millions of 802.11b cards and access points have been sold worldwide, creating an explosion of wireless networks. The benefits of 802.11b are that the required equipment is easy to set up, it's low-cost, and after you buy the gear, there's no extra charge for airtime on the equipment that you own (as with cell-based data services).

Besides working with access points, 802.11b devices can work in "ad-hoc" mode, meaning that they can connect directly to one another. Apple refers to this mode in its AirPort software as creating a "Computer-to-Computer" network. You can create this private network with another computer to transfer files, share an Internet connection, or to use iChat.

The 802.11b standard balances a slower theoretical top speed than either 802.11a or 802.11g (11 Mbps versus 54 Mbps) with a longer effective range (300 versus 150 feet). 802.11b radios share the 2.4 GHz radio band with other consumer electronics products such as cordless phones, microwave ovens, and Bluetooth devices. If you're in an area where two of these different types of devices are in use, you may suffer the effects of interference; for example, we own a 2.4 GHz wireless phone, and when we bring it into the same room as one of our 802.11b APs, we can hear a soft clicking noise on the phone, and the data throughput from the AP to our laptops drops. You'll find more about the details of 802.11b in Chapter 2.

802.11g. 802.11g gets 802.11a's 54 Mbps data throughput, while still being able to share the same wireless network with 802.11b users. Because 802.11g shares the 2.4 GHz band with 802.11b, it must be backward compatible. This combination of speed and backward compatibility led Apple to embrace 802.11g in January 2003, under the name AirPort Extreme. Apple replaced its AirPort Base Stations with new AirPort Extreme models, and released new AirPort Extreme cards for its newer CPUs (the new cards are a different form factor, so they can't be used to give older machines AirPort Extreme capabilities). The theoretical speed of 802.11g is 54 Mbps, with real-world throughput falling into the 20 to 30 Mbps range.

As of this writing (October 2003), the IEEE has recently finalized the 802.11g standard. What this means is that when you buy 802.11g hardware, it may or may not work well with 802.11g hardware from other manufacturers, at least until they roll out their standard-compliant updates. Our recommendation is to either stick with hardware from one manufacturer (usually Apple), or make sure that anything you buy can be upgraded via firmware to the standard. You should also ensure that your hardware is running the latest firmware version: check the manufacturer's web site to find out the latest version, then use the hardware's management software to check what version the hardware is running. See Chapter 4 for more information on how to manage Apple's AirPort Base Stations.

Now that the standard is final, the Wi-Fi Alliance has updated their logo program to show which products are a, b, and/or g. There are more details about 802.11g in Chapter 2.

Table 1-1 provides an overview of the different 802.11 protocols.

Table 1-1. 802.11x at a glance

Standard	Band	Speed	Distance	Apple support?
802.11b	2.4 GHz	11 Mbps	300 feet	Yes (AirPort)
802.11a	5 GHz	54 Mbps	150 feet	No
802.11g	2.4 GHz	54 Mbps	150 feet	Yes (AirPort Extreme)

It's important to keep a few things in mind when looking at these numbers:

- The theoretical top speeds listed in the table include all of the parts of the wireless signal, and that signal isn't just the data that you are sending and receiving. There is considerable overhead in the network signal, such as signaling the beginning and end of data packets, canceling out interference, and ensuring that transmissions are synchronized. This overhead reduces the theoretical speed of your data significantly: with 802.11b, you'll get about 6 Mbps at best, and because low-cost consumer gear doesn't quite live up to the theoretical maximum, your throughput is likely to be between 4 to 5 Mbps. There's an analogy to wired Ethernet: 10Base-T Ethernet is supposedly 10 Mbps, but in the real world, it's more like 7 to 8 Mbps.

- Real world numbers will always vary from the listed speed and distance. Sometimes, the numbers will vary widely, so don't be surprised if you don't get the performance implied by this chart.

- The speed of the connection decreases the further you get from the AP. You're not going to get maximum throughput when you're near the limit of its range. 802.11 devices are designed to automatically reduce their data throughput and maintain the connection as the distance between the base station and the wireless client increases.

- Nearly anything can diminish the signal strength and range. If your walls are thick, it's more likely that you won't be able to use wireless over long distances. We've heard stories about people with outside receivers whose signal strength differs depending on how many leaves are on the trees. There are a lot of variables, and what holds true in one situation may well not be the case in another location.

Bluetooth

If you think of 802.11x as a replacement for wired Ethernet networking, the goal of Bluetooth is to replace Universal Serial Bus (USB). See all those wires connecting your keyboard and mouse to your computer? In Apple's dreams, all of those will be connected wirelessly to your Mac via Bluetooth.

You can learn more about the specification at these sites:

http://www.bluetooth.com/
    Information site for users

http://www.bluetooth.org/
    Information site for developers

Figure 1-4 shows the Bluetooth symbol.

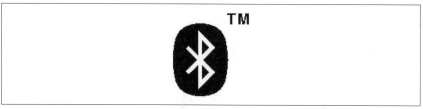

Figure 1-4. Symbol designating Bluetooth products

This dream is gradually becoming reality. In September 2003, Apple began shipping a Bluetooth mouse and keyboard. Microsoft's Bluetooth keyboard and mouse work with Mac OS X 10.2.6 or later (see Apple Knowledge Base article 107586 (*http://docs.info.apple.com/article.html?artnum=107586*). At the time of this writing (October 2003) several other hardware manufacturers, including Logitech, Bluetake, and Belkin had announced (but not yet shipped) Bluetooth mice or keyboards. Given that Apple just began shipping machines with Bluetooth built-in in Q1 2003, we expect that over time:

1. The cost of the Bluetooth chips will come down.

2. More machines will (obviously) be available that support Bluetooth.

Given these factors, we're willing to bet that many peripherals vendors will support Bluetooth within a year or two.

> So, why care about Bluetooth now? One of the coolest demonstrations of the future of Bluetooth is a Bluetooth cell phone such as the Sony Ericsson (*http://www.sonyericsson.com/*) T68i or P800, or the Nokia 3650 (*http://nokia.com*). One you've synced your contacts and appointments wirelessly between your Mac and your phone, you'll never again want to think about where your connection cable might be hiding.

The big advantage of Bluetooth over infrared is that it doesn't require line-of-sight transmissions: even if you have your Bluetooth phone tucked away in your purse or pocket, it can still interact with both your Bluetooth-equipped Mac and your Bluetooth headset. In fact, Bluetooth will allow you to use your cell phone without ever pulling it out of your pocket—you won't be able to tell the difference between the crazy person talking to himself and the cutting-edge gadget geek unless you get a good look at their ears.

The advantage of Bluetooth over RF (described in the following section) is that it requires only one Bluetooth adapter, no matter how many Bluetooth devices you hook up to any other given device. When Bluetooth input devices become widely available, switching from RF to Bluetooth will enable you to get rid of all the little receivers lined up next to your computer. A final advantage of Bluetooth over its predecessors is its range, which has a theoretical maximum of up to 10 meters, considerably better than RF.

This just scratches the surface of the how and what of Bluetooth, which will be covered thoroughly in Chapter 6, which is unsurprisingly titled "Bluetooth."

RF

Given the status of Bluetooth as not-quite-here-yet technology, many of the currently available wireless keyboards and mice are Radio Frequency (RF) devices, often working in the 900 Mhz range. Because RF requires a separate receiver for each wireless device (unless you buy a combination device, such as the ones from Logitech, *http://www.logitech.com/*) it's not a wonderful solution.

Infrared

Infrared was an early contender to RF and Bluetooth, and for a while it looked like infrared was going to be the winning wireless short-range technology. IR, also referred to as IrDA (*http://www.irda.org/*, short for Infrared Data Association, the body that creates the IR standards), works via infrared radiation to control external devices. Despite appearances, IR isn't completely dead on the Mac. If you need IR but have a newer Mac that shipped without IR support, it's possible to buy an adapter from MadsonLine (*http://www.madsonline.com/*) that connects via USB.

IR is currently used primarily for PDAs, some printers, and a few other accessories such as Keyspan's (*http://www.keyspan.com/*) Digital Media Remote. The latter comes with its own IR receiver, so it'll work with any USB-equipped Mac.

Infrared does have one major advantage over Bluetooth. To understand why, think about beaming information from one PDA to another at a crowded meeting. If more PDAs had Bluetooth, every PDA would be trying to talk to every other PDA within range. With IR and short distance line-of-sight, your PDA can easily figure out which other PDA it should be speaking to.

Table 1-2 compares short-range wireless options. Appendix A discusses both RF and IR in greater detail.

Table 1-2. Short-range wireless choices

Protocol	Band	Speed	Distance	Line-of-sight required?
IR	N/A	4 Mbps	3 feet	Yes
RF	Variable, depends on manufacturer's specifications			No
Bluetooth	2.4 GHz	1 Mbps	30 to 800 feet	No

Wireless Software

Wireless hardware is handy enough, but software adds even more functionality. Both Apple and third-party developers have written applications that take the wireless hardware and make it accomplish some pretty darn cool stuff.

Apple's Software

As might be expected with a technology that they're trying to evangelize, Apple has led the way with their own software. If you're not running at least Mac OS X 10.2 Jaguar, you'll want to upgrade, because it's a requirement for almost all of their "digital hub" applications.

iSync. Now that it's possible to hook up devices such as the Sony Ericsson T68i and the Palm Tungsten T (*http://www.palm.com/products/handhelds/ tungsten-t/*) via Bluetooth, you need iSync (*http://www.apple.com/isync/*), which helps you move your data to and from these devices.

That's not to say that iSync is only for wireless devices. It works equally well for those with wires, such as the iPod. But the specialized needs of Bluetooth devices require a specialized application. With iSync, you can synchronize the contents of your Address Book contacts and your iCal appointments to your Palm, your cell phone, or both. Chapter 6 covers iSync and how you can use it with Bluetooth.

iChat. Not just another chat client, iChat (*http://www.apple.com/ichat*) leverages OS X 10.2 and later to provide a superior chat experience. In addition to simply sending "how r u?" to people on your buddy list, you can share files and images, just by dragging them into the message window. In addition, your buddy list isn't limited to Mac users: you can also include anyone on AIM, America Online's instant messaging service.

Of course, iChat doesn't require that you be unwired—it works fine when you're hooked up to a network via Ethernet. But the combination of AirPort, Rendezvous, and iChat allows local wireless networks to do amazing things.

Rendezvous. Like iChat, Rendezvous is not so much about wireless networking as it is another way of looking at networking altogether. It works equally well over both wired and unwired networks.

Rendezvous started off as an Internet Engineering Task Force (IETF) proposal called Zeroconf, for "zero configuration." Their goal was to enable computers to connect to other computers seamlessly and easily, regardless of computer and OS make. Apple introduced this concept to the Mac in OS X 10.2 under the name Rendezvous. For more information, see the following URLs:

- *http://www.apple.com/macosx/jaguar/rendezvous.html*
- *http://www.ietf.org/html.charters/zeroconf-charter.html*
- *http://www.zeroconf.org/*

Any Rendezvous-enabled device on a network can find and talk to any other Rendezvous-enabled device. Going forward, this will let you set up networks that automatically know about all the other machines and printers on the network. You'll be able to carry an AirPort-enabled laptop into a room full of other computers, and share files without first having to spend years learning system administration.

Rendezvous and iChat work together, so you can chat with anyone on your local network, even if they're not on your buddy list. I've found this to be amazingly useful at tech conferences, where the audience can be chatting to each other (and heckling the speakers!) while looking like they're taking notes.

While Rendezvous is about zero configuration, that doesn't mean that there aren't a few things worth knowing about it, and those (along with iChat) will be covered in Chapter 7.

Third-Party Software

Applications by third parties range from the useful to the unethical to the possibly (depending on your jurisdiction) illegal. The latter group will be saved for Chapter 5.

One example of a useful application written by someone other than Apple is MobileSync, from Salling Software (*http://www.salling.com/*). While iSync is a great application if you happen to use iCal and Address Book, not everyone does. If you want to sync your Microsoft Entourage contacts and calendar with your Sony Ericsson cell phone via Bluetooth, you need MobileSync. Additionally, MobileSync works with IrDA if you don't have Bluetooth, and via serial cable if you don't have either.

The same developer has also produced Salling Clicker, a program that allows you to turn your Bluetooth-capable cell phone and Palm OS PDA into a remote control for iTunes, Apple's Keynote presentation program, and more. You'll find more about Salling Clicker in Chapter 6.

CHAPTER TWO

Wi-Fi in Your Mac

For most people, wireless networking means connecting to the Internet or to other computers without the bother of an Ethernet wire tethering your computer to a wall jack. As you'll see later in this book, there's a lot more to wireless technology than just Internet access, but in this and the next three chapters we'll cover Wi-Fi, the technology that you'll use most of the time to wirelessly connect your computer to other computers and to the Internet. Apple has branded its Wi-Fi hardware and software with the name AirPort (for 802.11b) and AirPort Extreme (for 802.11g).

Wi-Fi allows convenient wireless network access, which is equally useful at work, educational institutions, and in the home. At work, people can use their notebook computers anywhere in the office and still have access to all of the network services, including file servers, printers, and (of course) the Internet. In schools, students with notebook computers can move from classroom to classroom and remain connected. Home users have the freedom to move around and be connected anywhere in the house, without dealing with the cost and hassle of running wires through the walls.

About 802.11b and 802.11g

Before talking about the Wi-Fi hardware, let's take a look at the two different Wi-Fi standards in use on the Macintosh and some of the terminology associated with them. These standards are 802.11b and 802.11g. Both operate in the 2.4 GHz radio band, which is the part of the radio spectrum that the Federal Communications Commission (FCC) in the United States has allocated for unlicensed use by the public. These standards are developed and maintained by the Institute of Electrical and Electronics Engineers (IEEE). Table 2-1 compares 802.11b and 802.11g base stations.

As mentioned in Chapter 1, there is a third Wi-Fi standard, 802.11a, which runs at 54 Mbps and uses the 5 GHz radio band (so it is incompatible with 802.11b and 802.11g). Because Apple doesn't support 802.11a, we won't discuss it in this chapter.

Table 2-1. Comparing 802.11b and 802.11g base stations

	802.11b	802.11g
Frequency	2.4 GHz spectrum	2.4 GHz spectrum
Rated data rate	11 Mbps	54 Mbps
Typical real-world throughput	5 to 7 Mbps	20 to 25 Mbps
Range	Up to 300 feet	Up to 150 feet
Non-overlapping channels	Three (1, 6, 11)	Three (1, 6, 11)

As you can see from the table, 802.11g base stations have half the range of 802.11b, but the benefit is up to five times the data rate—as long as all of the units are 802.11g. 802.11g is backward compatible with 802.11b, meaning that 802.11g hardware can accept signals from the slower 802.11b hardware. When an 802.11b client connects to a 802.11g base station, the 802.11g equipment "steps down" in speed, and the 802.11g hardware's throughput drops from between 20 to 25 Mbps into the 14 Mbps range.

SSID

The Service Set Identifier, or SSID, is the name for the wireless network. All of the devices participating in a particular wireless network must specify this SSID. Base stations broadcast their SSID, and it is this network name that appears in the Finder's AirPort menu, as shown in Figure 2-1.

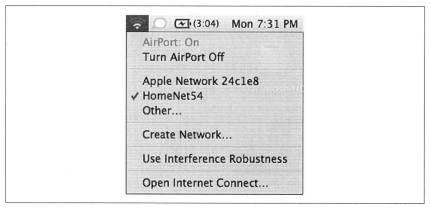

Figure 2-1. SSIDs for two different Wi-Fi networks in the Finder's AirPort menu

If you prefer, you can prevent your base station from broadcasting its SSID, which means that people who want to hook up to your network will need to know and enter the exact SSID in order to connect. It's commonly thought that this will enhance the security of your network, but at best, it may keep users from accidentally connecting to your network. This will not prevent a determined attacker, even a novice, from entering your network. Apple refers to networks that do not broadcast their SSID as *closed networks*.

Channels

The 802.11b and 802.11g standards define 14 channels. A *channel* is a particular frequency that a Wi-Fi client and base station use to communicate. Though there are 14 channels in the standards, the U.S. only uses channels 1 to 11, Europe uses channels 1 through 13, and Japan uses all 14 channels.

A channel represents the center frequency used by both the radio card and the wireless base station. Each channel occupies 22 MHz of the spectrum, beginning with Channel 1 at 2.412 GHz and ending with Channel 14 at 2.484 GHz. The frequency difference between each channel is 5 MHz, which means that each channel overlaps with other channels. Therefore, if you use multiple base stations with your network, you need to use each base station's management software to set the channels so that they do not overlap and interfere with each other. Figure 2-2 illustrates the 5 MHz frequency difference between each channel and 25 MHz used by 5 channels, which gives you 3 MHz of breathing room. So to avoid interference, you should manually set channels 1, 6, and 11 if you're using multiple base stations within range of each other.

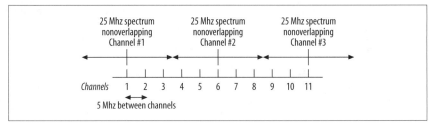

Figure 2-2. The non-overlapping channels in 802.11b and 802.11g

If you have only one base station serving a particular area (the likely situation at home and in a small business), you probably won't need to worry about setting your base station's channel. Each base station comes preset to use a particular channel, and all Wi-Fi cards can automatically find and select the correct channel needed to connect to the base station.

Security (WEP and 802.1X)

When you set up an AirPort Base Station, you are asked if you want to enable a password to connect to the base station. If you do, the base station turns on Wired Equivalent Privacy, or *WEP*. Clients that wish to connect to a base station with WEP turned on must enter the password to gain access to the network. WEP is a protocol that encrypts the data packets on a wireless network, making it more difficult (but by no means impossible; see Chapter 5 for more information) for unauthorized users to intercept and read that data. WEP uses a 64- or 256-bit shared-key algorithm to encrypt the data packets. WEP increases the security of your data, but there is a price to be paid: the encryption and decryption process reduces your effective data rates.

A more secure protocol is *802.1X*, a port-based access control mechanism that was originally designed for wired networks, but works for wireless as well. This mechanism controls a series of challenges and responses between the client machine and the base station, resulting in the authentication of the client by an authentication server. 802.1X support was introduced in Mac OS X Panther (10.3). You'll find more information about 802.1X in Chapter 5.

If you're a home or small office user, you should be able to use WEP for security, but we suggest changing your WEP key weekly. If you have a large network, or even a small one with large amounts of traffic, we suggest using 802.1X. The vulnerability of a WEP-protected system increases with the amount of network traffic.

Networking Modes

Your Macintosh can participate in a wireless network in one of two modes. The first, *ad-hoc mode*, is a wireless network in which two or more computers communicate directly with one another. Apple's name for this mode is a *Computer to Computer network*. In ad-hoc mode, there is no base station; the computers communicate in a peer-to-peer fashion. There's more information about setting up a Computer to Computer network in Chapter 3.

The second (and more common) mode is *infrastructure mode*, in which one or more client computers communicate with a wireless base station.

AirPort Cards

All of the computers that Apple has manufactured since 2000 are *AirPort-ready*, meaning that they contain an internal slot that can accept either an AirPort card or an AirPort Extreme card. These cards are the radio transceivers that transmit and receive the Wi-Fi signals. PowerBooks, iBooks, iMacs, eMacs, and Power Macintosh G4 desktops have internal antennas in their cases that plug into the cards. The all-aluminum case of the Power Macintosh G5 computers prevent the transmission of radio signals through the case, so these machines come with a small external AirPort antenna that plugs into the computer's rear panel.

The Original AirPort Card

The original AirPort card supports the 802.11b standard, for theoretical data transfer rates of up to 11 Mbps. In the real world, however, signal inefficiencies and networking overhead reduce the actual data throughput you'll get from 802.11b to approximately 6 Mbps at best, which is still plenty fast for Internet surfing and most network file transfers. Distance is also a factor with wireless: that 11 Mbps figure is for throughput close to the base station. As you get farther away, the signal will degrade to 5.5 Mbps, then 2 Mbps, 1 Mbps, and 512 Kbps before you lose the signal altogether.

The AirPort card is a special version of a PC card, similar to the cards used in the expansion slots of notebook computers such as Apple's PowerBooks. The card has a 16-bit interface running at 10 MHz, with an effective data throughput of approximately 20 Mbps. However, the AirPort card is specifically designed for the internal slots used in Apple's machines, and can't be used in regular PC card slots. Figure 2-3 shows the AirPort card.

Figure 2-3. The AirPort card supports only 802.11b

Table 2-2 lists the computers compatible with the AirPort card, with the annoyingly vague and nondescriptive terminology that Apple uses for each model.

Table 2-2. AirPort-ready Macintosh computers

Computer	Model
iMac	iMac (Slot loading)
	iMac (Summer 2000)
	iMac (Early 2001)
	iMac (Summer 2001)
	iMac (Flat panel)
	iMac (17-inch flat panel)
eMac	eMac
iBook	All clamshell models: iBook, iBook SE, iBook (FireWire), IBook SE (FireWire)
	iBook (Dual USB)
	iBook (Late 2001)
	iBook (14.1 LCD)
	iBook (16 VRAM)
	iBook (Dual USB)
	iBook (14.1 LCD 16 VRAM)
	iBook (Opaque 16 VRAM)
	iBook (16 VRAM)
	iBook (14.1 LCD 32 VRAM)
	iBook (Early 2003)
PowerBook G3	PowerBook G3 (FireWire)
PowerBook G4	PowerBook G4 (Titanium)
	PowerBook G4 (Gigabit Ethernet)
	PowerBook G4 (DVI)
	PowerBook G4 (1 GHz/867 MHz)
Power Mac G4	Power Mac G4 (AGP)
	Power Mac G4 (Cube)
	Power Mac G4 (Gigabit Ethernet)
	Power Mac G4 (Digital audio)
	Power Mac G4 (QuickSilver)
	Power Mac G4 (QuickSilver 2002)
	Power Mac G4 (Mirrored drive doors)

The $79 AirPort card is still available from Apple for use with the Macintoshes listed in the table. Newer Macs use the AirPort Extreme card.

The AirPort Extreme Card

Besides supporting the 802.11g standard, the $99 AirPort Extreme card is quite different from the older AirPort card. For one thing, it's physically much smaller; as Apple says, it's about half the size of a standard business card. The change in the card's form factor was necessary to support 802.11g's higher speeds. The AirPort Extreme card is a Mini-PCI card that connects to a full-speed PCI bus in AirPort Extreme–ready computers. This is a full 32-bit PCI 2.2 bus running at 33 MHz, offering throughput of around one gigabit per second. That's more than fast enough to handle 802.11g's rated 54 Mbps speed, and easily handles its effective 25 Mbps throughput. Figure 2-4 shows the AirPort Extreme card.

Figure 2-4. The AirPort Extreme card

AirPort Extreme's need for the Mini PCI bus is the reason there can't be an AirPort Extreme card for older AirPort-enabled systems; the AirPort slot for those systems, running at only 10 MHz, simply can't transfer the data fast enough.

AirPort Extreme was introduced in January 2003, and most new Macs announced since that date use AirPort Extreme, rather than AirPort. Table 2-3 lists Apple's AirPort Extreme–ready Macintoshes.

Table 2-3. AirPort Extreme–ready Macintosh computers

Computer	Model
iMac (Flat Panel)	iMac (17-inch 1 GHz)
	iMac (15-inch 1 GHz)
	iMac (17-inch 1.25 GHz)
eMac	eMac (ATI Graphics)
iBook G4	All models
PowerBook G4	PowerBook G4 (12-inch) (all models)
	PowerBook G4 (15-inch FireWire 800)
	PowerBook G4 (17-inch) (all models have built-in Airport Extreme)
Power Mac G4	Power Mac G4 (FW 800)
Power Mac G5	All models

Installing AirPort Cards

The AirPort and AirPort Extreme cards are designed to be user installable, and the only tools you usually need are a coin or a small screwdriver. Installation instructions differ for each type of Macintosh with an AirPort or AirPort Extreme slot, and there isn't enough room in this book to list the instructions for every model. Luckily, Apple's web site does provide such a list: the Customer-Installable Parts page, found at *http://www.info.apple.com/usen/cip/*, has a pop-up list from which you select your computer's model. This menu links to PDF files that show you how to install each of the customer-installable parts for your computer.

> It's often more convenient to view a PDF file right in a browser such as Safari than it is to use external helper applications such as Preview or Adobe Acrobat Reader. We like to use the free PDF Browser Plug-in, from Manfred Schubert. It's not as full-featured as an external program, but it can't be beat for quick viewing of PDF files on the Web. You can download it from *http://www.schubert-it.com/*.

Third-Party Connection Solutions

If you want to use Wi-Fi equipment from companies other than Apple, you have a few options, and some decisions to make. First you'll need to decide how you will connect the Wi-Fi equipment to your Macintosh. You have three choices:

- If you have a PowerBook with a PC card slot, you can use a third-party Wi-Fi card that supports 802.11b or 802.11g.

- You can use a USB-to-wireless adapter to add Wi-Fi capability to a desktop Mac that doesn't have an AirPort slot.

- Desktop Macs that don't have an AirPort slot but do have a free PCI slot can use PCI wireless cards.

Most of the time, if you have a Mac with an appropriate slot, it makes more sense to use Apple's AirPort or AirPort Extreme cards in your Macs, rather than other vendors' Wi-Fi cards. The Apple cards are usually more expensive than third-party cards, but they are installed internally, so they don't take up your notebook's PC card slot. Plus, the software driver to run the cards is built into Mac OS X or readily downloadable from Apple. But if you want to use Wi-Fi hardware from other manufacturers, their drivers are also available.

PC Cards

If you have a PowerBook with a PC card slot, you can use the slot to host a wireless card. Many manufacturers sell 802.11g and 802.11b cards that will work (see the "PC Card Drivers" sidebar for the software side of the hookup equation). These cards are usually less expensive than Apple's equivalent offerings, and smart shoppers can often find cards for half the price Apple charges. A fine example is the 802.11g-compatible Linksys WPC54G Wireless-G Notebook Adapter, shown in Figure 2-5.

Figure 2-5. The Linksys WPC54G 802.11g PC card adapter; photo courtesy of Linksys

You can see that the card has a gray cap at one end. This is the card's antenna, which projects from the side of the PowerBook. PC card wireless adapters can't take advantage of the internal antennas built into many PowerBook's cases. In the case of the Titanium PowerBooks, this is an advantage, as those notebooks have notoriously poor wireless range. See the "Extending the Titanium PowerBook's Range" section later in this chapter for more information on solving this problem.

PC Card Drivers

As long as you're running Mac OS X 10.2.6 or later and AirPort Update 3.1 or later, you can use any vendor's 802.11b or 802.11g wireless PC card based on the Broadcom or Intersil chip sets. That means that cards from Linksys, D-Link, Buffalo, Belkin, or Asante, among others, should work as soon as you plug them in. If you also have an AirPort card installed in the internal slot, you may need to remove it for the third-party card to work correctly.

To use the PC card in your PowerBook, simply insert it into the PC card slot on the side of the machine. After a moment, a PC card icon will appear in the menu bar, as shown in Figure 2-6.

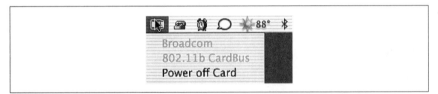

Figure 2-6. The PC card menu

The PC card menu shows the name of the PC card device, and allows you to turn the device off without removing it from the computer. To turn the device back on, however, you will need to remove and reinsert the PC card. Once the computer recognizes the card, you can use the regular AirPort software to join, create, or administer wireless networks, as detailed in the "Setting Up Your Mac to Use Wi-Fi" section later in this chapter, and in Chapter 3.

USB Adapters

If your Mac has a free USB port, you can use a wireless USB adapter to get the Mac on the wireless network. There are several devices that work with Mac OS X, including the D-Link DWL-122, shown in Figure 2-7. The DWL-122 plugs into any USB port and uses the AirPort software for configuration.

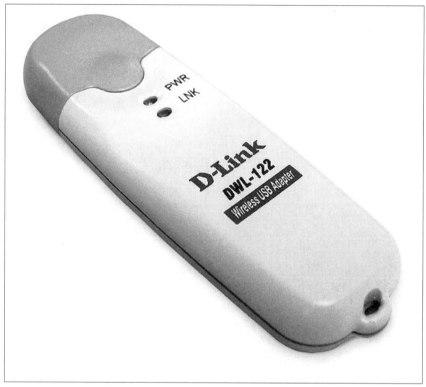

Figure 2-7. The DWL-122 wireless USB adapter; photo courtesy of D-Link

PCI Cards

Desktop Macs with PCI slots but no AirPort slots, such as the Blue and White Power Macintosh G3, can use a wireless network by opening the computer and installing a wireless PCI adapter, such as the Buffalo AirStation WLI-PCI-G54, shown in Figure 2-8.

As with PC cards, PCI card adapters are recognized by the system and used by the AirPort software; as long as you make sure that the PCI adapter is compatible with Mac OS X, you should have no problems using the adapter in wireless networks.

Setting Up Your Mac to Use Wi-Fi

Once you have your Wi-Fi client hardware installed, you need to set up your Mac to use it. You can do this in two ways. The easiest way is to use the AirPort Setup Assistant, which is a program that configures your Wi-Fi hardware and AirPort software with almost no input needed from you. The other way is to use the Internet Connect application and Network Preferences to set the AirPort preferences that you need.

Figure 2-8. The Buffalo Airstation WLI-PCI-G54 PCI adapter; photo courtesy of Buffalo

Using the AirPort Setup Assistant

You'll find the AirPort Setup Assistant in */Applications/Utilities/*. Follow these steps to set up your AirPort hardware:

1. Launch the AirPort Setup Assistant. The Introduction screen will appear, as shown in Figure 2-9.

2. Choose "Set up your computer to join an existing AirPort network."

3. Click Continue.

4. If there is more than one AirPort network available, as in Figure 2-10, choose which network you wish to join from the "Available AirPort networks" pop-up menu. If there is only one AirPort netowrk available, this pop-up menu will not appear.

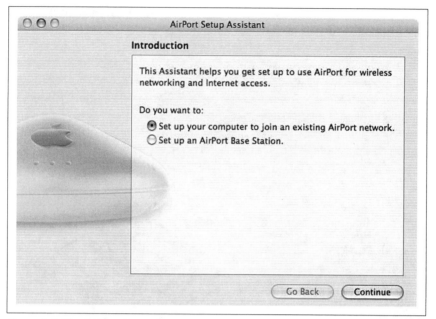

Figure 2-9. The AirPort Setup Assistant's Introduction screen

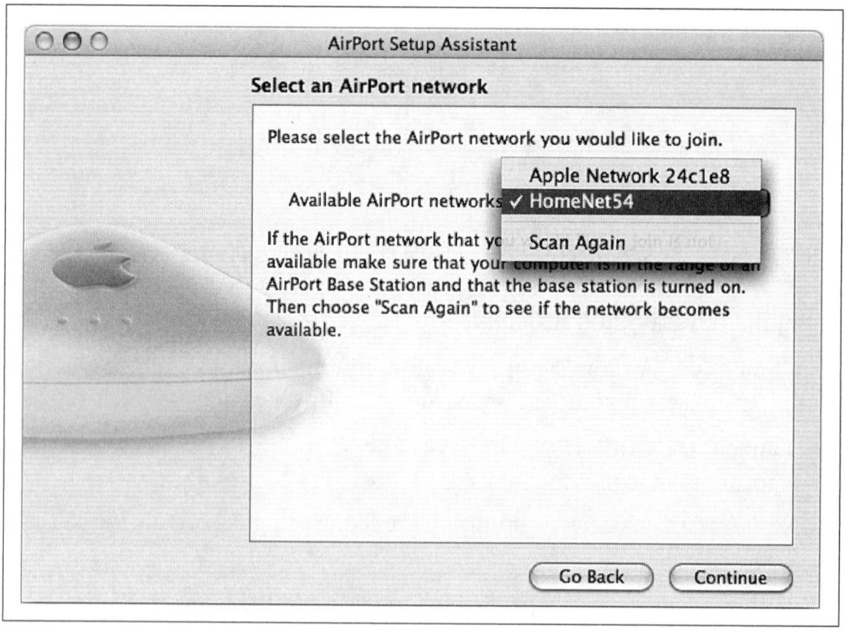

AirPort Setup Assistant

Select an AirPort network

Please select the AirPort network you would like to join.

Apple Network 24c1e8
Available AirPort networks ✓ HomeNet54

If the AirPort network that y   Scan Again
available make sure that your computer is in the range of an
AirPort Base Station and that the base station is turned on.
Then choose "Scan Again" to see if the network becomes
available.

Go Back   Continue

Figure 2-10. Choosing the AirPort network you want to join

5. Click Continue.

6. If the network you selected requires a password, the Enter Network Password screen will appear, as shown in Figure 2-11.

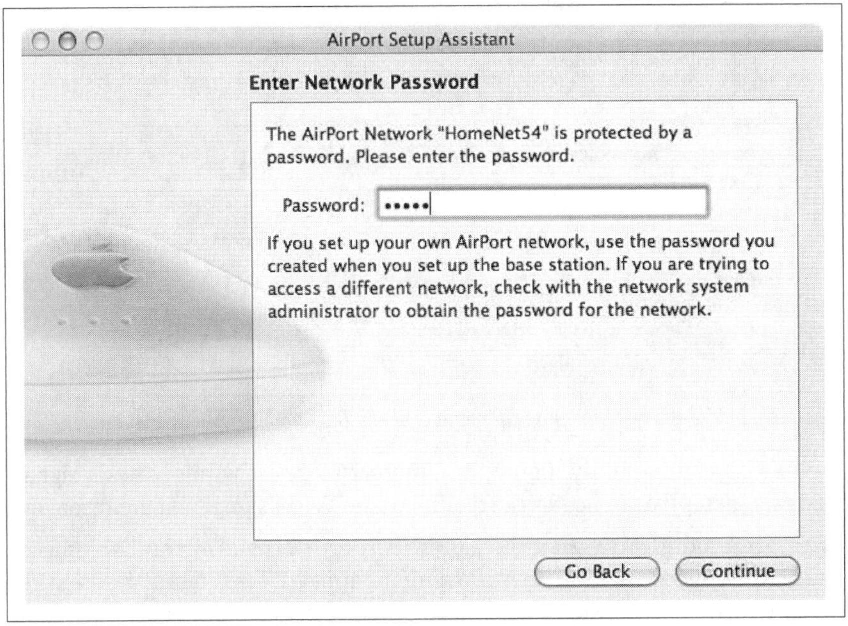

Figure 2-11. Entering the network password

7. Type the network password, then click Continue.

8. The Conclusion screen will appear, letting you know that the AirPort Setup Assistant is ready to configure your computer. Click Continue.

9. The AirPort Setup Assistant reports that it was able to make the connection to your selected network. Click Done.

Connecting to a Wireless Network Manually

To connect to a wireless network manually, use the Internet Connect application found in your Applications folder. You can also use the AirPort pane of Network Preferences for some settings.

Follow these steps to use Internet Connect:

1. Launch Internet Connect.

2. Click the AirPort button in the Internet Connect window's toolbar.

3. If AirPort is turned off, click the Turn AirPort On button.

4. From the Network pop-up menu, choose the network that you want to join, as shown in Figure 2-12.

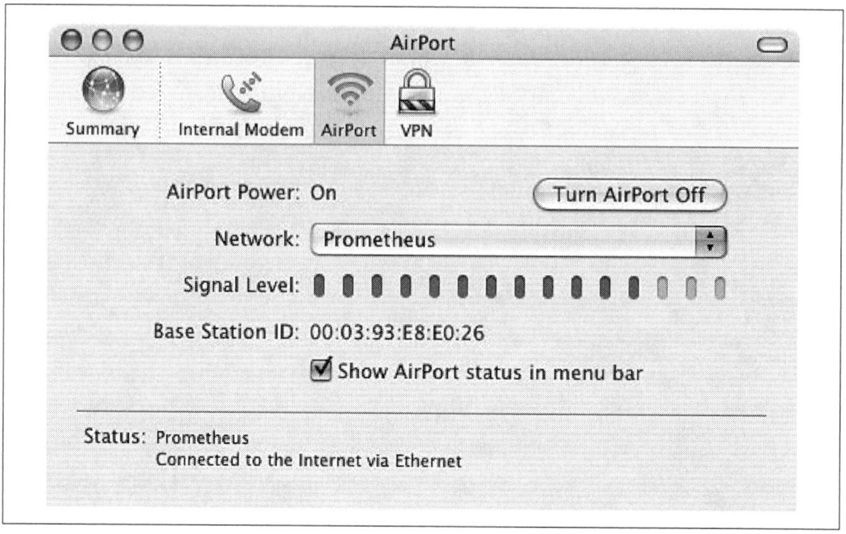

Figure 2-12. Use the Network pop-up menu to select the wireless network you want

As you can see in the figure, the Internet Connect window has a signal-level meter that indicates the quality of the Wi-Fi signal you are receiving.

5. It's a good idea to click the "Show AirPort status in menu bar" checkbox; doing so makes the AirPort menu appear. This menu shows available wireless networks and allows you to switch between them, as shown in Figure 2-13.

6. Choose File → Quit to leave the Internet Connect application.

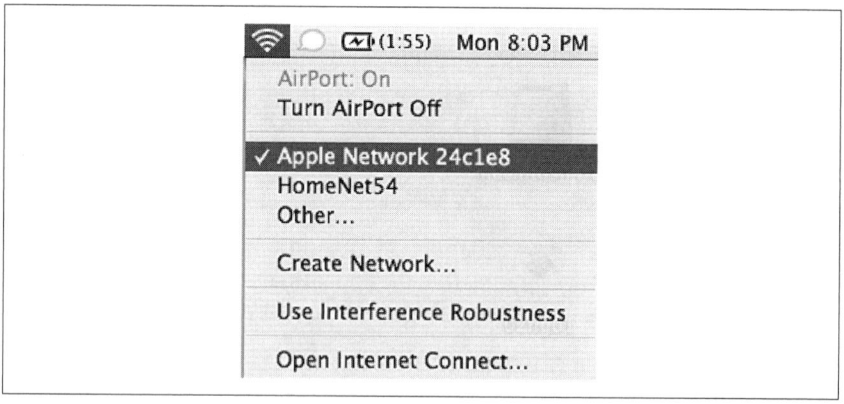

Figure 2-13. The AirPort menu: curved lines denote the wireless network's signal strength

To minimize interference from other 2.4 Ghz devices (such as cordless phones) that interfere with AirPort, you can select Use Interference Robustness from the AirPort menu. However, this may reduce throughput and range in exchange for increased reliability.

Follow these steps to use the AirPort pane of Network Preferences:

1. From the Apple menu, choose System Preferences. The System Preferences application will launch.

2. In the Internet & Network section, click Network. When the Network pane appears, set it to display Network Status, as shown in Figure 2-14.

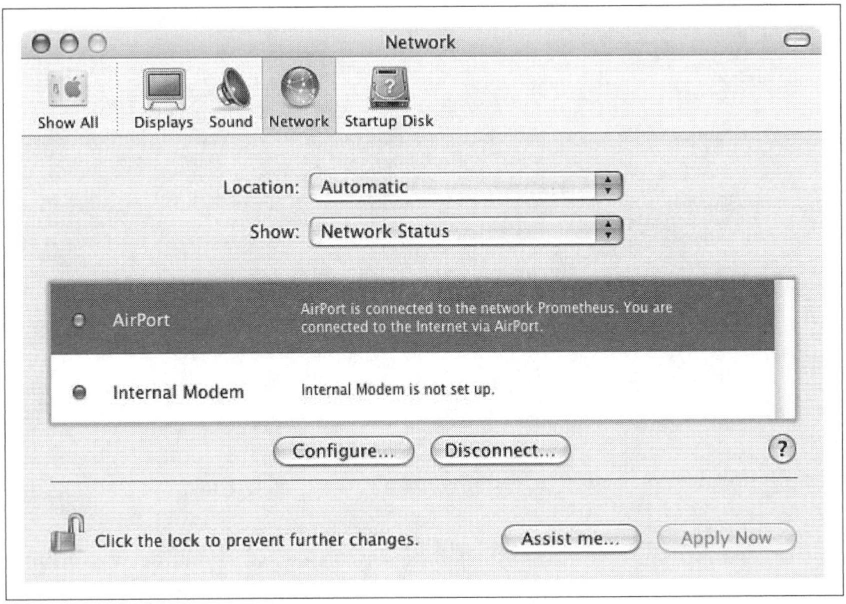

Figure 2-14. The Network Status screen of System Preferences

3. From the Show menu, choose AirPort (if it isn't already showing). The AirPort tab lets you choose to join a specific network by default, or any network, as shown in Figure 2-15.

4. Click TCP/IP. This tab, shown in Figure 2-16, shows the computer's IP address, subnet mask, and the router IP address that the computer has obtained from the wireless base station.

5. Click AppleTalk. The AppleTalk tab appears (Figure 2-17, page 33).

6. If you want to run AppleTalk over AirPort (used for some printers and some file sharing with older versions of Mac OS), click Make AppleTalk Active.

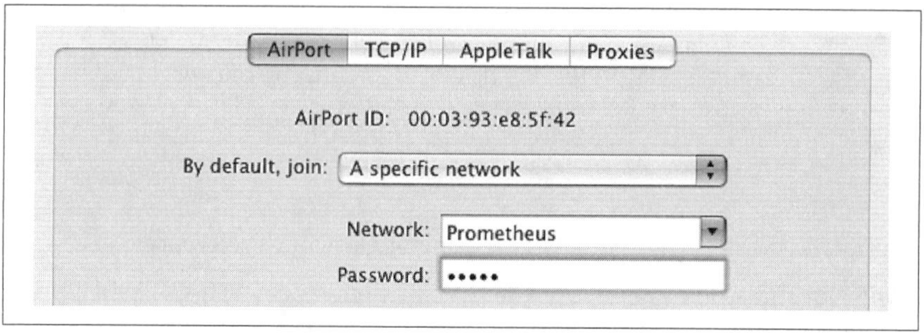

Figure 2-15. Setting a default AirPort network

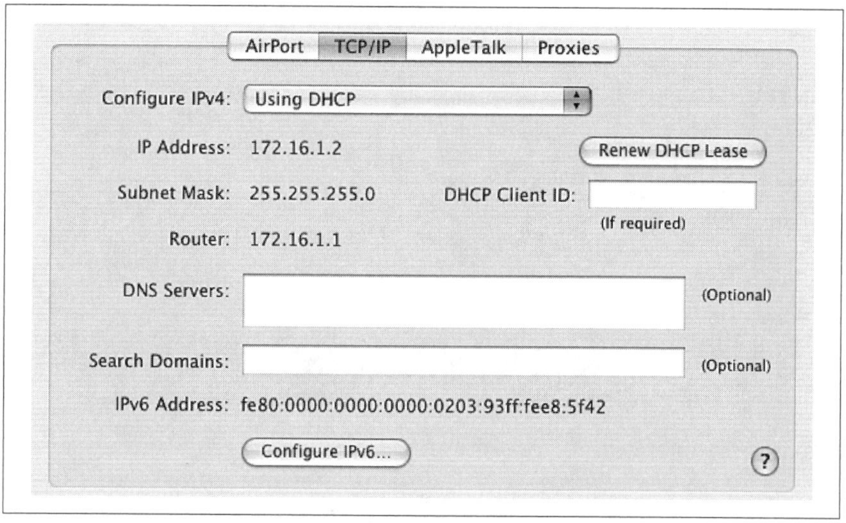

Figure 2-16. You can see the IP address information in the TCP/IP tab

Switching Between Wireless Networks

After you have set AirPort up, you will rarely need to make changes, if at all. Most often, you'll only need to switch between different wireless networks. For that task, you can use either the Internet Connect application or the Air-Port menu. It's usually easier to use the menu. Simply choose the wireless network you want and, if necessary, enter the password for the network.

Extending the Titanium PowerBook's Range

The Titanium PowerBook G4, aka TiBook, is a terrific laptop computer, but it has one major drawback: because of the titanium case, it has poor Wi-Fi reception. Poor reception translates mainly into limited range; when Dori first got her TiBook, Tom had an old blueberry clamshell iBook that could run rings around the TiBook in terms of Wi-Fi reception. The iBook could

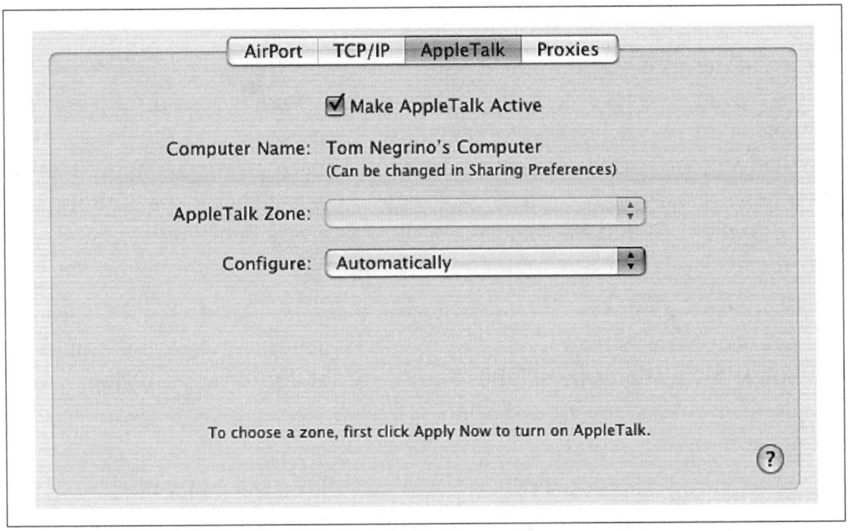

Figure 2-17. The AppleTalk tab of Network Preferences

stay connected to the living room's base station out on the front porch, back in the master bedroom, and even in the kitchen; in short, anywhere in or around the house. By contrast, the TiBook's range was about half the distance from the base station as the iBook's. There are a variety of techniques you can use to improve the reception of your TiBook, and we'll go through them from easiest to most difficult.

By the way, later-model TiBooks are an improvement over the original models, but the difference is not very large. Part of the problem with all models of the TiBook is the location of its built-in antennas: you can see them on either side of the computer as small plastic oblongs. The plastic is much more transparent to Wi-Fi signals than the metal titanium case, but because of their small size, reception isn't that great. The reception problems are greatly improved with the Aluminum PowerBooks, because the antennas in these machines are on the sides of the screen, where they are raised when the computer is in use. Apple also increased the size of the antennas in their later machines.

Orienting your laptop

When you're having problems with Wi-Fi reception on your TiBook, the easiest solution is to move closer to the base station. If that isn't feasible, you can try turning the laptop so that the antennas do a better job of receiving the Wi-Fi signal. Just turn the laptop 90 degrees in either direction and see if the signal strength improves. In really dodgy reception situations, we've found that turning our TiBook can mean the difference between staying connected—and not.

Checking the AirPort Card

Before trying more drastic measures, make sure that your AirPort card is seated correctly in its slot, and that the antenna wire is seated fully into the connector on the end of the AirPort card. It's possible that the person who installed the AirPort card didn't seat the connector properly, and a loose antenna wire can easily be fixed. Chances are good that if the AirPort card isn't properly inserted into its slot, AirPort won't be working at all, but it's easy to check while you're looking at the antenna connection.

1. Remove the battery, then remove the bottom case of your PowerBook G4 using the instructions for your model of PowerBook found at Apple's Customer-Installable Parts page, at *http://www.info.apple.com/usen/cip/*. You'll need a Torx T8 screwdriver, which you can find at most hardware stores.

2. Make sure that the AirPort card is seated all the way in its slot.

3. The antenna cable connector plugs into the port on the AirPort card. Make sure the connector is straight and inserted all the way into the port.

4. Reassemble the computer.

Squeezing the Battery Bay

We haven't had success with this technique ourselves, but after reading several reports that swear by it, we decided to include this tip. It may help your reception if you remove the battery, then press on the inside of the battery bay, which is near one of the antennas. This method apparently works because the antenna cable runs in a channel that secures it in front of the plastic antenna window on the sides of the computer. If the cable has shifted for some reason, it misses the window. Pressing on the inside of the battery bay pushes the antenna cable back into its channel and presumably back in front of the plastic window.

You're trying this procedure at your own risk: we are not responsible in any way if you break your laptop. We suggest using MacStumbler to get a numerical reading of your signal strength before and after the procedure, to make sure that any perceived improvement isn't just the placebo effect in action. Follow these steps:

1. Shut down the TiBook.

2. Turn the laptop over and remove the battery.

3. Locate the AirPort antenna on that side of the computer (it's the plastic strip on the side of the case outside the battery bay).

4. With your fingers, press on the inside of the battery compartment behind the antenna. Press gently but firmly: you're not trying to deform the case or anything. Press in several places in the general area, for about 10 seconds, as shown in Figure 2-18.

Figure 2-18. Pressing on the inside of the battery bay

5. Replace the battery, boot your Mac, and check your Wi-Fi reception.

Using a PC Card Wi-Fi Adapter

Perhaps the best solution to getting better Wi-Fi reception from a TiBook is to add a PC card wireless adapter. This route also allows you to add an 802.11g adapter to get better wireless speeds than an internal AirPort card (though because of the PC card's slot's throughput limitations, you will most likely get slower throughput than a PowerBook with an AirPort Extreme card). The main benefit to a PC card adapter, however, is the antenna that projects beyond the beautiful (but maddeningly radio-opaque) titanium case. Using this external antenna makes all the difference in receptivity, and the increased range is equal to that of iBooks and even a bit better than Aluminum PowerBooks.

You can find a wide range of PC card wireless adapters; no-name 802.11b cards sell from as little as $18. Branded cards cost about $40, and 802.11g cards go for between $30 and $80.

Many PC card adapters will work, as long as you are running Mac OS X 10.2.6 or later and AirPort software 3.1 or later. These versions of the system and AirPort software enabled support for third-party Wi-Fi adapters that are based on the Broadcom and Intersil chip sets.

Installing External Antennas

As mentioned in the last section, the largest improvement in Wi-Fi reception doesn't come from the PC card's radio receiver, but from the antenna that protrudes outside of the PowerBook's case. So why not dispense with a card and just add an external antenna? A few companies offer external antennas for PowerBooks, but we'll just talk about one, QuickerTek (*http:// www.quickertek.com/*). This company makes two antennas for the Power-Book G3 (Pismo) and PowerBook G4 (Titanium). The $50 Stub wireless antenna (shown in Figure 2-19) looks like a PC card antenna and snaps into the PC card slot. The company claims that you can get double the range of the standard internal antennas with the Stub. The $90 Whip wireless antenna (shown in Figure 2-20) has a claimed reception improvement of up to 10 times, and is an external antenna that mounts to the case of your PowerBook with Velcro.

Figure 2-19. The QuickerTek Stub external antenna

These antennas require you to open the PowerBook case, remove the cable connection to the internal antennas, then connect the new antenna's cable connection to the AirPort card. That cable is then threaded through the PC card slot and connected to the Stub or Whip antennas. While the Quick-erTek antenna is installed, you'll lose the use of the PC card slot. And naturally, installing them voids your Apple warranty (if you still have one in effect). Both antennas require that you already have an AirPort card.

Of these two antennas, the Stub should perform similarly to a PC card Wi-Fi adapter, which costs approximately the same as the Stub. If you don't

Figure 2-20. The QuickerTek Whip external antenna

already have an AirPort card, it's a no-brainer to skip the Stub and just get a PC card Wi-Fi adapter. The Whip is a bit more of a judgment call: if you need to use exceptionally weak Wi-Fi signals, the reception improvement of the Whip may be worth the price.

Hitching a Ride

Finally, there is one approach to wireless connectivity that isn't entirely wireless. If you are using two laptops in a place with weak wireless access, and only one of them can receive a usable signal, you can turn on Internet Sharing and connect an Ethernet cable between the two laptops. That way, both computers can share the wireless connection. We've used this approach in cases where Tom's PowerBook G4 (12-inch) was able to get reception, while Dori's TiBook could not.

 Incidentally, this approach allows more than one computer to be on the Net in wireless hotspots that use captive portals to limit access (and almost certainly violates the terms of service of the hotspot provider). See Chapter 4 for more information about hotspots and captive portals.

This technique is, in effect, the opposite of using AirPort Internet Sharing, which allows you to share a direct Ethernet connection over wireless. You'll find more about setting up AirPort Internet Sharing in Chapter 3.

Follow these steps to share a wireless connection via Ethernet:

1. Connect the two computers with an Ethernet cable. Most later-model Macintoshes, including all PowerBook G4 models and iBook (Dual USB and later), don't require an Ethernet crossover cable; to check if yours does, see *http://docs.info.apple.com/article.html?artnum=42717*.

2. On the computer that has the wireless connection, open System Preferences.

3. In the Internet & Sharing section of the System Preferences window, click Sharing.

4. Click the Internet tab, as shown in Figure 2-21.

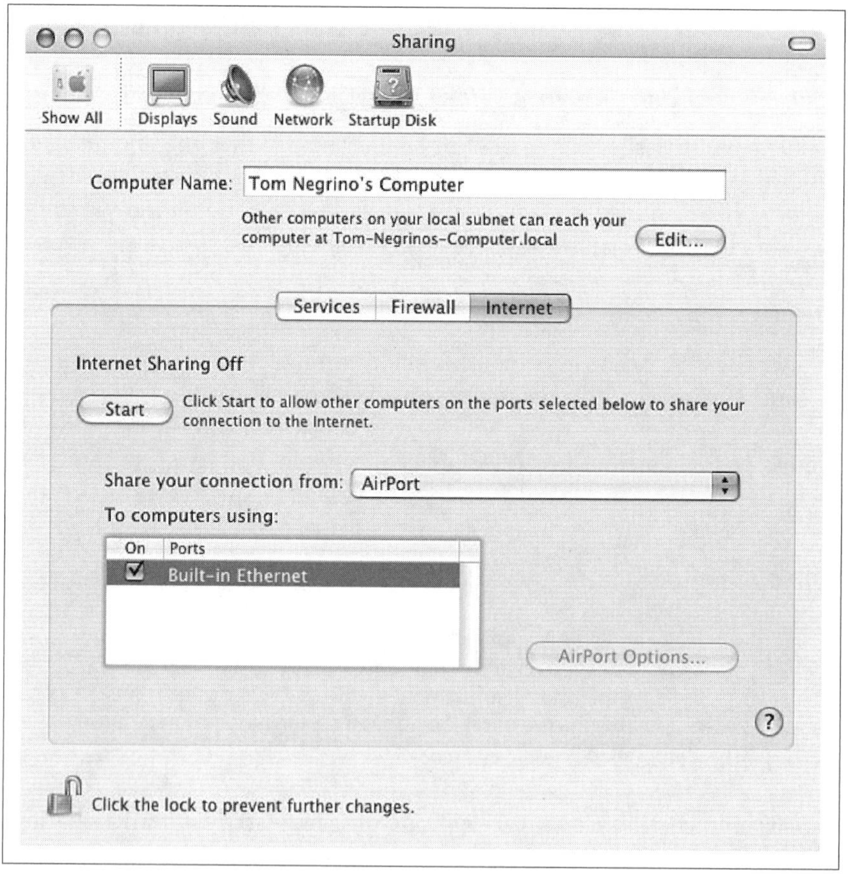

Figure 2-21. The Internet Sharing pane of System Preferences

5. In the "Share your connection from" pop-up menu, choose AirPort.

6. In the "To computers using" section, select the checkbox next to "Built-in Ethernet." The Start button will become active.

7. Click Start. An alert sheet will appear, asking if you're sure you want to turn on Internet sharing.

8. Click Start in the alert sheet. The window will show that Internet sharing is on and that you are sharing your AirPort connection.

9. On the computer that is connected via Ethernet, open System Preferences.

10. In the Internet & Sharing section of the System Preferences window, click Network.

11. Click the TCP/IP tab and choose "Using DHCP" from the "Configure IPv4" pop-up menu. You should now be able to use the other computer's wireless connection.

CHAPTER THREE

Making the Wi-Fi Connection

In Chapter 2, we discussed making the wireless connection on the client side. In this chapter, we'll discuss some networking basics: using and configuring wireless base stations to connect to the Internet, turning your Mac into a software base station using Internet Sharing, using wireless bridges to your wired Ethernet network, and extending the range of your wireless network using additional base stations as repeaters.

Setting Up a Wireless Network

Wireless networking has become so widespread that the cost of the hardware has plunged over the last few years. You can easily set up a wireless network at home for under $200 (if you use a third-party base station) or under $300 (if you go with Apple gear). For that amount, you can get wireless cards for one or two computers and a base station.

To set up your own wireless network, you'll need the following:

- A high-speed Internet connection (via DSL, cable modem, or satellite Internet) or a dial-up Internet connection (if your wireless base station includes a modem; Apple's AirPort Base Stations do)
- A wireless base station with router functionality
- A wireless card for each machine that wants to use the wireless network

A typical home/office network is shown in Figure 3-1.

Networking Principles

Before plunging into the details of setting up a wireless network, it's important to understand the fundamentals of networking, specifically Transmission Control Protocol/Internet Protocol, or *TCP/IP*, which is the networking

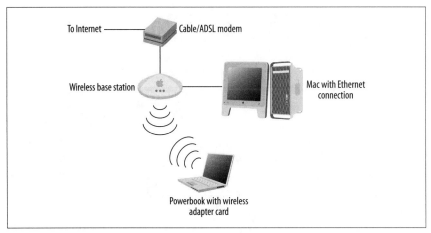

Figure 3-1. A typical wireless network setup

standard used by the Internet, as well as home and office connections. TCP/IP controls how data flows across the Internet and on Ethernet networks in your home or office.

TCP/IP

To understand TCP/IP, you'll need to know how computers identify one another, how they talk to other computers on the same network, and how they talk to machines on other networks or the Internet.

IP address. On a TCP/IP network, each computer has an *IP address*. This address uniquely identifies each computer (also called a *host*) on the network. An IP address contains four numbers separated by periods and looks like this: 192.168.1.1. IP addresses are all 32 bits in length, and are broken into four 8-bit parts. This allows each part to have numbers ranging from 0 to 255. The four parts are combined in a notation called *dotted quad*, which just means that each 8-bit value is separated by a period.

Assigning IP addresses isn't a simple matter of starting with the number 1 and counting upwards. There are really two parts to an IP address: the *network number*, and the *host number* within that network, as shown in Figure 3-2. By using two parts to an IP address, machines on different networks can have the same host number. However, because the network number of the two networks is different, the machines are uniquely identified (the machine numbers are the same, but the network numbers are different).

IP addresses are assigned on the basis of the size of the company or organization requesting them. In a small company, there is no need for many IP

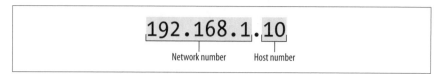

Figure 3-2. IP address components

addresses within the network. On the other hand, a large corporation or educational institution may have thousands of hosts needing IP addresses. IP addresses come in five *classes*, indicated by the value of the first byte of the IP address (the numbers before the first period in the address). The classes that we're interested in are Class A, Class B, and Class C. There are a Class D and Class E, but they have special purposes and are not used as part of the IP address numbering.

Class A
> 0 to 127: Each Class A network supports a maximum of 16,777,214 IP addresses. There are 125 possible Class A networks (3 network numbers are reserved).

Class B
> 128 to 191: Each Class B network supports a maximum of 65,534 IP addresses. There are 16,382 possible Class B networks.

Class C
> 192 to 223: Each Class C network supports a maximum of 254 IP addresses. There are 2,097,150 possible Class C networks.

Figure 3-3 shows the network number and host number used in each class of IP addresses.

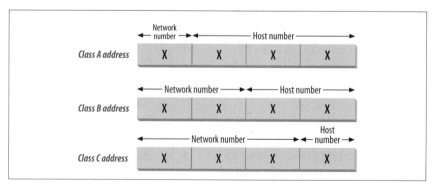

Figure 3-3. Network and host numbers in each IP address class

Some IP address ranges are reserved for special uses, and so are not assigned to any host:

0.0.0.0 to 0.255.255.255
127.0.0.0 to 127.255.255.255
169.254.0.0 to 169.254.255.255

There are four IP address blocks that are reserved for private networks (you'll probably use one of these for a home or small business network, especially if you have a router on your network). These private networks can be configured to see the outside world without letting the outside world see them (see the "DHCP and NAT" section later in this chapter):

10.0.0.0 to 10.255.255.255
169.254.0.0 to 169.254.255.255
172.16.0.0 to 172.31.255.255
192.168.0.0 to 192.168.255.255

When setting up a computer or a router, you will often have to enter a number called a *subnet mask*. There's a long explanation of subnet masks that is fascinating to network engineers and of almost no interest to the rest of us. Let's skip to the important part: if you have less than 255 hosts on your network (which will almost always be the case on a home or small business network) and you are using an AirPort Base Station or similar access point from another vendor, the subnet mask number will be 255.255.255.0.

Routers. A *router* is a hardware device that forwards data packets between networks. Typically, you'll use a router to connect your home or small business network to your Internet Service Provider's network and the Internet. For example, let's say that you have a high-speed DSL or cable modem connection. The service provider gives you a DSL modem or cable modem that hooks up to a phone line or coaxial cable. That modem has an Ethernet connector to which you can plug in a single computer, assuming you have not been saddled with a DSL or cable modem that uses a USB cable (and if you want to connect your access point to such a modem, you'll be out of luck, so talk to your ISP about replacing it). But if you have a network of computers that you want to share the high-speed connection, you'll need a router. You connect the router to your high-speed Ethernet connection, then connect the computers on your network to the router. That last connection, from your computers to the router, can use either a wired Ethernet network, or be wireless. Devices such as the AirPort Base Stations are combinations of routers and wireless access points, which is why they are sometimes called *wireless routers*.

Welcome to IPv6

The IP addresses referred to throughout this book are part of an IP addressing scheme called *IPv4*. This 32-bit scheme, which allows for approximately 4.3 billion hosts, worked great when the Internet was young; the original architects of TCP/IP didn't imagine that more hosts would be needed. However, around 1992 it became obvious that 4.3 billion IP addresses were just not going to be enough (some people think the world will run out of IPv4 addresses as soon as 2006), and the IETF (Internet Engineering Task Force, the folks concerned with the evolution of the Internet architecture) began the process of figuring out a larger IP addressing scheme. After years of work, the base specification for the new scheme, called *IPv6*, was released in 1998.

IPv6 expands the IP address size from 32 bits to 128 bits, which supports a vastly greater number of hosts. How many more? Approximately 340 undecillion, which is 340 followed by 36 zeros. This should do the trick. IPv6 is designed to allow every host on the Internet to have its own unique IP address, eliminating the need for NAT and other workarounds. Consequently, IPv6 will bring about the bright future we keep hearing about in which every car, mobile phone, and refrigerator will be hooked up to the Internet. IPv6 also has built-in security features that don't exist in IPv4.

IPv6 is not just of academic interest: it's being supported in most modern operating systems, and will become increasingly widespread in the next few years. Mac OS X has supported IPv6 since version 10.2 (Jaguar), and in 10.3 (Panther) the Network pane of System Preferences shows your machine's IPv6 address and allows you to configure that address (Figure 3-4). However, applications will need to be reengineered to take advantage of IPv6. Until browsers, email programs, and chat clients support IPv6, it will remain more promise than reality.

A Dynamic Host Configuration Protocol *(DHCP)* server, which is usually built into your router, automatically assigns an IP address to client computers when they log onto the network. This makes up for the fact that most DSL or cable-based home networks get only a single IP address from the provider, which would mean that only one machine could connect the Internet at any one time. Since that's no fun, most home routers also support Network Address Translation *(NAT)*. With NAT, the router uses that single IP address assigned by the Internet provider, and computers connected to the router are assigned IP addresses that are only valid within the local network (and are unusable on the Internet at large). For packets that are sent out to the Internet, the router translates the local IP addresses into the real IP address that the router has. When a data packet from the Internet arrives

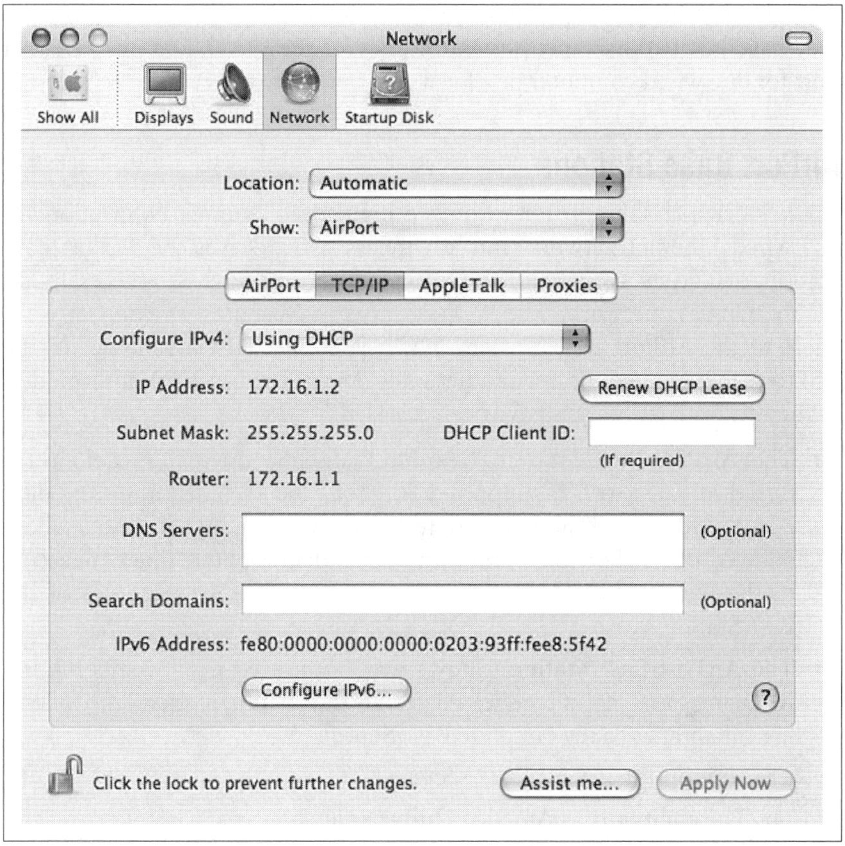

Figure 3-4. IPv6 IP address in Panther

for a computer on the local network, the translation process occurs in reverse, and the router sends the packet on to the correct local machine.

Because computers that are using a DHCP server to get their IP addresses can have those addresses change every time the computer logs onto the network, those addresses are known as *dynamic IP addresses*. It's fine to use dynamic IP addresses inside your network, because your router keeps track of how to get data packets to each computer on the network. Addresses that don't change are called *static IP addresses*.

Routers with switches. Many non-Apple wireless routers also contain *switches* or *hubs*, which allow you to plug more than one computer into the router via Ethernet. Most home routers with switches have four Ethernet ports for direct Ethernet connections to computers, plus a fifth port that connects to the *WAN* port (Wide Area Network, in this case the connection to the DSL or cable modem). The Apple Base Stations do not contain switches; instead, they have just two Ethernet ports: one port for the WAN, and one Ethernet port for one wired computer or a local area network (*LAN*).

AirPort Base Stations

Apple's original solution for turning a high-speed Internet connection (or any wired Ethernet network) into a wireless network was the AirPort Base Station. It (and its successors) serves as a router and a wireless access point for the wireless network. The AirPort cards in Macintoshes connect wirelessly to the AirPort Base Station, which is connected via Ethernet to the DSL or cable modem, or a wired network. As of October 2003, four models of the AirPort Base Station have been released:

- The **AirPort Base Station (Graphite)** was the original model, introduced in July 1999. It supported 802.11b, and included a 56K modem and a 10-Base-T Ethernet port to connect to the WAN. The modem allowed the AirPort Base Station to use a dialup phone line connection to the Internet. The "Graphite" designation refers to the color of the Base Station's case.

- The **AirPort Base Station (Snow)** was introduced in November 2001, replacing the Graphite model. Also an 802.11b unit, it added the following capabilities to the Graphite Base Station:

  a. Support for 128-bit WEP security

  b. The ability to use America Online as an ISP

  c. A second, 10/100-Base-T Ethernet port for connection to a local area network (it still had the 10-Base-T Ethernet port for connecting to the WAN)

  d. A built-in firewall to protect the LAN from unauthorized access from the Internet

  e. RADIUS support (RADIUS is a scheme that allows central management of user access via an authorization server)

  The AirPort 2.0 software was released along with the Snow Base Station, allowing the Graphite units to add America Online and 128-bit WEP support.

- The **AirPort Extreme Base Station** was introduced in January 2003, and replaced the Snow units. This was Apple's first foray into the newer 802.11g standard (which it calls AirPort Extreme), and was released before that standard was finalized, necessitating a firmware upgrade in July 2003 for true 802.11g support.

Using External Antennas

The AirPort Extreme Base Station (with modem and antenna port) lets you use third-party external antennas to extend the range of the base station. Dr. Bott (*http://www.drbott.com*) sells two antennas that we tested and found to work well:

- The $100 ExtendAIR Omni (Figure 3-5) is an omnidirectional antenna that adds a 3.5 dBi boost to the Wi-Fi signal. That boost, along with the omnidirectional coverage, gives a respectable improvement in range and throughput.

- The ExtendAIR Direct (Figure 3-6), a $150 antenna, provides a 6.5 dBi boost in the signal in a relatively narrow 70-degree beam, designed to boost Wi-Fi signals in large rooms and long hallways. The Direct allowed us to effectively connect to the AirPort Extreme Base Station in our house from our office, which is in a room above a detached garage.

Apple uses the same antenna connector on the AirPort Extreme Base Station and the Power Macintosh G5, which require an external AirPort antenna due to their aluminum cases. As a result, both antennas also work with the G5s. Those computers come with a stub external AirPort antenna, but a larger external antenna improves reception.

Another company, QuickerTek (*http://www.quickertek.com*), makes the $129 AntennaKit, which is an external 5 dBi omnidirectional antenna that can be installed on either model of the AirPort Extreme Base Station or on the Air-Port Base Station (Snow). This antenna requires opening the Base Station's case to attach the antenna and a bracket, and drilling a small hole in the case for an antenna wire.

Besides the faster data rate, the AirPort Extreme Base Stations add wireless bridging, which allows you to use up to four additional AirPort Extreme Base Stations to extend the reach of your wireless network (see the "WDS Tab" section later in this chapter). Another new feature is USB printer sharing, which allows all of the computers on the wireless network to share the use of a printer that is connected to an AirPort Extreme Base Station. Finally, one model of the AirPort Extreme Base Station allows the use of an external antenna to improve the reception range of the Base Station.

Figure 3-5. The ExtendAIR Omni external antenna

There are two models of the AirPort Extreme Base Station:

a. The $199 **AirPort Extreme Base Station** does not include a 56K modem, and does not have a connector for an external antenna. It's a good choice for the remote unit when you're setting up wireless bridging.

b. The $249 **AirPort Extreme Base Station (with modem and antenna port)** has, as you might have already guessed, a 56K modem and an antenna connector. Because of the external antenna connector, it works well as the main base station when you are doing wireless bridging.

Setting up an AirPort Extreme or AirPort Base Station

Getting your wireless network on the air is a two-step process. First, there's the physical setup of the hardware. Then you'll need to configure the AirPort Base Station using the AirPort Setup Assistant or the AirPort Admin Utility.

Figure 3-6. The ExtendAIR Direct external antenna

Connecting the hardware. There are three basic connection scenarios for the AirPort Base Station hardware, described next and illustrated in Figure 3-7:

- If all of the clients using an Apple Base Station will be wireless and you have high-speed Internet access, hookup is pretty simple: just run an Ethernet cable from the output of the DSL or cable modem to the WAN port of the Base Station.

- If you have *just one* computer that needs to connect with a wire, with the rest wireless, make the hookup as described in the previous bullet, and then connect the wired computer to the LAN port on the Base Station.

- If you are using an AirPort Base Station and you want to have multiple computers that *don't* have wireless cards access the Internet through the base station, you will also have to purchase an Ethernet switch or hub, plug the wired computers into it, then connect the switch or hub into the base station's LAN port. The DSL or cable modem is then connected to the base station's WAN port.

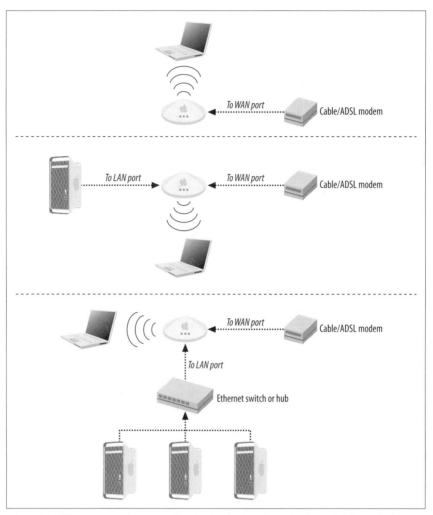

Figure 3-7. Three connection scenarios for the AirPort Base Station: with just wireless clients (top); with one wired client and one or more wireless clients (middle); or with a network of wired clients and wireless clients (bottom)

Base station setup. The easiest way to set up an AirPort Extreme or AirPort Base Station is to use the AirPort Setup Assistant, which walks you through the basic steps in just a few minutes. You can also use the AirPort Admin Utility, which is a tool that lets you configure virtually every aspect of the base stations. Look for more information on the latter utility in the "Using the AirPort Admin Utility" section later in this chapter.

To set up an AirPort Extreme Base Station using the AirPort Setup Assistant, follow these steps (setting up prior models is similar, but may not be exactly the same):

1. Launch the AirPort Setup Assistant, which you'll find in */Applications/ Utilities/*.

2. On the Introduction screen, click "Set up an AirPort Base Station," then click Continue.

3. If your base station is not running the latest firmware for its particular model, the AirPort Setup Assistant will offer to update the firmware, as shown in Figure 3-8. Your choices are Update or Quit, so click Update.

   The Setup Assistant will download the firmware, and then the Base Station will reset itself and the "Select an AirPort network" screen will appear.

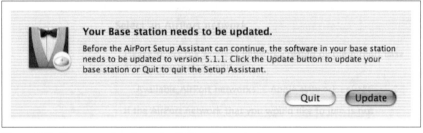

Figure 3-8. Firmware alert from the AirPort Setup Assistant

4. If more than one AirPort network is available, as in Figure 3-9, you should choose which network you wish to join from the Available AirPort networks pop-up menu. If only one AirPort network is available, this pop-up menu will not appear.

> In the figure, you'll note that the network name, "Apple Network 24c1e8," is a bit odd. It has that name because new or just-reset Apple Base Stations use the name Apple Network with the end of the Base Station's MAC address (the MAC address is an Ethernet hardware address) appended to it.

5. Click Continue.

6. On the next screen, you'll be asked if you are using America Online as your Internet Service Provider. The Assistant is really asking if you will be connecting to America Online using the Base Station's modem and a phone line. If that's the case, click "I am using America Online," then enter dial-up phone numbers and phone settings in the fields that will appear (Figure 3-10). Then click Continue and skip to Step 8.

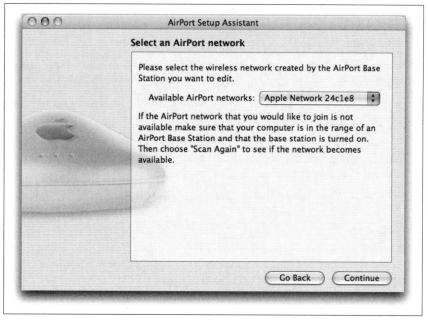

Figure 3-9. *Choosing a base station*

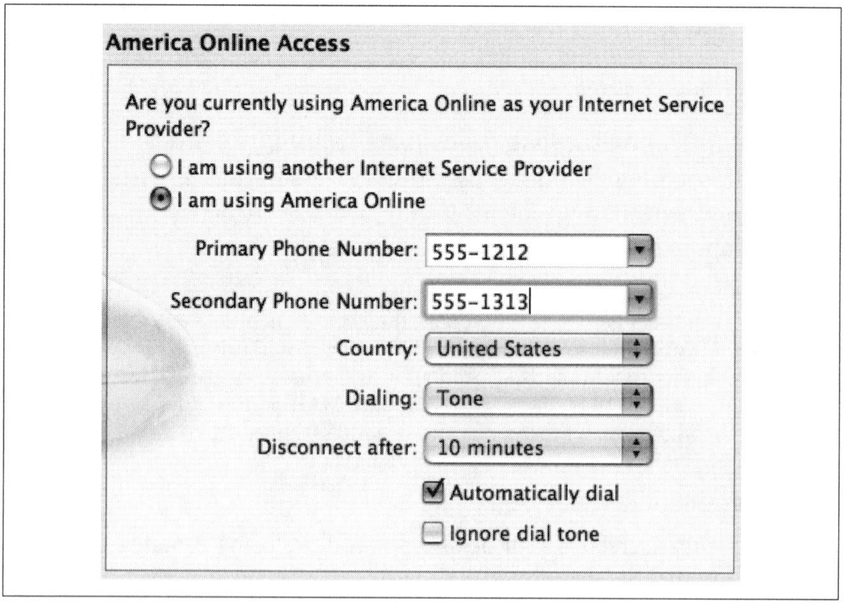

America Online Access

Are you currently using America Online as your Internet Service Provider?

○ I am using another Internet Service Provider
◉ I am using America Online

Primary Phone Number: 555-1212

Secondary Phone Number: 555-1313|

Country: United States

Dialing: Tone

Disconnect after: 10 minutes

☑ Automatically dial

☐ Ignore dial tone

Figure 3-10. *America Online phone settings*

If you'll be using America Online via a broadband connection, don't choose "I am using America Online" in this step. Instead choose "Cable Modem or DSL using static IP or DHCP" or "Cable Modem or DSL using PPP over Ethernet (PPPoE)" in Step 7. Then you'll need to set up your AOL software to use either a "Broadband" or "LAN/ISP" connection, depending on your version of the AOL software.

7. If you are not using America Online dial-up access, the Internet Access screen will appear, as shown in Figure 3-11. Choose from one of the displayed choices.

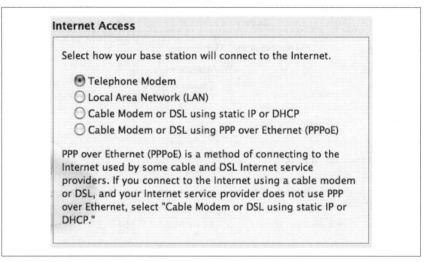

Figure 3-11. Internet Access screen

a. Choose Phone Access if you will be using the AirPort's 56K modem to dial in to an ISP. Clicking Continue will then take you to the Modem Access screen, shown in Figure 3-12.

In the Modem Access screen, you will need to enter your ISP's phone number and your account information. When you're done, click Continue.

b. Choose Local Area Network (LAN) if your base station is connected to an Ethernet network. Clicking Continue will then take you to the Ethernet Access screen, shown in Figure 3-13. Most of the time, you will be able to leave the default choice in the Configure Base Station pop-up menu, "Using DHCP." If your network administrator instructs otherwise, choose "Manually," then fill in the IP Address, Subnet Mask and Router Address fields. When you're done, click Continue.

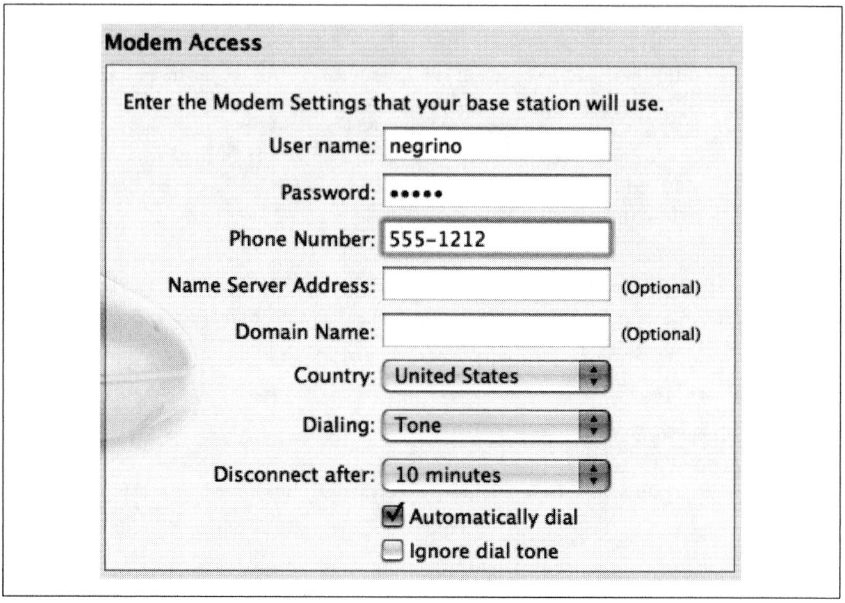

Modem Access

Enter the Modem Settings that your base station will use.

User name:	negrino
Password:	•••••
Phone Number:	555-1212
Name Server Address:	(Optional)
Domain Name:	(Optional)
Country:	United States
Dialing:	Tone
Disconnect after:	10 minutes

☑ Automatically dial

☐ Ignore dial tone

Figure 3-12. Modem Access screen

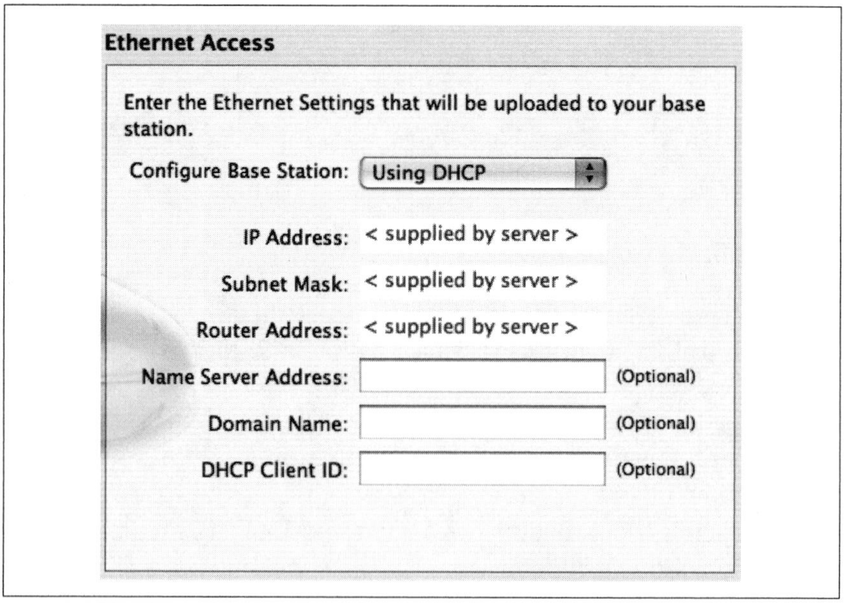

Ethernet Access

Enter the Ethernet Settings that will be uploaded to your base station.

Configure Base Station:	Using DHCP
IP Address:	< supplied by server >
Subnet Mask:	< supplied by server >
Router Address:	< supplied by server >
Name Server Address:	(Optional)
Domain Name:	(Optional)
DHCP Client ID:	(Optional)

Figure 3-13. Ethernet Access screen

c. Choose Cable Modem or DSL using static IP or DHCP if your base station is connected to a high-speed connection. Clicking Continue will then take you to the Ethernet Access screen; follow the instructions in 7b. When you're done, click Continue.

d. Choose Cable Modem or DSL using PPP over Ethernet (PPPoE) if your base station is connected to a high-speed connection and your ISP has specified this sort of connection. PPPoE is an alternative method of connecting a cable or DSL modem that requires you to enter some additional information. Clicking Continue will take you to the PPPoE Access screen, as shown in Figure 3-14. Enter the information given to you by your ISP, then click Continue.

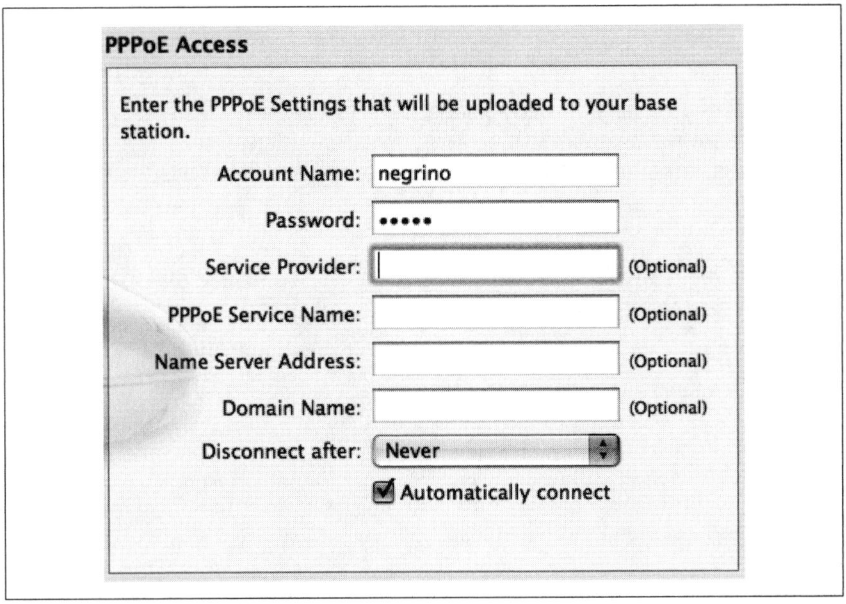

PPPoE Access

Enter the PPPoE Settings that will be uploaded to your base station.

Account Name:	negrino
Password:	•••••
Service Provider:	(Optional)
PPPoE Service Name:	(Optional)
Name Server Address:	(Optional)
Domain Name:	(Optional)
Disconnect after:	Never

☑ Automatically connect

Figure 3-14. PPPoE Access screen

8. The Network Name and Password screen (Figure 3-15) allows you to enter information about the wireless network. Enter the Network Name; this is the name that people will see in the AirPort menu when they connect to your network.

 The Network Name is another name for the base station's SSID.

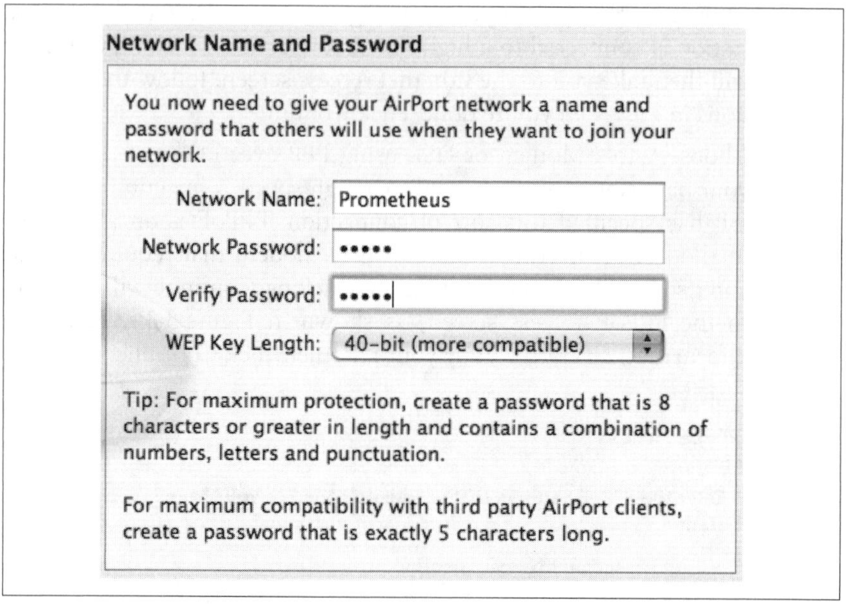

Network Name and Password

You now need to give your AirPort network a name and password that others will use when they want to join your network.

Network Name:	Prometheus
Network Password:	•••••
Verify Password:	•••••|
WEP Key Length:	40–bit (more compatible) ⬍

Tip: For maximum protection, create a password that is 8 characters or greater in length and contains a combination of numbers, letters and punctuation.

For maximum compatibility with third party AirPort clients, create a password that is exactly 5 characters long.

Figure 3-15. Network Name and Password screen

Enter the Network Password twice; this password will need to be entered by clients to connect to the network. From the WEP Key Length pop-up menu, choose either 40-bit or 128-bit. Then click Continue.

By default, WEP is turned on by the AirPort Setup Assistant, which enables encryption and slightly enhances security of your network. See Chapter 5 for more information about WEP. You can turn WEP off with the AirPort Admin Utility, discussed later in this chapter.

9. The Base Station Password, shown in Figure 3-16, lets you choose whether or not you want the password that will be used by the AirPort Admin Utility to be the same as the network password. As it says on the screen, if you're setting up a home network, it's often easier to use the same password, though it is obviously less secure. Make your choice, then click Continue.

10. The Conclusion screen tells you that the AirPort Setup Assistant is ready to configure the base station. Click Continue.

The base station is updated, then automatically resets. Click Done to leave the AirPort Setup Assistant. You're ready to use your new wireless network!

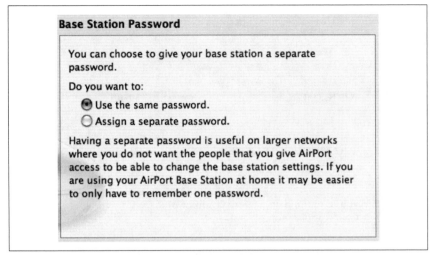

Base Station Password

You can choose to give your base station a separate password.

Do you want to:

⦿ Use the same password.

◯ Assign a separate password.

Having a separate password is useful on larger networks where you do not want the people that you give AirPort access to be able to change the base station settings. If you are using your AirPort Base Station at home it may be easier to only have to remember one password.

Figure 3-16. Base Station Password screen

Setting Up USB Printer Sharing

Both models of the AirPort Extreme Base Station include a USB port that allows the wireless clients to share a printer connected to the base station with a USB cable. A large number of (mostly) inkjet and PostScript printers will work with wireless printer sharing. Here's how to set up the printer for wireless access.

 You must be running Mac OS X 10.2.3 or later to use USB printing with an AirPort Extreme Base Station. The instructions below are for Mac OS X 10.3 (Panther).

1. Before you work with the base station, make sure that your computer can print to the USB printer. Connect your computer directly to the printer with a USB cable, then print a test page from any application.

2. Connect the USB cable from your printer to the AirPort Extreme Base Station.

3. Make sure that the network name for the AirPort Extreme Base Station is selected in the AirPort menu.

4. Open the Printer Setup Utility, found in */Applications/Utilities/*. The application's main window appears, as shown in Figure 3-17.

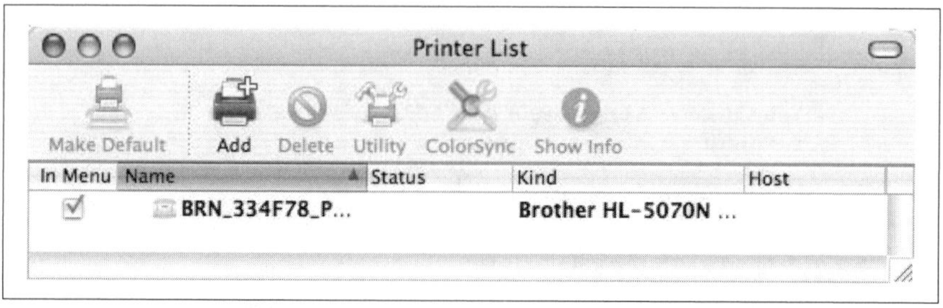

Figure 3-17. Printer Setup Utility

The Printer Setup Utility first appeared in Mac OS X 10.3. If you're running an earlier version of Mac OS X, use the Print Center application.

5. Click the Add button. The Add sheet appears.

Not all printers are compatible with AirPort Extreme Printer Sharing; check out the list at *http://www.apple.com/AirPort/printcompatibility.html* to see if your printer is on the list. On the other hand, it's worth trying your printer even if it isn't on the list; it may work anyway.

6. From the upper menu, choose Rendezvous. The sheet changes to show the name of the printer connected to the AirPort Extreme Base Station.

7. Click to select the printer in the sheet. The name of the AirPort Extreme Base Station appears next to Location at the bottom of the sheet, as shown in Figure 3-18.

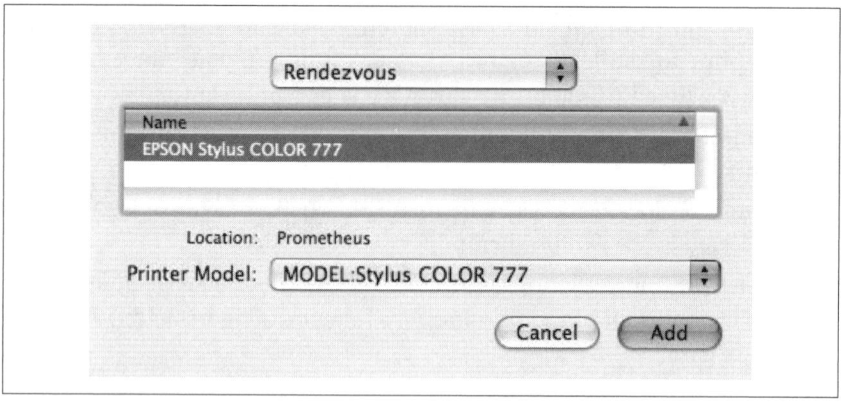

Figure 3-18. Selecting the shared printer

8. If necessary, choose your printer from the Printer Model pop-up menu.

9. Click Add. The new printer will appear in the Printer List.

10. Quit the Printer Setup Utility, then print a test page.

Printer error and status messages may not be available when you're printing wirelessly. For example, you may not receive "Out of Paper" messages from your printer.

If you're not using the LAN port on an AirPort Base Station (Snow) or an AirPort Extreme Base Station because you have only wireless clients on that base station, you can feel free to plug in an Ethernet-capable printer. The base station will serve as a bridge from the wireless network to the printer.

Using the AirPort Admin Utility

For detailed configuration of any of the AirPort Base Stations, you'll need to turn to the AirPort Admin Utility. This program lets you select and configure any of the Apple Base Stations on your network (and a few older base stations from Lucent or Orinoco). In this section, we'll run through the different screens of the AirPort Admin Utility and discuss the settings on each screen. We'll be administering an AirPort Extreme Base Station; prior models have fewer settings, and the AirPort Admin Utility shows a correspondingly smaller set of options when used with those models. But many of the settings are common to all models, so you may find discussion of the features you're interested in even if you have a Graphite or Snow Base Station.

To administer an AirPort Extreme Base Station, follow these steps:

1. Launch the AirPort Admin Utility, found in */Applications/Utilities/*. The application's main window appears, as shown in Figure 3-19. The utility scans the network for all available base stations.

2. In the list, select the base station that you want to administer.

3. Click Configure.

4. Enter the password for the base station, then click OK. The Summary screen for the base station appears, showing some of the basic settings for the base station, as in Figure 3-20.

   The AirPort Admin Utility has two simplified screens, Name and Password, and Internet Connection, which have commonly accessed settings. These settings are also available on the detailed screens available from Show All Settings.

5. Click Show All Settings. The detailed settings (discussed in the following sections) appear.

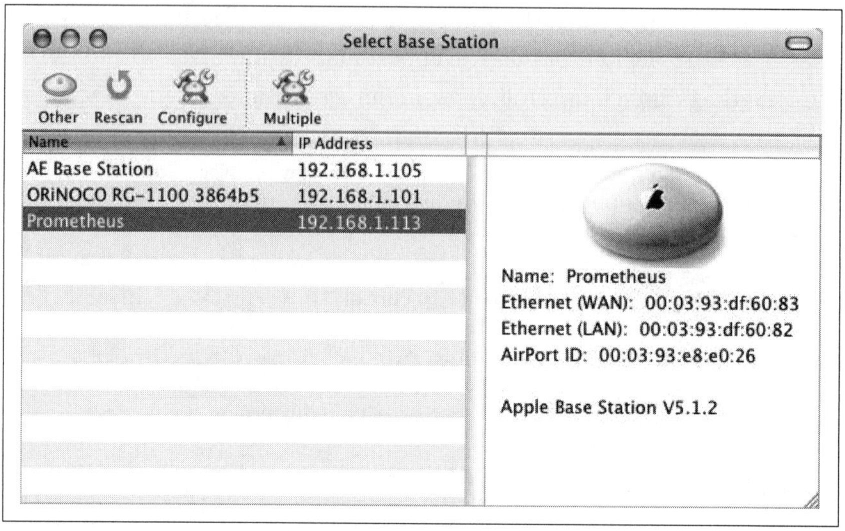

Figure 3-19. AirPort Admin Utility screen

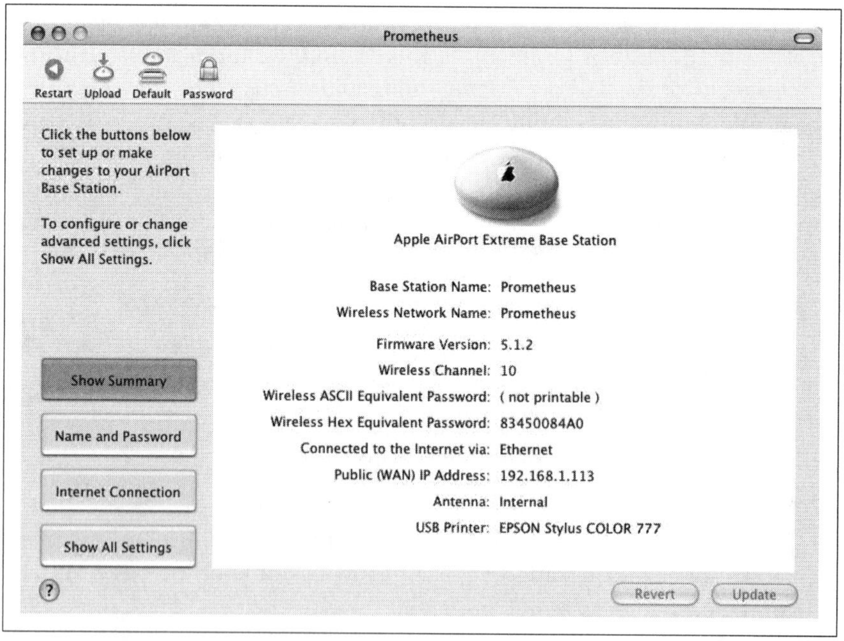

Figure 3-20. AirPort Admin Utility Summary screen

AirPort Tab

The AirPort tab of the AirPort Admin Utility, shown in Figure 3-21, allows you to change the names and passwords for the base station and wireless network.

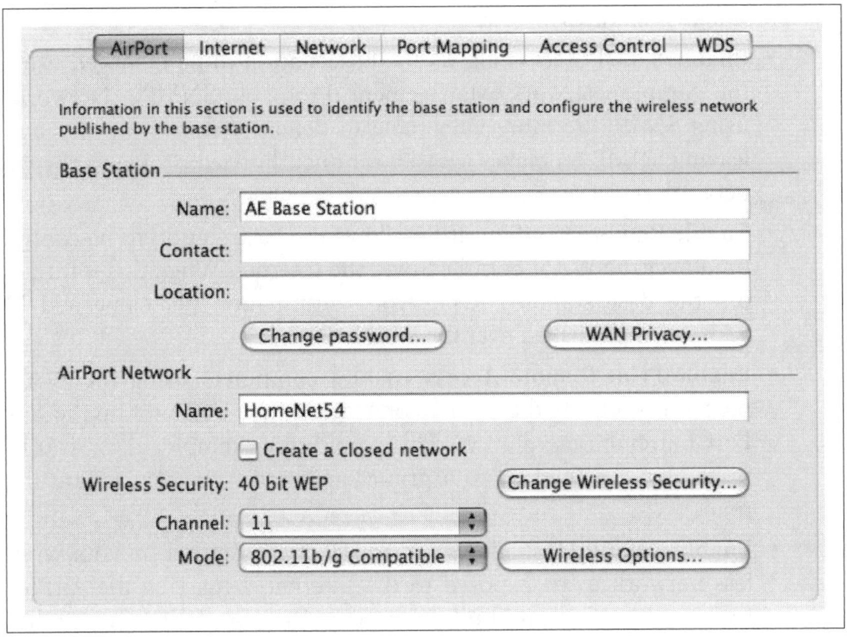

Figure 3-21. AirPort tab

Things to know about this screen:

- The Base Station Name is the name used by the AirPort Admin Utility.
- The AirPort Network Name is another name for the SSID. It is the name that shows up in the AirPort menu on client machines.
- In the Base Station section, clicking the WAN Privacy button brings up a sheet that allows you to enable or disable certain access features sent over the WAN port, as shown in Figure 3-22.

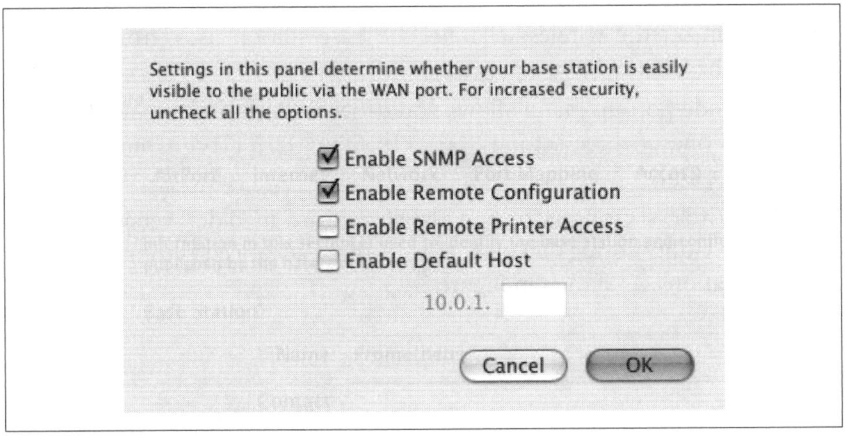

Figure 3-22. WAN privacy settings

These access features include:

- **Enable SNMP Access** allows the base station to be managed using the Simple Network Management Protocol (SNMP). Networks using SNMP are more vulnerable to denial-of-service attacks, and leaving SNMP on makes it easier for unauthorized people to change network settings.

- **Enable Remote Configuration** allows the base station to be configured over the WAN port, i.e., over the Internet. When this is turned on, the base station's Rendezvous information (its name and IP address) is published over the WAN port.

- **Enable Print Remote Access** enables computers using the WAN port to print using the printer connected to the USB port on the AirPort Extreme Base Station. This would, for example, allow you to print over the Internet to a printer at home while you are on the road.

- **Enable Default Host** allows you to select a computer on your wireless network to be exposed to the Internet, bypassing the AirPort Extreme Base Station's built-in firewall. On base stations from other manufacturers, this feature is often referred to as the *DMZ host*.

- The "Create a closed network" setting turns on or off the broadcast of the AirPort Network Name (SSID). If this setting is turned on, clients will have to manually type in the name of the wireless network to gain access to it.

- To enable encryption for the Base Station, click the Change Wireless Security button. From the resulting sheet, you may then set one of four levels of security, which are, in increasing order of security strength, WEP 40-bit, WEP 128-bit, WPA Personal, and WPA Enterprise. The WPA settings are available only on AirPort Extreme Base Stations.

- You can set the wireless channel the base station uses, from 1 to 11, using the Channel pop-up menu.

- The Mode pop-up menu allows you to set an AirPort Extreme Base Station to one of three settings: 802.11b Only, 802.11b/g Compatible, or 802.11g Only.

- The Wireless Options button (labeled More in older versions of the Admin Utility) brings up a sheet with three advanced settings and their explanations, as shown in Figure 3-23.

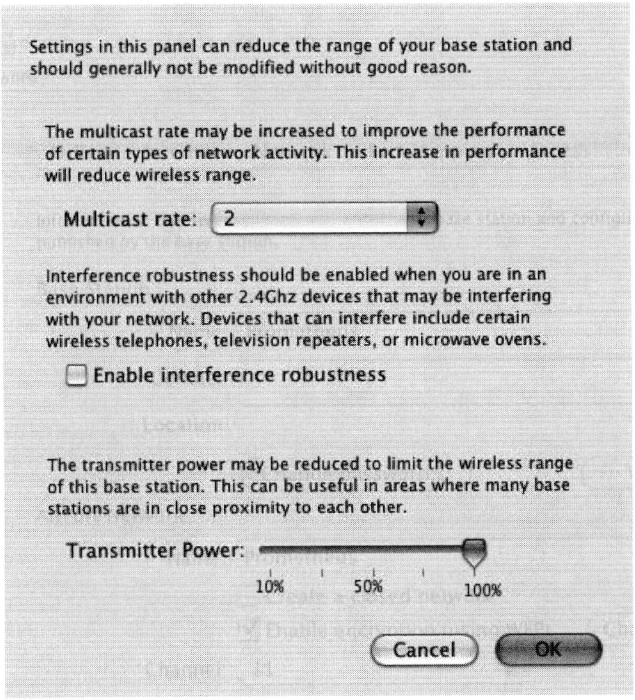

Settings in this panel can reduce the range of your base station and should generally not be modified without good reason.

The multicast rate may be increased to improve the performance of certain types of network activity. This increase in performance will reduce wireless range.

Multicast rate: 2

Interference robustness should be enabled when you are in an environment with other 2.4Ghz devices that may be interfering with your network. Devices that can interfere include certain wireless telephones, television repeaters, or microwave ovens.

☐ Enable interference robustness

The transmitter power may be reduced to limit the wireless range of this base station. This can be useful in areas where many base stations are in close proximity to each other.

Transmitter Power:

10%   50%   100%

Cancel   OK

Figure 3-23. Advanced AirPort settings

Internet Tab

The Internet tab, shown in Figure 3-24, is where you enter the settings needed to connect to your ISP.

Things to know about this screen:

- The contents of the screen change according to the choice made in the "Connect using" pop-up menu. The choices are:
  - **Ethernet** is chosen when connecting to a DSL or cable modem over the WAN port.
  - **Modem (V.90)** is chosen when you are using the base station's modem to connect to an ISP at 56 Kbps.
  - **Modem (V.34)** is chosen when you are using the base station's modem to connect to an ISP at 28.8 Kbps.
  - **PPP over Ethernet (PPPoE)** is chosen to connect to some DSL or cable modem ISPs.
  - **America Online (AOLnet, V.90)** is chosen when you are using the base station's modem to connect to America Online at 56 Kbps.

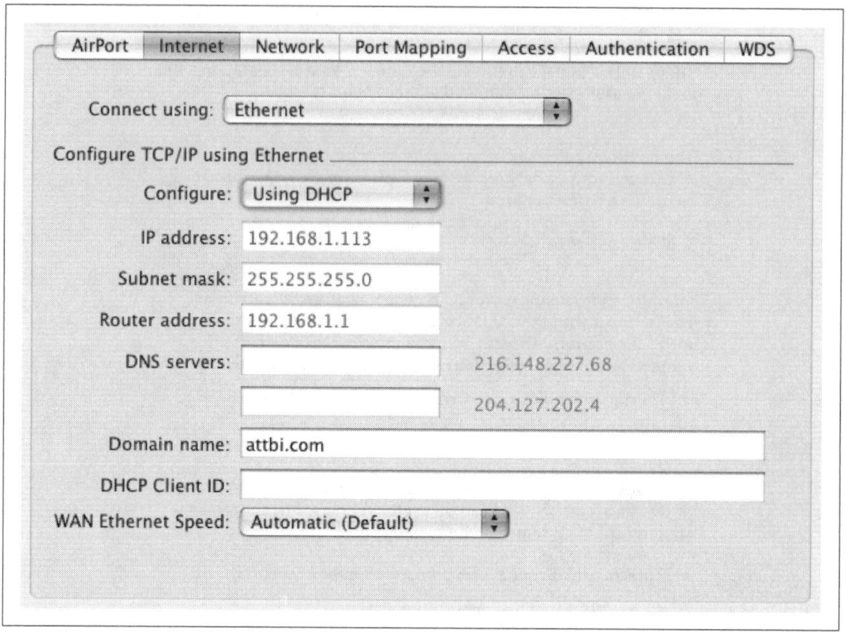

| AirPort | Internet | Network | Port Mapping | Access | Authentication | WDS |

Connect using: [Ethernet   ⬍]

Configure TCP/IP using Ethernet _____

Configure: [Using DHCP   ⬍]

IP address: [192.168.1.113]

Subnet mask: [255.255.255.0]

Router address: [192.168.1.1]

DNS servers: [   ]   216.148.227.68

[   ]   204.127.202.4

Domain name: [attbi.com   ]

DHCP Client ID: [   ]

WAN Ethernet Speed: [Automatic (Default)   ⬍]

Figure 3-24. The Internet tab

- **America Online (AOLnet, V.34)** is chosen when you are using the base station's modem to connect to America Online at 28.8 Kbps.

- **America Online (DSL)** is chosen when you are using America Online as your ISP over a DSL connection.

- **AirPort (WDS)** is chosen when the base station is part of a Wireless Distribution System. See the "WDS Tab" section later in this chapter for more information.

Network Tab

The Network tab, shown in Figure 3-25, controls how the base station's Internet connection is shared with its wireless clients. Things to know about this screen:

- Deselecting "Distribute IP addresses" will turn off the base station's DHCP server, and wireless clients will be able to access the Internet only if they set up their TCP/IP settings manually, and if the ISP provides multiple IP addresses. Deselecting this setting is rarely done.

- You can choose the IP numbering for your wireless network from the pop-up menu under "Share a single IP address (using DHCP and NAT)." You can choose to begin your numbering at one of three address blocks: 10.0.1.1 (the default choice), 172.16.1.1, or 192.168.1.1.

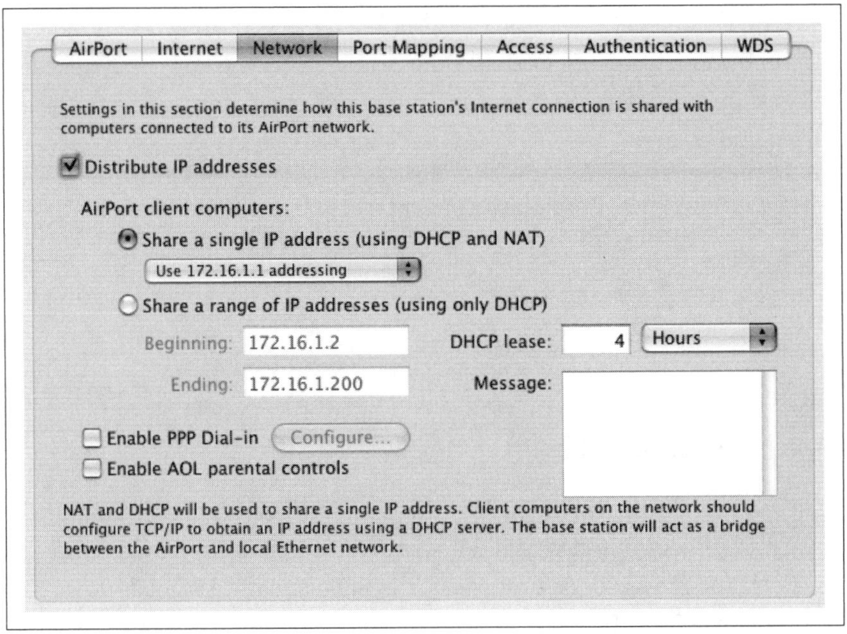

```
AirPort    Internet    Network    Port Mapping    Access    Authentication    WDS

Settings in this section determine how this base station's Internet connection is shared with
computers connected to its AirPort network.

☑ Distribute IP addresses

   AirPort client computers:
      ⦿ Share a single IP address (using DHCP and NAT)
         [ Use 172.16.1.1 addressing        ◆]
      ○ Share a range of IP addresses (using only DHCP)

      Beginning: [ 172.16.1.2 ]        DHCP lease:   [   4 ] [ Hours    ◆]

         Ending: [ 172.16.1.200 ]         Message:  [                      ]
                                                     [                      ]
   ☐ Enable PPP Dial-in  ( Configure... )            [                      ]
   ☐ Enable AOL parental controls                    [                      ]

   NAT and DHCP will be used to share a single IP address. Client computers on the network should
   configure TCP/IP to obtain an IP address using a DHCP server. The base station will act as a bridge
   between the AirPort and local Ethernet network.
```

Figure 3-25. Network tab

- The "Share a range of IP addresses (using only DHCP)" setting turns off Network Address Translation (NAT) and should only be used if you are prepared to have your wireless clients use a specific range of IP addresses that have been assigned by a network administrator.

- "Enable PPP Dial-in" will cause the base station's modem to answer telephone calls. This enables you to dial into the wireless network using a modem. Apple recommends that you use this feature with a dedicated telephone line. If you enable this setting, you'll need to use the Configure button to set up a username and password for the base station.

- The "DHCP lease" setting controls the amount of time a dynamic IP address will be valid for a computer on the wireless network. The default lease time is four hours.

Port Mapping Tab

The Port Mapping tab allows you to use a wireless client as a web, FTP, or AppleShare server. This ensures that requests are properly routed to the server. In order to use port mapping, you must configure TCP/IP manually on the computer that is running the server (so that it has a permanent IP address).

To set up port mapping, follow these steps:

1. On the Port Mapping tab, click the Add button. The Port sheet appears, as shown in Figure 3-26.

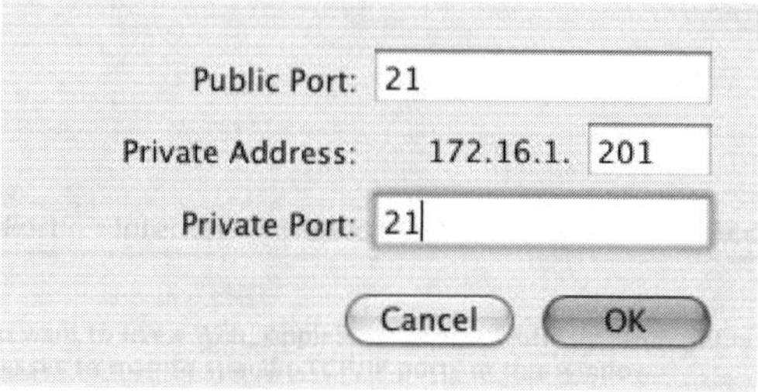

Figure 3-26. Setting port mapping

2. Enter the Public Port, which is the port number that other computers will use to access the server.

3. Enter the Private IP Address, which is the manually assigned, private IP address of the server.

4. Enter the Private Port, which is the port that will be used on the server to provide the service. In most cases, it can be the same number as the public port.

5. Click OK. The new port assignment will appear in the Port Mapping screen, as shown in Figure 3-27.

Access Tab

This tab lets you restrict access to your base station by the MAC (Media Access Control) address of the client. You'll find further discussion in Chapter 5, in the "MAC Address Filtering" section.

Authentication Tab

This tab handles setting up your base station to support centrally managed user authentication using a RADIUS server. This is discussed in depth in Chapter 5, in the "RADIUS and the AirPort Base Station" section.

WDS Tab

The WDS tab allows you to set up the AirPort Extreme Base Station as part of a Wireless Distribution System. This allows you to extend the range of

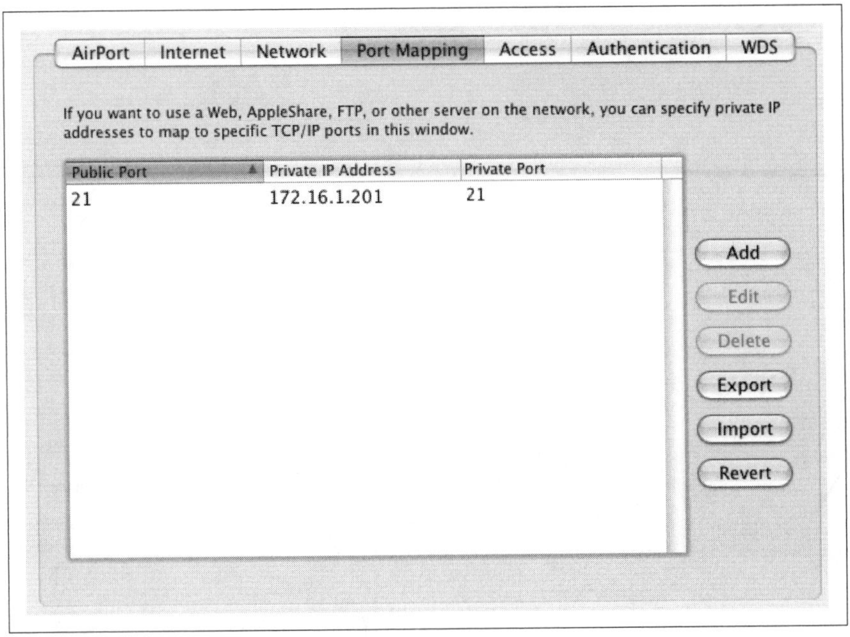

AirPort	Internet	Network	Port Mapping	Access	Authentication	WDS

If you want to use a Web, AppleShare, FTP, or other server on the network, you can specify private IP addresses to map to specific TCP/IP ports in this window.

Public Port ▲	Private IP Address	Private Port
21	172.16.1.201	21

Add

Edit

Delete

Export

Import

Revert

Figure 3-27. The Port Mapping tab

your AirPort wireless network by using multiple AirPort Extreme Base Stations. There are three possible components to a WDS:

- A *main base station* is connected to the Internet and shares its Internet connection with remote and relay base stations.

- A *remote base station* shares the main base station's Internet connection.

- A *relay base station* shares the main base station's Internet connection and passes on the connection to other remote or relay base stations.

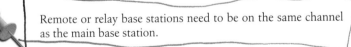

Remote or relay base stations need to be on the same channel as the main base station.

The remote and relay base stations act as wireless bridges to the main base station, as illustrated in Figure 3-28. By using a WDS, you can share a single high-speed Internet connection over a much wider area, such as in a school or office, breaking the 150-foot effective range of a single AirPort Extreme Base Station. A main base station can support up to four remote base stations and one relay base station in a WDS.

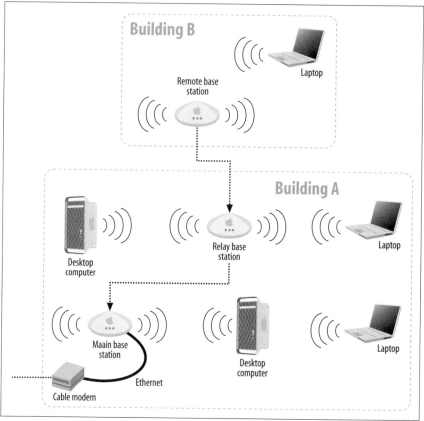

Figure 3-28. Diagram of a WDS

To set up a WDS, follow these steps:

1. Begin by using the AirPort Admin Utility to configure the main base station (the one that has the high-speed Internet connection).

2. Click Show All Settings, then click the WDS tab, shown in Figure 3-29.

3. Select "Enable this base station as a WDS," then choose "main base station" from the pop-up menu.

4. Click the Plus button to scan for other base stations that are in range of the main base station. A sheet will appear with the found base stations. Select the one you want, as shown in Figure 3-30, then click OK.

   If you want to set up the remote base station manually, deselect "Auto configure as a WDS remote base station."

5. Click Update at the bottom of the AirPort Admin Utility window to save your changes.

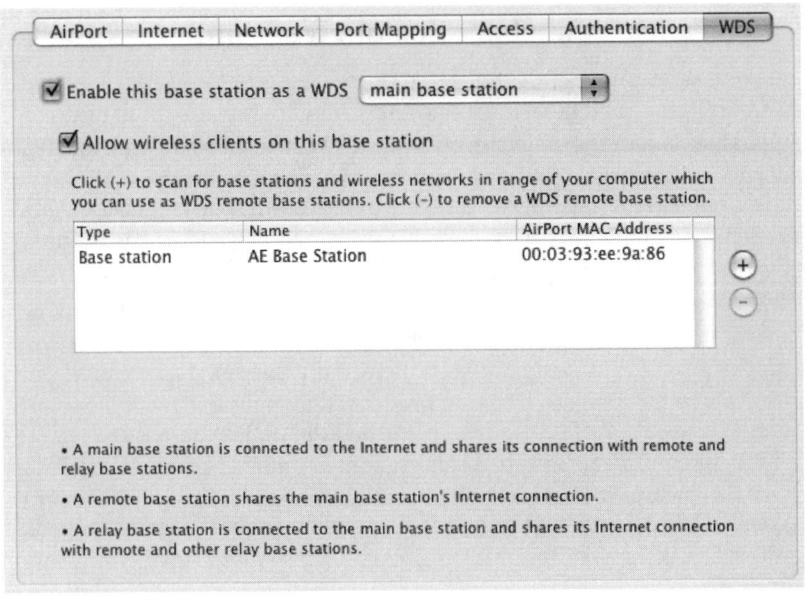

Figure 3-29. WDS tab

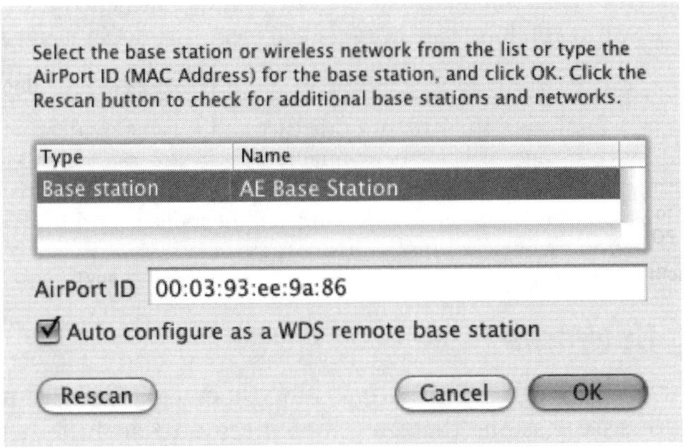

Figure 3-30. Selecting the remote base station

A Cheaper Remote WDS Unit

Because WDS is part of the IEEE 802.11 standard, it is being added to hardware from several different manufacturers (though because those manufacturers have not tested for interoperability, WDS-enabled boxes from different manufacturers may not work together). If you want to set up a WDS, you could purchase several AirPort Extreme Base Stations, but at $200 each (you probably wouldn't want the more expensive model as a remote base station), the costs can quickly mount up.

The Buffalo WLA-G54C AirStation 54 Mbps Compact Repeater Bridge, shown in Figure 3-31, is an inexpensive ($99) 802.11g wireless bridge that supports WDS and can work with the AirPort Extreme Base Station as a remote base station. You'll have to configure the Apple unit as the main base station using the AirPort Admin Utility, and the Buffalo unit as the remote base station, using its web-based configuration utility. The WLA-G54C can even accept an external antenna for improved reception. And at half the price of an AirPort Extreme Base Station, it makes a lot of sense to use it as a remote WDS station.

There is an alternative method to extend your network wirelessly if you have base station equipment that doesn't support WDS and you want to add a wireless segment to an Ethernet network. Look to a wireless bridge product such as the Linksys WET54G. It plugs into Ethernet and acts as a wireless-to-wired bridge. It can't be configured as an access point, however, and it costs $150, so as solutions go, the WET54G isn't as cost-effective as just buying an inexpensive bridge/base station.

Roaming Networks

A WDS extends your wireless network, but you can get similar functionality with multiple base stations that are all connected to an Ethernet network. This creates a single wireless network, called a *roaming network*. Roaming networks use the same Network Name (SSID) and password for all of the base stations on the network, allowing clients to move freely between the coverage areas of each base station. One benefit of a roaming network is that you can use more than five base stations (you're limited to five in a WDS) to create your wireless network and extend your wireless network's coverage.

Figure 3-31. The Buffalo WLA-G54C wireless bridge/access point

A roaming network has one DHCP server and cannot use NAT, so you'll need to assign a range of IP addresses for the DHCP server to hand out to the wireless clients.

To set up a roaming network, follow these steps:

1. Connect all of the base stations to the same subnet on your Ethernet network and use the AirPort Admin Utility to give them all the same Network Name and password.

2. On the base station that you've selected to be the DHCP server, go to the Network tab of the AirPort Admin Utility.

3. Select "Share a range of IP addresses (using only DHCP)," then enter the beginning and ending range of IP addresses that you want to use for the wireless network (if necessary, discuss what address block to use with your network administrator), as shown in Figure 3-32.

Share a range of IP addresses (using only DHCP)	
Beginning: 172.16.1.100	DHCP lease:
Ending: 172.16.1.200	Message:

Figure 3-32. Setting an IP address range

4. Click Update to save your configuration changes on the base station that is the DHCP server.

5. Use the AirPort Admin Utility to turn off Internet sharing on all the other base stations by deselecting "Distribute IP addresses" on those base stations.

Internet Sharing (Software Base Stations)

One of the nicest things about Mac OS X and AirPort is that you don't need a base station to share an Internet connection wirelessly. When we travel, both of us bring our PowerBooks. One of us hooks up to the hotel's broadband Internet connection with an Ethernet cable and shares that connection with the other PowerBook via AirPort. No more fighting over the broadband connection when we're on the road!

When using Internet Sharing in Mac OS X, you will typically share your connection between two different network ports. For example, you can share the Ethernet connection with computers using AirPort, as in the next example. This was called a *software base station* in previous versions of the AirPort software.

On more than one occasion, we've looked in the AirPort menu when we're in a hotel room or at a conference and found someone else's Internet sharing wireless network. If they have not password-protected the network, you can use their connection (though it might not be that polite to use bandwidth another person has paid for without their knowledge).

To set up Internet Sharing, follow these steps:

1. Connect the computer that will be sharing its connection to the high-speed connection.

2. Choose Apple → System Preferences.

3. Click Sharing.

4. Click the Internet tab. The Internet Sharing screen appears, as shown in Figure 3-33.

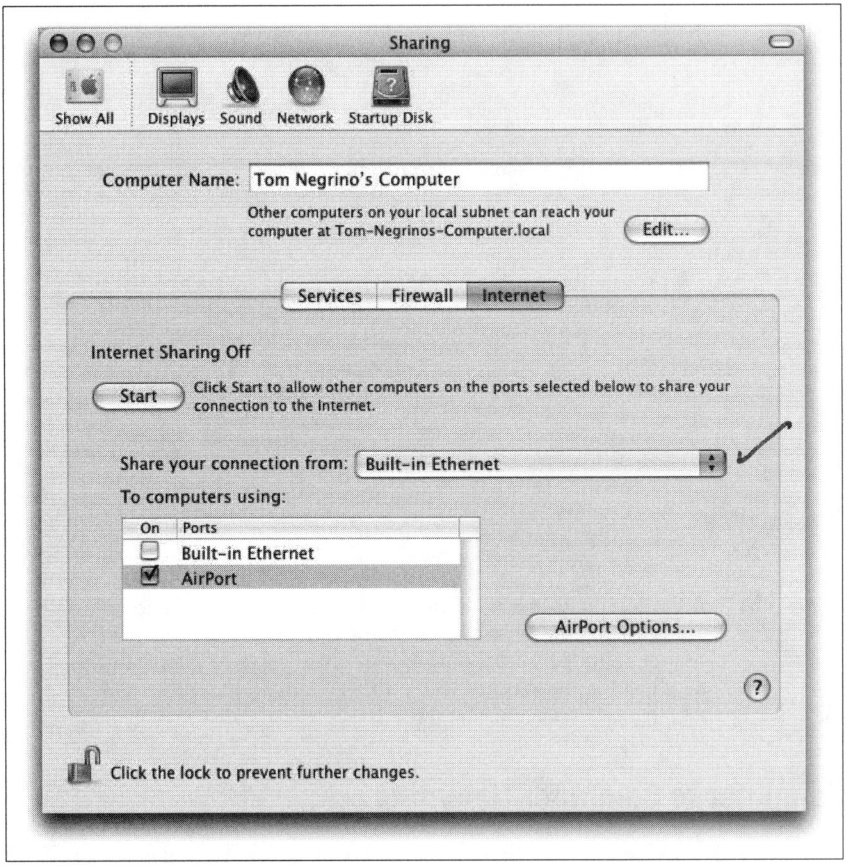

Figure 3-33. The Internet Sharing screen

5. From the "Share your connection from" pop-up menu, choose Built-in Ethernet.

6. In the "To computers using" list, click the On checkbox next to Air-Port. The Start button will be enabled.

7. (Optional) Click AirPort Options. The Options sheet appears, as shown in Figure 3-34.

8. (Optional) If you want, set the channel for wireless sharing and turn on WEP, click "Enable encryption (using WEP)" and enter the password twice. You can choose to use a 40-bit or 128-bit WEP key; the higher number is marginally more secure. Click OK to close the Options sheet.

9. Click Start. An alert sheet will appear, asking if you really want to turn on Internet Sharing.

10. Show the computer who's the boss by clicking Start. After a moment, Internet Sharing turns on.

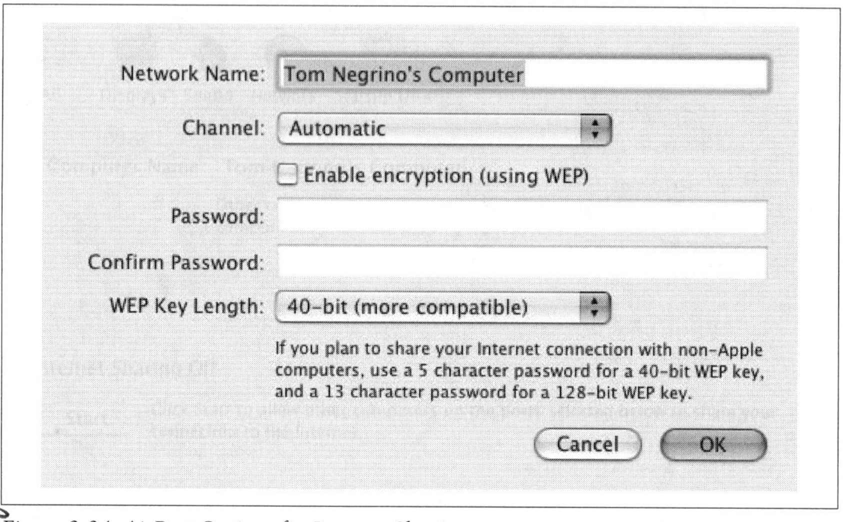

Figure 3-34. AirPort Options for Internet Sharing

If the computer that is sharing the Internet connection goes to sleep, the connection will be lost and you will have to turn Internet Sharing back on again. Prevent this from happening by adjusting the settings in the Energy Saver panel of System Preferences to delay sleep mode.

Computer to Computer Networks

When needed, you can connect your Mac via Wi-Fi directly to another computer wirelessly. Most companies call this an ad-hoc connection, but Apple calls it a Computer to Computer Network. You can use this kind of connection to transfer files between computers, to use iChat AV, or to play multiplayer games without the bother of wires. As befits a connection that you're setting up on the fly, it's easy to set up a Computer to Computer Network. Follow these steps:

1. From the AirPort menu, choose "Create network." The Computer to Computer dialog will appear, as shown in Figure 3-35.

2. Enter a name for the network. By default, it will be your computer's name as listed in the Sharing panel of System Preferences.

3. Choose the channel for the network from the pop-up menu, or leave it on Automatic, which uses channel 11.

4. If you want to enable WEP for the connection, click Show Options. The window expands to show the WEP settings.

5. Select "Enable encryption (using WEP)."

```
┌─────────────────────────────────────────────────────────┐
│         ╭──────────────────────────────────────────╮      │
│         │           Computer to Computer           │      │
│         ├──────────────────────────────────────────┤      │
│         │  Please enter the following information to create a  │
│         │  Computer to Computer Network:           │      │
│         │                                          │      │
│         │    Name: │ Tom Negrino's Computer      │ │      │
│         │                                          │      │
│         │  Channel: │ Automatic (11)          │ ⬍ │      │
│         │                                          │      │
│         │        ☑ Enable encryption (using WEP)   │      │
│         │                                          │      │
│         │  Password: │ ••••••••••••            │    │      │
│         │                                          │      │
│         │   Confirm: │ ••••••••••••            │    │      │
│         │                                          │      │
│         │   WEP key: │ 128-bit                │ ⬍ │      │
│         │                                          │      │
│         │  The WEP key must be entered as exactly 13 ASCII  │
│         │  characters or 26 HEX digits.            │      │
│         │                                          │      │
│         │  ( Hide Options )    ( Cancel )  ( OK )  │      │
│         ╰──────────────────────────────────────────╯      │
└─────────────────────────────────────────────────────────┘
```

Figure 3-35. Computer to Computer dialog, displaying WEP options

6. From the WEP key pop-up menu, choose the bit length for the WEP encryption.

 If you choose the 40-bit key length, your password must be exactly 5 characters long. If you choose the 128-bit key length, your password must be exactly 13 characters long.

7. Enter the password, then enter it again to confirm you typed it correctly.

8. Click OK. The Computer to Computer Network will start.

9. To join your Computer to Computer Network, other Macs should select the network name from their AirPort menus. Windows or Linux users should use their regular methods of connecting to a wireless network.

Third-Party Base Stations

Of course, Apple isn't the only manufacturer making base stations. You can easily find dozens of base stations from many different companies. But should you use them in your wireless network? In a Windows-centric world, will base stations from other manufacturers play well with Macs?

The answer to both questions is "Yes, mostly." The main benefit to using a third-party base station is a lower cost to set up your wireless network: if you shop around, you can find 802.11g base stations selling for under $100, and 802.11b units for under $70. Given the price differential, it makes sense to spend a few more dollars and get the 802.11g units, even if you currently have only 802.11b clients.

Another big benefit to non-Apple gear are features that Apple doesn't offer. The most obvious is that there are many units that include both a wireless router and an Ethernet switch. This is a perfect solution for many people: they have two or three or four Ethernet devices that need to get on the Internet, plus they want wireless networking. For example, let's look at Dori's setup in her office. She has a PowerBook G4, which is her main computer, plus a PC minitower under the desk. Most of the time she runs her Power-Book in a dock, using Ethernet to connect through a router to her DSL connection to the Internet. The PC also needs Net access, and her printer requires an Ethernet connection, too. Just to make things interesting, when the weather's nice, she likes to sit outside in the garden and read email and surf the Web wirelessly. When Tom brings his PowerBook to her office, he sometimes needs to send files to Dori's computer, and who wants to snake Ethernet cables across the office?

The solution was to get a wireless router with an Ethernet switch, in this case the Netgear MR814, which is an 802.11b base station with a 4-port Ethernet switch. All of her wired gear is plugged into the switch ports, and the router's WAN port is connected to the DSL modem. If she had bought an AirPort Base Station, she would have also had to invest in a separate Ethernet hub or switch to connect all her gear. With the solution she chose, she saved money *and* clutter.

Many third-party base stations other than the higher-end AirPort Extreme Base Station support external antennas, and there are often more and cheaper antenna choices available for them.

The Not-So-Good News

As enticing as it may seem to buy non-Apple base stations, there are some significant drawbacks. Software is the biggest problem. Most base stations, including the AirPort Base Stations, contain software in semi-permanent memory, called *firmware*. This software runs the base station, and can be updated as new features are introduced. Sometimes these firmware updates are very important. For example, Apple released the AirPort Extreme Base Station in January 2003, months before the 802.11g standard was finalized by the IEEE. The initially shipping units were compatible with a draft of the 802.11g standard. When the standard was finalized in the summer of 2003,

Apple updated the AirPort Admin Utility, which downloads a firmware update to the AirPort Extreme Base Station to make it compliant with the final 802.11g standard. Firmware updaters are also often released to fix bugs.

The problem is that most third party manufacturers make their firmware updater available only as Windows programs. That's fine if you have a PC on your network (or if you own a copy of Microsoft Virtual PC), but if you don't, you may not be able to update your base station's firmware. One possibility is to purchase from companies that do have Mac OS X firmware updaters (or that use a web browser to apply firmware updates), including D-Link (*http://www.dlink.com*), Netgear (*http://www.netgear.com*), Mac-Sense (*http://www.macsense.com*), or Asante (*http://www.asante.com*).

Configuring Third-Party Base Stations

Apple's AirPort Base Stations use the AirPort Admin Utility for configuration, but most other manufacturers prefer a web browser–based configuration program. These base stations let you use your favorite browser to change their settings.

When you connect to these base stations (using a URL that you find in the product's user manual), you're presented with an interface to the base station's settings. Figure 3-36 shows the configuration utility for the Linksys WRT54G wireless router, accessed by the Safari browser. Other manufacturers' utilities are similar. Follow the instructions in the user manuals to configure your base station.

> If you have a base station that uses a web browser–based interface, and you use Safari as your browser, make sure that you have turned off the Safari → Block Pop-Up Windows feature while you are configuring the base station. Some manufacturers use a pop-up window to confirm parts of the configuration process—if you have pop-ups blocked, you may think (as we did until we figured it out) that configuration wasn't working, when it really was.

Here are some tips that will make configuring your third-party base stations easier:

- Save a PDF of the user manual on your computer's hard disk. Sooner or later you'll need it. If you need it when you're having problems with the base station, you might not have Net access and won't be able to download the user manual from the manufacturer's web site.

- Bookmark the base station's configuration web page in your browser. These devices use numeric addresses, such as *http://192.168.1.1*, and you might not remember the right number.

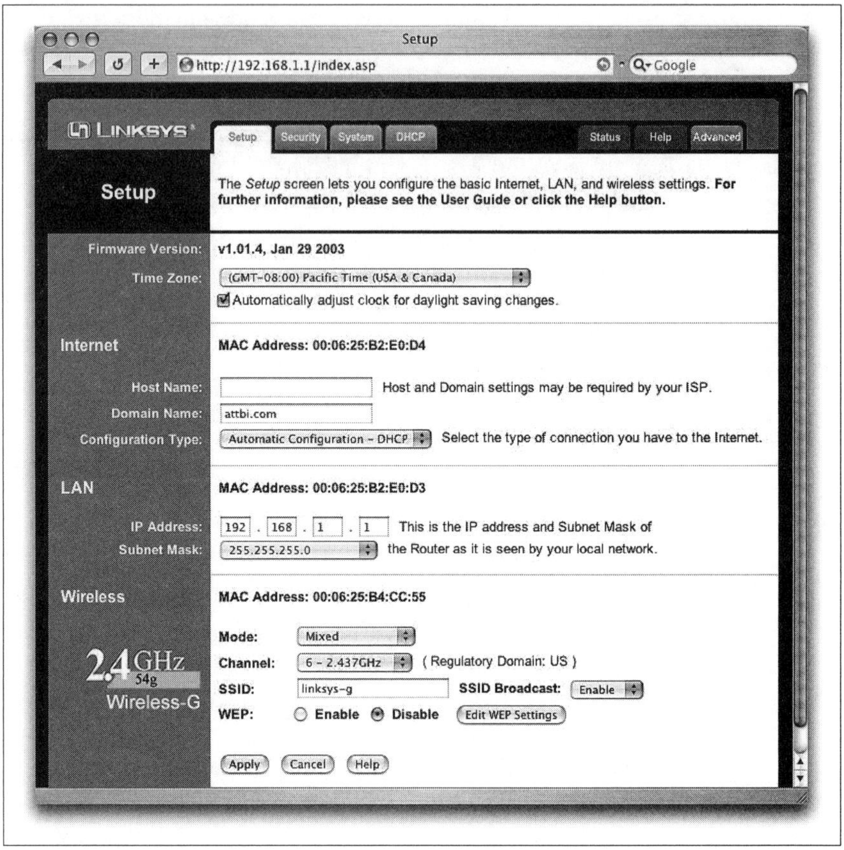

Figure 3-36. The Linksys configuration utility

- Change the base station's default SSID, username, and password. You would be appalled at how many base stations are running with the factory settings, virtually begging mischief makers to reconfigure them on the sly.

- Once you change them, keep track of the base station's username and password.

- If you do need to reconfigure the device, and you can't remember the password, you can reset the base station, which reloads the factory settings, including the default username and password. You'll lose any custom settings you made, however.

Wi-Fi on the Road

Now that you've learned what you can do with Wi-Fi, it's time to find Net access on the road. One of the biggest benefits of equipping your Mac with Wi-Fi is being able to take advantage of the wireless access that's available outside your home or office.

The major difference between using Wi-Fi in your home or office and using it on the road is that you can't simply open up your laptop and find your usual broadband network. Instead, you'll need to track down connectivity, and helping you to do that is the goal of this chapter.

One word of warning: no one has yet figured out how to consistently make money selling wireless connectivity to travelers. It sometimes seems as though even-numbered days of the month are devoted to press releases from new wireless access companies announcing their arrival, while odd-numbered days mark the demise of other companies. In other words, while this book mentions a number of companies that are currently alive and kicking, remember that the Wi-Fi access market is constantly changing. By the time you read this, the business models of the companies we mention may be different, or they may even have gone out of business.

Finding a Hotspot

A *hotspot* is, simply enough, any place that allows you to get wireless connectivity via Wi-Fi. The hardest part of getting connected on the road can sometimes be finding a hotspot, and the simplest way to get connected is to find a for-fee public hotspot.

Public Networks

There are a number of web sites that can help you find public networks:

http://www.80211hotspots.com/
http://www.wifinder.com/
http://www.hotspots.cc/

You'll occasionally get different results from each of these lists, although they all attempt to be comprehensive. When we searched each site for our nearby city of Santa Rosa, California, all showed the same six T-Mobile HotSpot locations at various Starbucks. A check of the T-Mobile HotSpot site (*http://locations.hotspot.t-mobile.com/*), however, showed seven Starbucks hotspots, and checking the Intel Centrino Hotspot Finder (*http://www.intel.com/products/mobiletechnology/hotspots/finder.htm*) showed an eighth T-Mobile HotSpot location (at a Borders Books and Music) that T-Mobile HotSpot didn't even appear to know about.

Finding the one independent hotspot required checking Surf and Sip (the wireless access provider for that hotspot, *http://www.surfandsip.com/*) or Boingo Wireless at *http://www.boingo.com/*, an aggregator that includes Surf and Sip; more about aggregators later in this chapter).

Wi-Fi ZONE (*http://www.wi-fizone.org*) is a new Wi-Fi Alliance project that aims to certify hotspots in the same way that the alliance currently certifies Wi-Fi equipment. When their Wi-Fi Finder is up and running, they plan to provide a worldwide database of all certified hotspots, which will allow users to look in one place for hotspots instead of several. In addition, you'll be ensured that the place selling you bandwidth has met certain criteria, including security and support. Figure 4-1 shows the Wi-Fi ZONE logo.

Figure 4-1. After the service is launched, this logo will signify a Wi-Fi ZONE certified hotspot

Fee-based wireless ISPs. Wireless ISPs (referred to as WISPs), generally contract with local venues such as cafés, coffee houses, hotels, and airports. The venue gets a cut of the proceeds, and the WISP maintains the network and handles the billing.

WISPs range in size from T-Mobile HotSpot (*http://www.t-mobile.com/hotspot/*), which at this writing has more than 2,700 locations across the United States, to Cafe.com (*http://www.cafe.com/*), which has just a dozen or so locations in southern California.

T-Mobile HotSpot is commonly found in Starbucks and at Borders Books and Music locations, which means that they are nearly ubiquitous across the U.S. In airports, they have contracts for wireless service at airport club lounges run by American, Delta, and United. When this chapter was written (October 2003), T-Mobile HotSpot offered four different payment plans:

- Unlimited National Annual subscription plan: $30 per month with an annual contract ($20 a month if you are a T-Mobile cellular customer).
- Unlimited National month-to-month subscription plan: $40 per month, payable month-to-month with a minimum one-month commitment requirement.
- Wi-Fi DayPass: $10 for unlimited minutes during a 24-hour period.
- Wi-Fi Metered Plan: $0.10 per minute, with a minimum user session of 60 minutes per login.

All of these plans include unlimited amounts of data transfer, a recent and welcome change. Because your usage is not metered by the amount of files that you transfer, you can upload or download everything you need without worrying that you will be charged extra for heavy use.

> If you're having problems using T-Mobile HotSpot service, it might be because you're using Mozilla or Safari as your web browser. It's not a problem with the browser; it's that you probably have those browsers' ability to block pop-up windows turned on. T-Mobile HotSpot uses a pop-up window that appears when you log on, and you need to use it to log out of the network when you're done. If you block pop-ups, you won't get the log out window. Just turn the pop-up blocker off when you log in, and things should go fine.

Signing up for most WISPs is simple: take your laptop to the hotspot and launch your web browser. As soon as you try to go to any web site, you'll automatically be taken to the WISP's signup or login page, referred to as a *captive portal* (shown in Figure 4-2). This is where you'll be prompted to sign up and enter your credit card information.

Figure 4-2. A captive portal page from a local Starbucks equipped with T-Mobile HotSpot service

When Dori first started using hotspots on the road, she frequently wanted to send and receive email. She often found herself beating her head against the wall trying to figure out why it wasn't working. The reason was that because she wasn't using web-based email, she never reached the captive portal page—after all, the web browser displays it. So if you're having trouble sending or receiving email at a hotspot, try launching your browser. If a captive portal page appears, you most likely have the same problem. Just sign up or log in, and your email should work fine. But until you pass through the captive portal, your email ports are blocked.

If you're looking for a wireless ISP in your neck of the woods, a good place to start is BrainHeart Capital's mammoth worldwide list of WISPs (*http://www.brainheart.com/main.asp?pageID=020503*).

Community networks. Another type of WISP is the community network, generally founded by a group of people who figure that they've already got wireless access set up, so why not share it? If you've been unwired for a while and don't understand why there aren't just hotspots available everywhere you want to connect, you'll fit right in with these folks.

Your best bet for finding a community network is in one of the larger cities on the west coast. If you live in Portland, Oregon or Seattle, Washington, you're in luck. They're not the only places with community networks though, so it can be worth checking out Portland's Personal Telco's list of wireless communities (*http://www.personaltelco.net/index.cgi/WirelessCommunities*) to see if there might be one available where you're traveling.

Even if a network is community-based, you may still have to either sign up or pay for access to that network (although it is frequently free). As before, find a network via AirPort, launch a browser, and see if you're presented with a captive portal. If you are, read the rules and log in; if not, you're online.

If you're intrigued and thinking about setting up your own community network, you'll want to take a look at Rob Flickenger's book, *Building Wireless Community Networks*, Second Edition (O'Reilly). You might also want to check out NoCat.net (*http://www.nocat.net/*), makers of Linux-based NoCatAuth, a software application that handles registration and authentication for your potential wireless users. Another good source for community network information is the web site of one of the largest, Seattle Wireless (*http://www.seattlewireless.net/*).

The fun thing about wireless community networks is that you can get them started for a surprisingly small amount of money, certainly under $500. A few inexpensive base stations, some antennas to beam signals between the base stations, a bit of ingenuity, and you're on your way. An old PC running Linux rounds out the system if you want to run the NoCat.net authorization software. Otherwise, you can just run a completely open network.

Aggregators. If you're frequently on the road, it can be a pain to have to deal with multiple WISPs. The one at your hotel probably isn't the same as the one at the airport, and each WISP charges their own access fee and has their own signup and login process. Solving this problem is where an *aggregator* comes in.

The theory behind aggregators is that you can set up an account with a single company—the aggregator—who has already cut deals with multiple WISPs, allowing you to use all of their locations. The aggregator handles billing you, and you get a single signup process. The largest and best known

WISP aggregator is Boingo Wireless, who contracts with everyone from the small Surf and Sip (mentioned earlier in the "Public Networks" section) to the large Wayport (*http://www.wayport.com/*), which has numerous hotspots in airports and hotels.

Boingo provides software that will not only connect you to their affiliated hotspots, but will also sniff them out for you. Because it's one company handling the support and billing, you don't need to keep changing your settings—the Boingo software handles it all for you.

Boingo's current pricing structure has two individual options, which each charge based on what they refer to as "Connect Days." A Connect Day lasts 24 hours, starting from whenever you first get onto any hotspot on their system. However, that day applies only to usage at that same hotspot, so spending an hour online at the airport and another hour online in your hotel room counts as two Connect Days. Their two individual plan options are:

- Boingo As-You-Go: This pay as you go plan has an initial charge of $8, which includes two Connect Days that can be used at any time. Additional usage is another $8 per Connect Day.

- Boingo Unlimited: All-you-can-eat connectivity for $22/month for the first year, climbing to $40/month thereafter.

The bad news? As of this writing, Boingo's software does not support Macs; it only works with Windows and some PocketPC devices. Mac support "soon" has been promised since day one, but shipping always seems to be sometime next quarter. At last check, Boingo said that Mac OS X support would arrive in late 2003, but we're writing this in October and it isn't here yet. We'll be happy when they finally ship their software, but we're not holding our breath.

Another aggregator is iPass (*http://www.ipass.com/*), which already has Mac OS X software for their service. The company is focused more on selling its services to businesses than to end users who want quick wireless access, but that could change: iPass has cut a preliminary deal with Cometa Networks, a joint venture of AT&T, Intel, and IBM that promises to deploy more than 20,000 hotspots covering the 50 largest cities in the United States.

Private open networks. Remember that screenshot of the MacStumbler application (*http://www.macstumbler.com/*) back in Chapter 1 that showed several networks that were findable from the comfort of someone's Manhattan living room?

It's possible (although ethically questionable) to piggyback on anyone else's wireless network if they haven't turned on security.

In Figure 4-3, MacStumbler shows two open networks, both of which are completely available to anyone within range who wants to use them (the key is that it says No in the WEP column). Assuming that you have the AirPort icon in your menu bar, all you have to do is choose the SSID of the AP you want from the pull-down menu, and you're on.

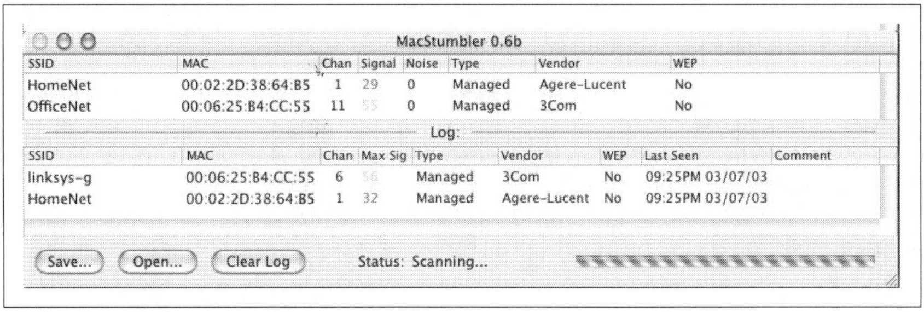

SSID	MAC	Chan	Signal	Noise	Type	Vendor	WEP
HomeNet	00:02:2D:38:64:B5	1	29	0	Managed	Agere–Lucent	No
OfficeNet	00:06:25:B4:CC:55	11	55	0	Managed	3Com	No

Log:

SSID	MAC	Chan	Max Sig	Type	Vendor	WEP	Last Seen	Comment
linksys–g	00:06:25:B4:CC:55	6	56	Managed	3Com	No	09:25PM 03/07/03	
HomeNet	00:02:2D:38:64:B5	1	32	Managed	Agere–Lucent	No	09:25PM 03/07/03	

Save...   Open...   Clear Log   Status: Scanning...

Figure 4-3. MacStumbler finding open networks

It's possible to see networks on the road that appear open (because WEP is not turned on) but that are still inaccessible to casual use. That may be because the AP is using MAC address control for its wireless clients. MAC, in this case, doesn't refer to Macintosh, but to the hardware address of the Wi-Fi cards in the client computers. This MAC address is unique for each Ethernet device on the network. Most APs allow you to filter access to the wireless network based on a list of MAC addresses. The AP can be set to allow access to just those MAC addresses that are listed, or to allow access to any client except the listed addresses.

Another access scheme for protecting wireless networks is known as 802.1x. It's a protocol that allows only one TCP/IP port on the wireless network to be accessed by a wireless client. That port is used only for authorization of the client; if the client passes authorization, they get access to other ports on the network (subject to the limits set by the network administrator) so that they can now use the network for email, web access, etc.

If you leave your network unprotected by any sort of access control, many people will assume that it is a public network, or at least that you don't mind if they use your network freely. The moral of this story: if you don't want people you haven't specifically authorized to ever use your network, turn WEP on, or use MAC address control. Chapter 5 covers the various methods you can use to protect both your Mac and your AP from others.

Wondering how to find the MAC address for your computer? Open System Preferences, then click on the Network icon. Make sure that the Show menu is displaying either Built-in Ethernet or AirPort. If it's Ethernet, choose the "Ethernet" tab, and the MAC address will be displayed as the Ethernet ID, as shown in Figure 4-4. If it's AirPort, choose the "AirPort" tab and the MAC address will be displayed as the AirPort ID.

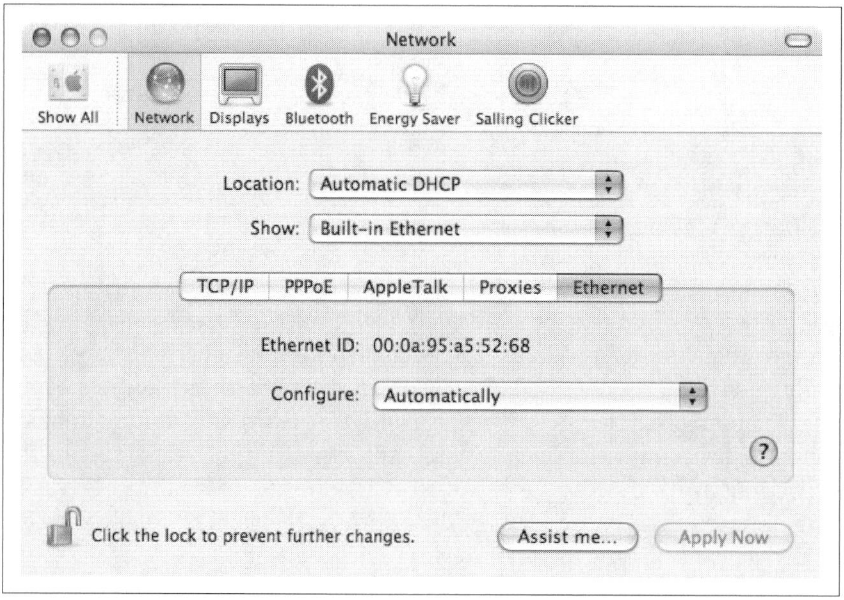

Figure 4-4. You can locate your computer's MAC address in the Network pane of System Preferences

Wardialing, wardriving, warwalking, and warchalking. The 1983 movie *War Games* gave rise to the phrase "wardialing," which referred to the lead character's hobby of setting up his modem to dial numbers until it found a computer to connect with. In the 20 years since, wardialing has given way to wardriving, warwalking, warchalking, and massive confusion about the prefix "war." Too many lazy journalists have assumed that if a word starts with "war," it must refer to an attack. In response, some people have attempted to create a back-formation that "war" stands for "Wireless Access Reconnaissance." It's a cute renaming, but as it hasn't caught on, the confusion and bad reputation persist.

As you might guess from the names, wardriving consists of driving in a car, running MacStumbler (or its equivalent for the OS being used), and waiting to see what wireless networks show up. Warwalking is similar, but on foot instead of by car. Depending on where you are, the number of hotspots you find with either method can vary from few to none (in our neighborhood in the boondocks) to jam-packed (in major techie cities such as San Francisco, New York, and Seattle).

Warchalking came about after Matt Jones, a designer and wireless aficionado from the United Kingdom, decided that it was a pain to always walk around with his laptop open. He figured it'd be simpler if warwalkers wrote a symbol in chalk (see Figure 4-5) on the wall nearest the signal to describe the type of AP available.

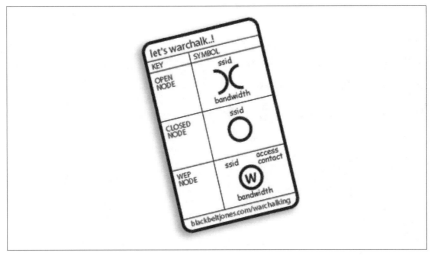

Figure 4-5. Warchalking symbols

He borrowed the idea from hobo chalk language, in which hobos would write a code by someone's door advising future hobo visitors as to whether that house was worth a visit. In this case, the chalk marks signify whether the AP is open or closed, the password (if available), and how fast the bandwidth is. See *http://www.warchalking.org/* to learn more about warchalking. While there was a lot of talk about this method when it was first introduced, warchalking marks are usually made by people advertising their own APs—it's rare to come across one in the wild. Consequently, we still haven't left the days of walking around with a laptop.

That's not to say that MacStumbler doesn't have any uses besides the sneaky ones. It's a great help if you're trying to figure out where to position your home AP, as just moving it a few feet often extends the range dramatically (which can be very helpful if you still have an old TiBook). In addition, before the introduction of Rendezvous and iChat, MacStumbler was used as an early type of chatting system. At the July 2002 Macworld Expo keynote, audience members changed their local network names continuously as a way of providing real-time commentary on the keynote. Anyone with a copy of MacStumbler could read along with the ad-hoc chat and see such edifying comments as "No AirPort access? WEAK!", "Typical Apple PR disaster", and "Newsflash: Jobs to wear black" (along with many less printable examples).

 Our personal recommendation for finding free bandwidth while traveling: look for a local Apple store (*http://www.apple.com/retail/*). They always have plenty of bandwidth, and they're happy when Mac users come into the store and demonstrate how useful Wi-Fi really is.

Ethics and Legalities of Open Networks

Open networks are still a gray area in both law and ethics, as no laws have been enacted that control how they should and should not be used. There are any number of opinions as to their legality and ethicality, so you'll have to decide for yourself.

Opening your network

Whether it's legal to open your network to the public, or even to selected friends, depends entirely upon your ISP user agreement. Unfortunately, not every ISP has been clear about sharing access (especially with older agreements), but you can almost always find something on their web site describing usage policy. While some ISPs explicitly allow you to share the wealth, others explicitly ban it. If you're with one of the latter, you'll need to weigh the benefits of opening your network against the chances of being caught.

In any event, if you do choose to make your network open to others, consider giving your network a name that makes your intentions clear. For example, you could name your network something like "Public HomeNet," or "Use My Bandwidth, Please." You can also set up a Mac with a web server on your local network that is Rendezvous-enabled, so that visitors using Safari can easily find it. On that local site, you can include information about your wireless network, and a bit about you. See Chapter 8 for more information about using web sharing as a billboard for your WLAN.

Using open networks

You're on the road, need access to the Internet, and find an open network where someone hasn't enabled encryption! What do you do?

This is an area on the edges of the legal frontier, and many people disagree about what's proper when it comes to using open (but not explicitly shared) networks. The arguments for and against piggybacking on someone's AP usually come down to analogies: is borrowing bandwidth like listening along with your neighbor while they have their radio on, or is it more like breaking into their apartment while they're out and making copies of their CDs?

Two examples from the front lines:

The World Wide War Drive group (*http://www.worldwidewardrive.org/*) organizes an irregular national search for unsecured APs, with the goal of teaching owners how to secure their wireless networks. Their page on ethics specifically requests that participants *not* connect to any of the open hotspots that they find.

On the other side, the legality FAQ at Warchalking.org argues that using open networks is both legal and moral (*http://www.warchalking. org/story/2002/9/22/223831/236*). After all, if the owner doesn't want their network to be used by the public, all they have to do is turn on WEP to make their intent clear.

The jury is still out on this one, and we aren't qualified to give legal advice—you'll have to decide for yourself where you stand.

CHAPTER FIVE

Security

With no physical boundaries, can wireless networks be secure? Can they be locked down sufficiently to satisfy security-conscious users? Because of fundamental flaws in the initial wireless security standard, the answer is complicated. In this chapter, we explain the security issues inherent in the 802.11 family and the various ways you can secure a wireless network.

Secure Wireless Computing

Before we get into the gory details of Wi-Fi LAN security, let us make one thing clear: *Wired Equivalent Privacy (WEP)*, the security protocol used by most 802.11 networks at the time of this writing, is fundamentally flawed. Though we talk about WEP in much more detail later in this chapter, here is a quick rundown of WEP's flaws:

- All users in a wireless network share the same secret key, and a secret key is no longer a secret if more than one person knows it.

- The implementation of WEP makes it very susceptible to attacks by hackers. It is not a matter of whether it can be cracked, but a matter of how soon. The flaws in WEP have been proven both in theory *and* practice.

Although WEP has its flaws, it's worth using to discourage unauthorized users from connecting to your access point. If you need stronger security, you'll have to rely on other techniques to provide it. In the first part of this chapter, we assume that you are connected to a wireless network (with or without WEP), and that you want to securely access the network (even for simple tasks such as surfing the Web or reading your email). There are three ways for you to improve the security of your wireless communications.

Virtual Private Networks (VPN)

A VPN allows you to remotely access a private network as though you were connected to it physically. Moreover, the entire communication channel is protected by encryption. So if you are connected to a VPN server wirelessly, the packets transmitted between your computer and the VPN server (including the access point) are encrypted by the VPN connection, which is much more secure than using WEP. An added bonus is that most VPN solutions have stronger authentication than that available in WEP.

Secure Shell (SSH)

SSH lets you initiate a shell session (similar to Telnet) or exchange files with a remote server, with all information exchanges encrypted. When not using a VPN, SSH is an excellent option for securely connecting to another computer.

Firewalls

If you connect to public networks where your fellow users are unknown and untrusted, a good firewall can provide some degree of security. Mac OS X includes basic firewall capabilities; there are third-party firewall applications available that have more features.

After this, we'll cover the details of Wi-Fi security and the various technologies that are in use (or have been proposed) for securing wireless networks.

Virtual Private Networks

Imagine you are out of the office and need to access a printer or file server on the office network. Unless you dial in to the company's server, it isn't possible for you to access the network resources in the office. Even if you can overlook the slow speed in using a dial-up line, it is not a cheap alternative, especially if you are overseas.

A Virtual Private Network (VPN) allows you to establish a secure, encrypted connection to the office's network, all through a public network such as the Internet. Using a VPN, you can work as though you are connected to your company's network—even if you're out of the office. There are two main types of VPNs:

User-to-Network

This type allows a client to use a VPN to connect to a secure network, such as a corporate intranet. Your Mac communicates with the network as if it were present at that site or on the same network segment.

Network-to-Network

This type connects two networks via a VPN connection. This method effectively combines two disparate networks into one, eliminating the need for a Wide Area Network (WAN). It also reduces the need for the user to do anything to securely access the other network. It's often transparent, and acts as an encrypted bridge between two networks.

Tunneling

Tunneling is the process of encapsulating packets within other packets to protect their integrity and privacy during transit. A tunnel performs such tasks as encryption, authentication, packet forwarding, and masking of IP private addresses. Figure 5-1 shows a tunnel established between two computers through the Internet. Think of a tunnel as a private link between the two computers: whatever one sends is only visible to the other, even though it is sent through a public network like the Internet.

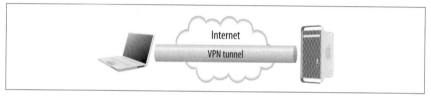

Figure 5-1. A tunnel established between two computers in a VPN

The following section discusses some tunneling protocols available for VPNs.

Accessing a VPN Server

In this section, we will show you how you can connect your Mac securely to your corporate VPN server.

1. Double-click the Internet Connect application located in the */Applications* folder.

2. Select File → New VPN Connection, or click on the VPN icon (see Figure 5-2).

3. Select the kind of VPN connection supported by your host (as shown in Figure 5-3) and click Continue.

4. Enter the server address (check with your administrator for the VPN server address), as well as the account name and password that you use to log on to the VPN server. Enable the "Show VPN status in menu bar" checkbox to display the VPN icon in the menu bar (see Figure 5-4; the icon is located on the left side of the menu bar). Click Connect to connect to the VPN server.

Summary
Summary
USB Bluetooth Modem Adaptor
Internal Modem
AirPort
VPN
AirPort: MyAirPortNetwork
Connected to the Internet via Ethernet

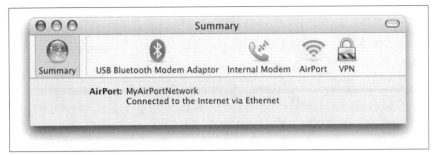

Figure 5-2. Locating the VPN icon in Internet Connect

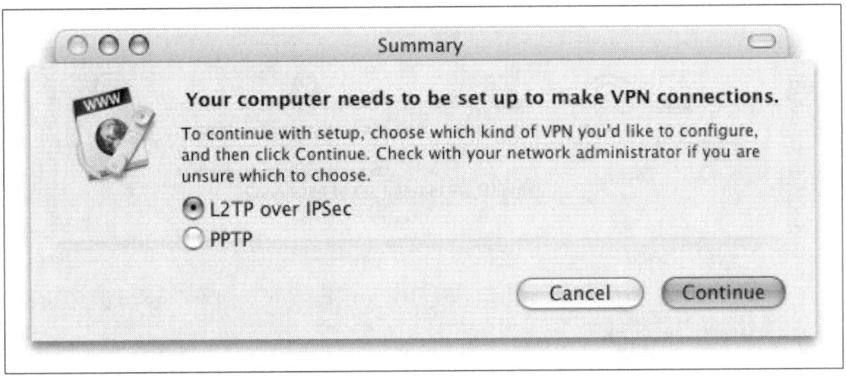

Summary
WWW
Your computer needs to be set up to make VPN connections.
To continue with setup, choose which kind of VPN you'd like to configure, and then click Continue. Check with your network administrator if you are unsure which to choose.
L2TP over IPSec
PPTP
Cancel
Continue

Figure 5-3. Selecting the type of VPN connection supported by your company

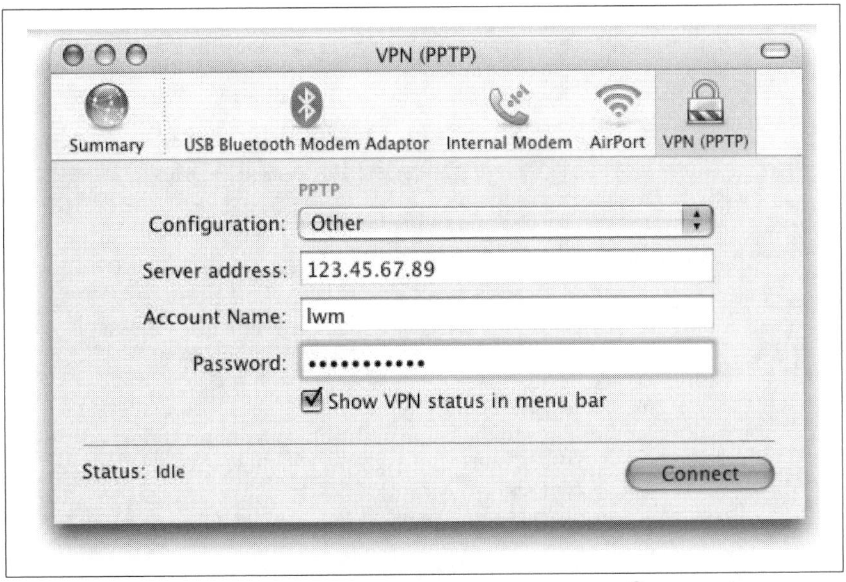

VPN (PPTP)
Summary
USB Bluetooth Modem Adaptor
Internal Modem
AirPort
VPN (PPTP)
PPTP
Configuration: Other
Server address: 123.45.67.89
Account Name: lwm
Password: •••••••••••
Show VPN status in menu bar
Status: Idle
Connect

Figure 5-4. Supplying the login information for the VPN server

5. To configure multiple VPN connections, go to File → New VPN Connection....

6. You can find the newly created VPN connections in System Preferences → Network (see Figure 5-5).

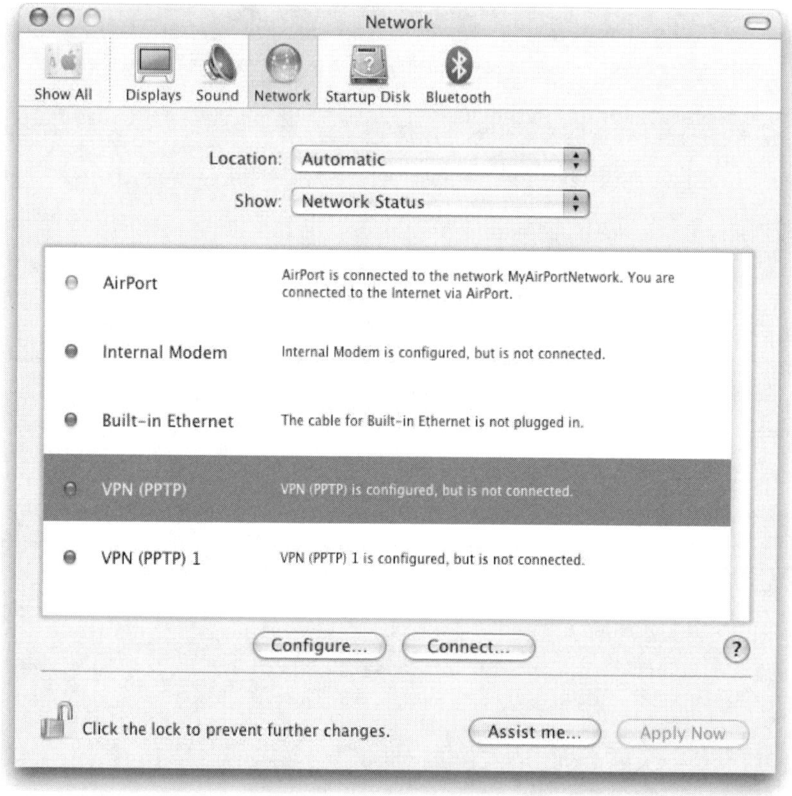

Figure 5-5. The VPN connections as listed in System Preferences

If your company or institution requires the use of a proxy server for Internet access, you'll need to configure your Mac for it, since all Internet traffic will go through the VPN while you are connected (if the remote network does not allow direct connections to the Internet, the only way out is through the proxy). To configure a proxy server, double-click on the VPN connection shown in Figure 5-5, and select the Proxies tab to configure that connection's Proxy server settings.

Secure Shell (SSH)

If you need to connect to Unix or Linux servers, you may be familiar with utilities such as *Telnet* and *FTP*. Telnet lets you connect to a command prompt on a machine over the network. The FTP utility transfers files between your machine and a remote server.

If you are using either Telnet or FTP to connect to a sensitive server, but you aren't using a VPN, you're exposing your password to anyone who can access the network you're connected to (perhaps you're on a public network at a wireless hotspot?), the network where the remote server resides, and any network in between.

> Anonymous FTP, in which you use your email address as a password, is not a concern. This is because, as the name implies, all remote users are treated as anonymous guests, and, if the remote FTP server is configured properly, are accorded no privileges that could be abused.

If the remote server supports it, you can use the SSH protocol to work with a remote machine's command prompt (replacing Telnet) or securely transfer files using *scp* or *sftp* (replacing *rcp(1)* and FTP).

Mac OS X includes an SSH client and server based on OpenSSH (*http://www.openssh.org/*). The SSH server can be enabled by checking the Remote Login option in System Preferences → Sharing.

You can run the SSH client by typing the command ssh *user@hostname* in the Terminal application, which is located in */Applications/Utilities*, as shown here:

```
Doris-Computer:~ dori$ ssh dori@as220.org
dori@as220.org's password:  ********
Linux gumzilla 2.2.20 #1 Sat Apr 20 11:45:28 EST 2002 i686 unknown

Copyright (C) 1993-1999 Software in the Public Interest, and others

Most of the programs included with the Debian GNU/Linux system are
freely redistributable; the exact distribution terms for each program
are described in the individual files in /usr/doc/*/copyright

Debian GNU/Linux comes with ABSOLUTELY NO WARRANTY, to the extent
permitted by applicable law.
You have mail.
Last login: Wed Sep 10 16:05:55 2003 from m018f36d0.tmodns.net
dori@gumzilla:~$ cd src
dori@gumzilla:~/src$ ls -l
```

```
total 48
drwxr-xr-x   2 dori   dori    4096 Jun  3 03:06 MyDocuments
-rwxr-xr-x   1 dori   dori   15645 Mar 23 15:57 blosxom_2_0_rc2.cgi
-rw-r--r--   1 dori   dori    5572 Apr 25 19:30 blosxom_2_0_rc2.zip
-rwxr-xr-x   1 dori   dori     960 May 14 09:28 newblog
drwxr-xr-x   4 dori   dori    4096 Mar 23 23:29 writeback
-rw-r--r--   1 dori   dori    9199 Mar 24 16:05 writeback.zip
dori@gumzilla:~/src$ logout
Connection to as220.org closed.
```

You can use *scp* (secure copy) and *sftp* (secure FTP) as well. To copy a file with *scp*, use scp *filename user@hostname*: *path*, as in scp secret_document. doc dori@as220.org:MyDocuments/.

To use *sftp*, specify the *user@hostname*, and log in with your password. You can then use ftp commands such as *put* (to upload a file to the server) and *get* (to download a file from the server):

```
Doris-Computer:~ dori$ sftp dori@as220.org
Connecting to as220.org...
dori@as220.org's password:  ********
sftp> cd MyDocuments
sftp> put secret_document.doc
secret_document.doc                        100%    0    0.0KB/s   --:--
ETA
sftp> get super_secret.doc
super_secret.doc                           100%    8    0.0KB/s   00:02
sftp> quit
Doris-Computer:~ dori$
```

For more information, consult the *ssh* manpage (run the command man ssh in Terminal).

Firewalls

A *firewall* keeps remote users from connecting to your computer, while letting you connect to remote servers. A Mac OS X system includes a number of services, such as file sharing, that a remote attacker can potentially use to access your system. When you are on the road, you should enable Mac OS X's firewall, because other users on the wireless network will be able to access your computer if you don't.

To enable the firewall on your Mac OS X computer:

1. Open System Preferences.
2. Click on the Sharing icon under the Internet & Network group.
3. The Sharing window is displayed (see Figure 5-6). Click on the Firewall button.

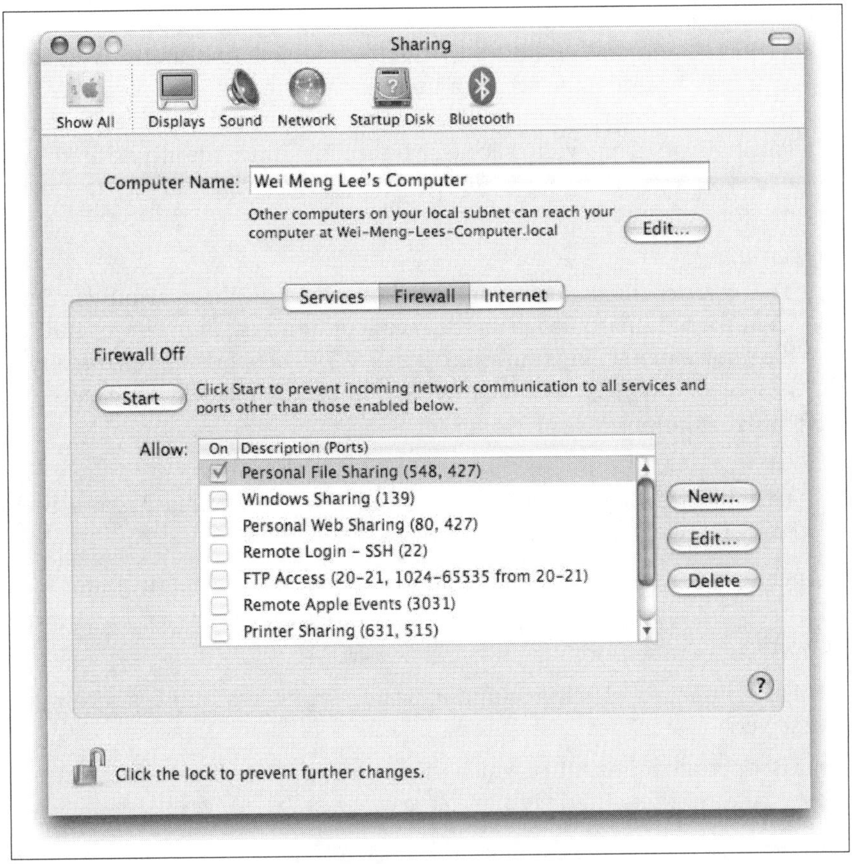

Figure 5-6. Enabling Mac OS X's firewall

4. To start Mac OS X's firewall, click Start. Check the services you want to run so that Mac OS X's firewall can allow access to the corresponding ports. Any services that are not checked will have their access blocked.

Wi-Fi Security

Now that we've covered some ways to secure your wireless connection, we'll get into the details of Wi-Fi security. A secure network should (ideally) have the following:

Authentication
This is the process of verifying the identity of a user and making sure that she is who she claims. When you log in to your Mac OS X computer, you are being authenticated via the username and password. In a Wi-Fi network, authentication comes into play when the access point has to determine whether a machine can connect to it.

Authorization

> This is the process of allowing or denying access to a specific resource. You may be authenticated as a user, but you may not be authorized to use certain feature. For example, suppose you are at a wireless hotspot and have used up your allotted connection time: the network knows who you are, but won't authorize you to access the Internet until you pay for more minutes.

Confidentiality

> This ensures the privacy of information that is being transmitted. Only an authorized party (such as the recipient of an email message) can see the information being transmitted. In a Wi-Fi network, confidentiality is supported by protocols such as WEP and 802.1X, which encrypt the data that moves through the air.

Integrity

> This ensures that the information you have transmitted has not been tampered with en route to its destination.

Authentication, authorization, confidentiality, and integrity are also addressed by other systems on your network, just as they are on a wired network:

- Passwords can be used to authenticate users when they log into a file server.
- User permissions control which files a given user has access to.
- Web and email communications can be secured with SSL.
- Network traffic can be tunneled through a VPN.

Wi-Fi has two main authentication schemes (see Figure 5-7): cryptographic and non-cryptographic.

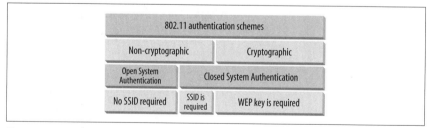

Figure 5-7. Authentication schemes

Under the non-cryptographic scheme, you can authenticate in one of two ways: with or without an SSID. If a wireless network allows clients to connect to it without specifying an SSID, it is known as *Open System Authentication*.

In Apple's terminology, an SSID is known as the Wireless Network Name. In this chapter, we'll use the two terms interchangeably.

For *Closed System Authentication*, two methods are possible: one using an SSID and one using a cryptographic key.

In an Open System Authentication scheme, there is no encryption performed on the packets transmitted between the client and the access point. The client does not need any SSID to join a network. This is the simplest mode, as the configuration is straightforward and does not require any administration.

In the Closed System Authentication scheme, a client needs to specify an SSID that is identical to that specified by the access point in order to join the network. In addition, a shared key may also be used to encrypt the data packets transmitted between the client and the access point. In 802.11, the encryption method is known as Wired Equivalent Privacy (WEP), which we discuss in the next section.

To connect to a network in a closed system, a client must fulfill one or several of the following criteria:

1. The SSID of the client must match that of the access point. If a wireless access point has SSID broadcast turned on, your Macintosh should be able to detect its presence and allow you to connect to it. If the SSID broadcast is turned off, then the client must manually enter the SSID in order to associate with the access point. Getting associated with the access point is the first step in joining a network. Using an SSID to prevent people from accessing your network is not effective, since the SSID is often guessable and can be "sniffed" by network tools such as KisMAC (more on this later).

 There are actually two steps to gaining network access. The first is *associating with the access point*, which means that the access point is willing to talk to your machine. The second step is *joining the network*, which usually means that your machine has been assigned an IP address and can talk to other hosts on the network. Unless we need to specifically discuss one or the other of these steps, we'll use *connected* to mean that the client has been associated with the access point and joined the network.

2. Some access points use MAC address filtering to prevent clients from associating with them. You can enter a list of MAC addresses in order to allow (or deny) association with the access point, usually through a

web-based configuration interface on the access point. Apple AirPort or AirPort Extreme Base Stations use the AirPort Admin Utility to set up MAC address association. Even if a client has the correct SSID, if its MAC address is not listed in the allow-list of the access point, it cannot be associated with the access point. Again, using MAC address filtering to prevent unauthorized access to the network is not foolproof—an unauthorized user can easily change his network card's MAC address to that of an authorized client. And often someone sniffing your wireless network knows the MAC addresses of Wi-Fi cards that appear to be authorized, so this will clearly only keep the casual and unskilled out of your network.

3. If WEP encryption is used on a wireless network, the client must specify the same WEP key as the one entered in the access point. Using a WEP key protects the data that is exchanged between the client and the access point. It also has the side effect of preventing unauthorized access to the network, since a client needs the WEP key to encrypt and decrypt the exchanged packets. However, it has been proven that WEP is not secure and the WEP key can easily be recovered by an attacker using freely available tools.

Wired Equivalent Privacy (WEP)

The main goal of WEP is to provide confidentiality of data packets, with a secondary function of granting authorization to a wireless network. This is, however, not the originally intended design goal of WEP (see the section on 802.1X later in this chapter). Although WEP was initially designed to safeguard the confidentiality of the data in a wireless network, it has been proven to be insecure. Here are some of the more important security concerns regarding WEP:

- The use of a shared static key is a major concern, since everyone uses the same static key to secure their communications. As soon as the key is made known, the network is no longer secure. Some access points use a passphrase to generate keys, which makes it easier to guess the key, since people tend to use familiar terms for passphrases.

- A significant component of the WEP system is its *initialization vector*, which is used to increase the unpredictability of the encryption scheme. This vector is relatively small and, as a result, the same vector comes up from time to time—especially on a busy access point where a lot of data is being transferred. When WEP uses the same vector more than once, it creates the opportunity for an attacker to discover the WEP key and bypass the security.

- If an eavesdropper obtains the key, he may be able to forge the identity of a legitimate user and intercept and reroute the transmitted data.

- Due to the export regulations of the United States, the 802.11 standard called only for 40-bit WEP. Most vendors introduced longer key lengths for their products, making them proprietary and often not interoperable. Apple's base stations can use either a 40-bit or 128-bit WEP key. Even so, since WEP is not a well-designed cryptographic system, having extra key length does not make your communications more secure.

Still, using WEP is better than no encryption at all, especially if you are protecting a small office or home network where there's not a lot of network traffic. Frequently changing your WEP keys is a very good idea. If you only want to use WEP to protect your network, you must change your WEP key as often as feasible to provide as little exposure as possible. Harvesting weak packets to attack WEP can be a lengthy process on networks with little traffic.

Enabling WEP on an AirPort base station. To enable WEP for your wireless network, open the AirPort Admin Utility and do the following:

1. Click on the Name and Password button.
2. Under the Wireless Network Name checkbox, check the Enable encryption (using WEP) checkbox.
3. Click on the Change password... button.
4. Select the length of the WEP key (40-bit or 128-bit) and enter a password (see Figure 5-8). Click OK.

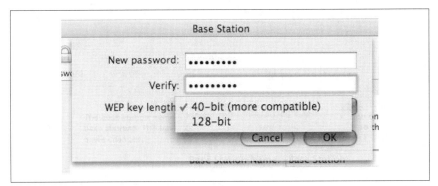

Figure 5-8. Entering a password to generate the WEP key

5. Click on the Update button to save the changes to the AirPort base station.

You can enter any string for the password, regardless of the size of the WEP key that you have selected. The AirPort base station will then internally generate a WEP key based on the password and the key size that you have selected.

Connecting Non-Macintosh Computers to a WEP-enabled AirPort Base Station. Since the AirPort Base Station uses a password to generate the WEP key, non-Macintosh computers connecting via the AirPort Base Station need to know that WEP key.

To get the WEP key generated by the AirPort Base Station, use the AirPort Admin Utility, select Base Station from the menu, then choose the "Equivalent Network Password…" item. Alternatively, the main screen of the AirPort Admin Utility should also display the WEP key if WEP is enabled (see Figure 5-9).

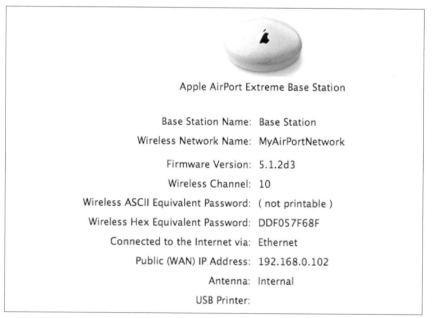

Figure 5-9. Getting the WEP password

For Windows users, note that you need to change the Network Authentication type from Open to Shared. If you don't change this setting, you may have trouble connecting to the AirPort base station (see Figure 5-10).

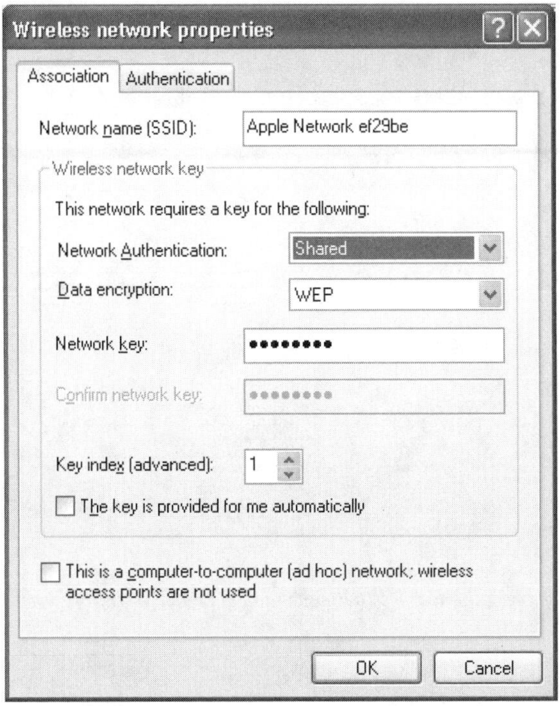

Figure 5-10. Changing the Network Authentication type on a Windows computer

Connecting your Mac to a Non-AirPort Base Station. If you are connecting to a non-AirPort base station and have WEP enabled, be careful when you specify your WEP password in the System Preferences → Network window (see Figure 5-11).

You should prefix your WEP keys with a "$" sign. For example, if the WEP key is "1234567890," then you should enter "$1234567890." The "$" sign tells AirPort that you are sending the WEP keys directly, and that it doesn't need to translate the password into its WEP equivalent.

Connecting to a WEP-enabled AirPort base station. To connect to a WEP-enabled AirPort base station, click the AirPort icon on the menu bar and select the wireless network to join. You will be prompted to enter the password (see Figure 5-12).

There are a number of options for entering the passwords:

Password
Use this option to enter the password that you have specified in your AirPort base station.

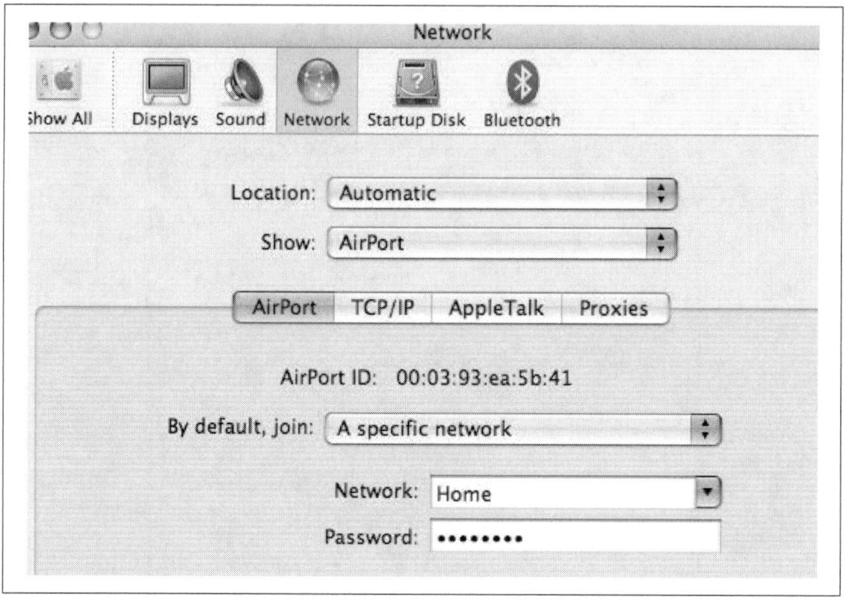

Figure 5-11. Specifying the wireless network password in System Preferences

Figure 5-12. Entering a password to join a WEP-protected wireless network

40-bit hex

Use this option to enter the WEP key that is generated by your AirPort base station. The size of this key is 10 hexadecimal digits.

40-bit ASCII

Use this option if the password in your base station is 5 characters long.

128-bit hex

Use this option to enter the WEP key generated by your AirPort base station. The size of this key is 32 hexadecimal digits.

128-bit ASCII

Use this option if the password in your base station is 16 characters long.

LEAP

Use this option if you are connecting to an access point that uses the Cisco authentication protocol known as LEAP.

 Users of earlier versions of Mac OS X should enter their username and password in the following format: <User Name/ Password>. Note that the two angle brackets are mandatory.

802.11i

A long-term solution to resolve WEP's inadequacies lies in the hands of the IEEE workgroup TGi (*http://grouper.ieee.org/groups/802/11/Reports/tgi_ update.htm*), who expect to complete the 802.11i specifications at the end of 2003.

The 802.11i specifications will address:

Use of 802.1X for authentication

The 802.1X specification is a framework for mutual authentication between a client and the access point. It may also use a RADIUS-based authentication server and one of the Extensible Authentication Protocol (EAP) variations. 802.1X uses a new key for each session; hence it replaces WEP's static key.

Use of the Temporal Key Integrity Protocol (TKIP)

TKIP will be used as a short-term solution to WEP's flaws. It uses 128-bit dynamic keys that are utilized by different clients. Because of the changing keys, intruders would not have time to collect enough packets to compromise the security scheme.

Use of the Advanced Encryption Standard (AES)

The full implementation of 802.11i will utilize the AES encryption system for enhanced encryption in access points. However, use of AES requires changes in the chipsets used in wireless devices. Thus, at the time of this writing, no wireless devices support AES.

The 802.11i specification is tentatively called WPA2. See the next section for more details.

Wi-Fi Protected Access (WPA). While the industry is waiting for the 802.11i specification to be ratified, the Wi-Fi Alliance has addressed the present need for secure wireless communication by introducing *Wi-Fi Protected Access (WPA)*. WPA is also known as WPA1, while 802.11i is known as WPA2. WPA is a subset of the 802.11i standard and will be forward compatible with it. The key components of WPA are:

802.1X
> See the next section for a detailed discussion of 802.1X.

TKIP technologies
> TKIP addresses WEP's limitations by using dynamic keys and a much longer initialization vector (meaning that the chances of reusing the same vector within a short period of time are reduced).

As this book was going to press, Apple released the AirPort 3.2 Update, which features their first implementation of WPA. This version enabled WPA encryption for AirPort Extreme Base Stations and AirPort Extreme cards only. It is expected that a later update will extend WPA protection to the original AirPort cards, but there may not be a WPA upgrade for AirPort Base Stations.

Apple's WPA implementation embraces two flavors of WPA. WPA Personal allows you to enter a password of between 8 and 63 text characters, or 64 hexadecimal characters. WPA Enterprise lets the user have their name and password verified by an external RADIUS authentication server. If you want to enable WPA encryption on your network—and it is markedly more secure than WEP—you should know that Apple's 3.2 AirPort software allows only all-WEP or all-WPA networks; you can't mix and match clients using different forms of encryption. If you're on an all–AirPort Extreme network, it's a good idea to upgrade to WPA. If you have a mixed AirPort and AirPort Extreme network, we recommend that you check to see if later versions of the AirPort software have been released that support WPA for the AirPort clients before you enable WPA.

Table 5-1 shows the differences between WPA and WEP.

Table 5-1. Comparing WPA to WEP

	WPA	WEP
Key length	128-bit	40-bit to 232-bit
Key type	Dynamic key; per-user, per-session, per-packet keys	Static shared key; used by everyone in the network
Key distribution	Automatic key distribution	Each user must type in the key
Authentication	Uses 802.1X and EAP	Uses WEP key for authentication; flawed

802.1X Authentication

The 802.1X specification is a port-based network access control mechanism: when a client is authenticated, the port (a connection between a client machine and an access point) is granted access; if not, access to the port is denied. Although 802.1X was originally designed for Ethernet networks, it can be applied to wireless networks as well.

This is how 802.1X works (see Figure 5-13):

1. The *supplicant* (the client that wants to access a network resource) connects to the *authenticator* (whose resource is needed).

2. The authenticator asks for credentials from the supplicant and passes the credentials to the *authenticating server*.

3. The authenticating server authenticates the supplicant on behalf of the authenticator.

4. If the supplicant is authenticated, access is granted.

Figure 5-13. Authenticating a supplicant in 802.1X

In a wireless network, a wireless client needs to connect to an access point; in this case, the wireless access point is the authenticator. The authenticator can maintain a database of users and their respective passwords. However, this is a huge administrative task, especially in a large network. So an access point can be connected to a *RADIUS* (*Remote Authentication Dial-In User Service*) server, which will maintain the database of users and perform authentication on behalf of the access point. This is as shown in Figure 5-14.

Using a RADIUS server only takes care of the authentication aspect of security. What about confidentiality? Packets traveling between the wireless clients and the access point must be encrypted to ensure confidentiality.

When a client is validated at the RADIUS server, an authentication key is transmitted to the access point. (This key is encrypted; only the access point can decrypt it.) The access point then decrypts the key and uses it to create a new key specific to that wireless client. That key is sent to the wireless client, where it's used to encrypt the master global authentication key to the wireless client. To address WEP's shortcoming of a fixed key, the access point will generate a new master authentication key at regular intervals.

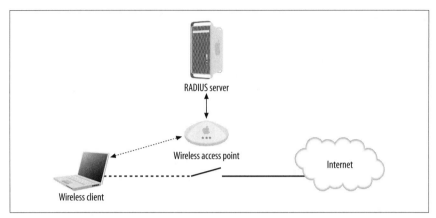

Figure 5-14. Using 802.1X authentication in a wireless network

Using 802.1X in Mac OS X. Connect to an access point secured using 802.1X:

1. Double-click the Internet Connect application located in the */Applications* folder.

2. Select File → New 802.1X Connection. The 802.1X panel appears (Figure 5-15). From this point on, you can configure 802.1X by clicking the 802.1X icon.

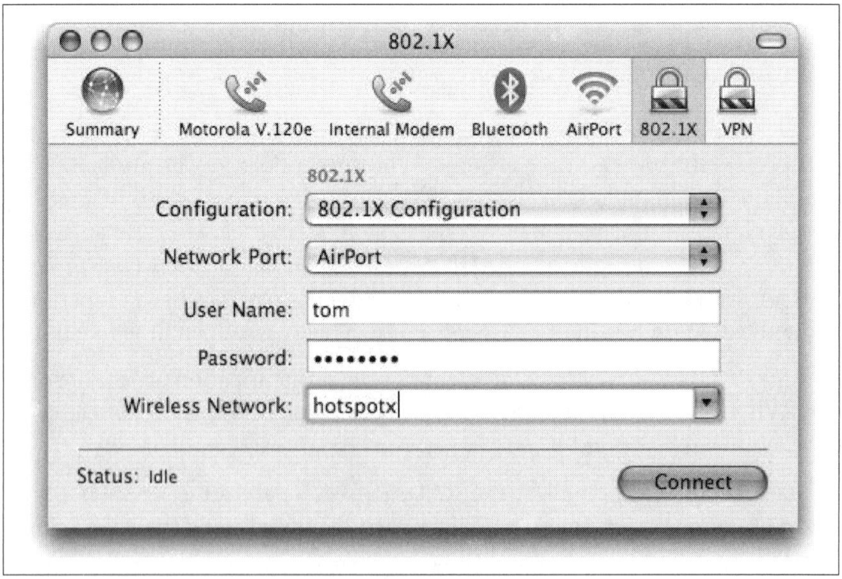

Figure 5-15. Configuring 802.1X in Internet Connect

3. Be sure that AirPort is selected as the Network Port, and then fill in the User Name, Password, and Wireless Network fields. You can choose the wireless network name from the drop-down menu or type one in.

4. Click Connect. If you have the correct user ID and password and are authorized, you will be connected to the network. If not, contact the administrator of the wireless network.

5. When you close Internet Connect, you'll be prompted to supply a new 802.1X configuration name. Your username and password, as well as the wireless network name, will be saved.

6. You can reconnect in the future by simply selecting the wireless network from the AirPort menu; a keychain dialog will appear asking for permission to access the saved 802.1X configuration. You can also reconnect by opening Internet Connect, clicking the 802.1X icon, selecting the configuration, and clicking Connect.

802.1X and RADIUS . To use 802.1X on your own network, you will need a RADIUS server to perform user and password authentication, and an access point that supports 802.1X. Although AirPort base stations (with the exception of the Graphite base station) support RADIUS authentication with the latest version of the AirPort software, they do not (at the time of this writing) support 802.1X. The RADIUS authentication included with AirPort performs simple MAC address-based authentication of computers on your network and, as noted earlier, MAC addresses are easily spoofed.

There are inexpensive access points on the market that support 802.1X. We tested 802.1X with a D-Link 900AP+ ($79) and FreeRadius (an open source RADIUS implementation available from *http://www.freeradius.org/*) running on a Linux backend server. FreeRadius can also be compiled for Mac OS X or Mac OS X Server.

RADIUS and the AirPort Base Station. This section explains how to configure your AirPort base station to authenticate the MAC addresses of client machines against a RADIUS server.

1. Using the AirPort Admin Utility, click on the Show All Settings button and then the Authentication button (see Figure 5-16).

2. Select Default from the RADIUS drop-down list.

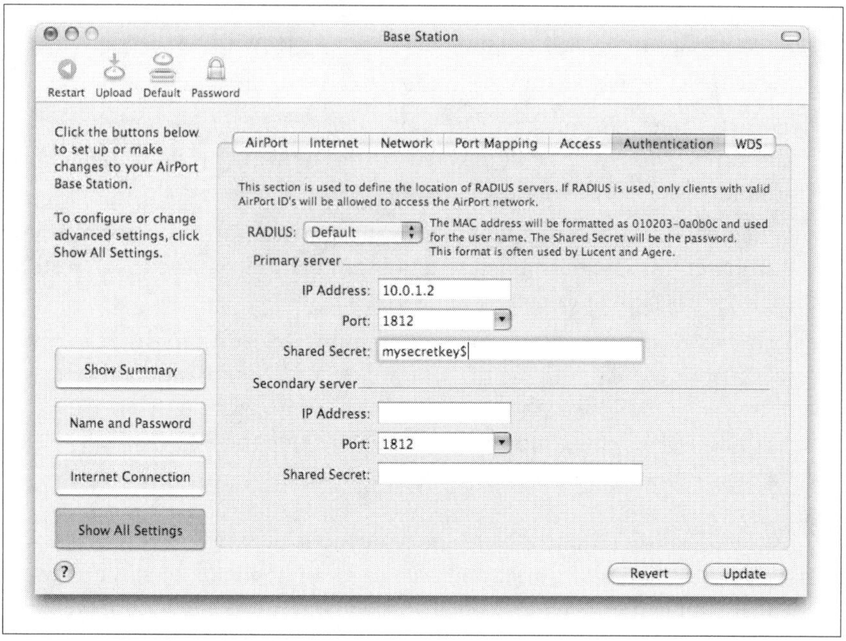

Figure 5-16. Specifying RADIUS server information

The RADIUS drop-down list contains two options: Default and Alternate. If you choose Default, the client's MAC address will be formatted as 010203-0a0b0c and used as the username on the RADIUS server. The shared secret is used as the password.

If you choose Alternate, the client's MAC address will be formatted as 0102030a0b0c and used as both username and password at the RADIUS server.

AirPort does not allow users to specify their username and password for RADIUS authentication.

3. Enter the IP address and port number of the RADIUS server. You'll also need to enter a shared secret that is entered at the RADIUS server as well.

4. You can also configure a secondary RADIUS server in case the first one fails.

Are 802.11 Networks Really Secure?

One of the problems with wireless security is that you don't need expensive tools to break into a wireless network. All you need in your toolbox is a computer, a wireless card, some suitable software, and perhaps a good antenna for receiving wireless signals.

The following is a list of software that you can use to detect wireless networks, sniff wireless packets in transit, and much more. These tools have numerous legitimate uses, such as detecting unauthorized access points, intrusion detection, network traffic analysis, and debugging networked applications such as a web server.

MacStumbler (http://www.macstumbler.com/)
MacStumbler is a free application that allows you to detect the presence of wireless networks. Using MacStumbler, you can obtain information about a particular access point: the SSID used, whether WEP is enabled, and so on. Coupled with a GPS receiver, you can also pinpoint the location of an access point. MacStumbler is often used for wardriving, site surveys, and detecting rogue access points. Figure 5-17 shows MacStumbler scanning for wireless networks.

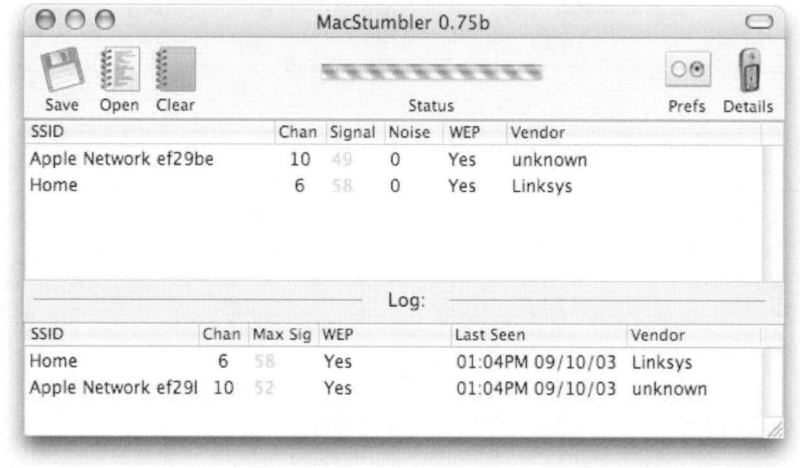

Figure 5-17. MacStumbler scanning for wireless networks

iStumbler (http://www.istumbler.net/)
iStumbler is another free tool that is similar to MacStumbler, but seems to be updated more frequently.

KisMAC (http://freshmeat.net/projects/kismac/)
KisMAC is very similar to the popular Windows and Unix package Kismet. It is a passive wireless scanner that sends no probes of its own, which means it is sneakier and less invasive than other tools such as MacStumbler. KisMAC (and Kismet) are silent and generally more useful than other software of its kind.

HenWen (http://seiryu.home.comcast.net/henwen.html)

HenWen is a network security package for Mac OS X that makes it easy to configure and run Snort, a free, open source Network Intrusion Detection System (NIDS). HenWen simplifies setting up and maintaining software that will scan the network for undesirable traffic that a firewall may not block. Everything you need is bundled in; no compiling or command-line configuration is necessary.

Snort Mac OS X (http://www.securemac.com/macosxsnort.php)

This is the Mac OS X command-line version of Snort, a packet sniffer and NIDS.

AiroPeek NX (http://www.airopeek.com/)

AiroPeek is a wireless LAN analyzer from WildPackets that runs on Windows. It is an extremely powerful wireless LAN analyzer that many security professionals use (be forewarned, this package costs $3,499!). AiroPeek is able to sniff raw wireless packets transmitted through the air, which is why protecting your wireless network with 802.1X, a VPN, SSH, or even WEP is important. AiroPeek can easily sniff unencrypted data packets.

Ethereal (http://www.ethereal.com/)

Ethereal is a free network protocol analyzer for Unix and Windows computers. It is similar to AiroPeek in that it allows you to sniff wireless (and wired) packets in transit. Many network protocols are susceptible to sniffing in this manner. For example, Telnet and FTP both send passwords as plaintext (for secure alternatives, see the section "Secure Shell (SSH)," earlier in this chapter).

Common Security Features on Access Points

Most wireless access points provide some degree of protection against unauthorized access to the network. Here are a few common features found in most consumer access points:

Disabling SSID broadcast

Disabling SSID broadcast causes the access point to suppress the broadcast of SSID information to wireless clients. In order to join the wireless network, a wireless client must manually specify the SSID that the network uses, or it will not be able to associate with the access point.

MAC address filtering

Most access points support MAC address filtering by allowing only network cards with the specified MAC addresses to be associated with them. In a small network, this is feasible but it becomes administratively prohibitive in a large network. Note that MAC address filtering authenticates a device, not a user.

IP filtering

IP filtering works just like MAC address filtering, but instead filters computers based on IP addresses.

802.1X

As 802.1X gains acceptance, expect to see support of 802.1X in consumer access points, not just enterprise-level access points. Check with your vendor to see if your access point supports 802.1X authentication (or can be upgraded to do so via a firmware upgrade).

The following sections cover some of the common techniques used for securing wireless networks, and rate their effectiveness.

MAC address filtering. While MAC address filtering can prevent unauthorized network devices from gaining entry to a network, there are two problems with it:

1. The device is authenticated in MAC address filtering, not the user. Hence if a user loses the network card, another user who picks it up is able to gain access to the network without any problem. Because AirPort cards are internal, this is less of a concern than if you are using a PC Card wireless adapter; you might not immediately notice that the PC Card is missing, but you're sure to notice if your PowerBook is gone.

2. MAC addresses can easily be spoofed. For example, you can impersonate the MAC address of another machine on a Linux system using the *ifconfig* utility, a network configuration utility. For this to work, you need a wireless card that allows you to change the MAC address. Although the Mac OS X version of *ifconfig* supports this capability, your mileage may vary with an AirPort card.

To enable MAC address filtering, use the AirPort Admin Utility and click on the Show All Settings button. You should see the window shown in Figure 5-18.

If the list is empty, all clients can connect to the AirPort base station. If the list has at least one item, then all clients are denied access except for those in the list.

You can import (or export) a list of clients to whom you want to allow access. The access control list is a text file containing the MAC address and description of individual computers (separated by a tab). Figure 5-19 shows one example.

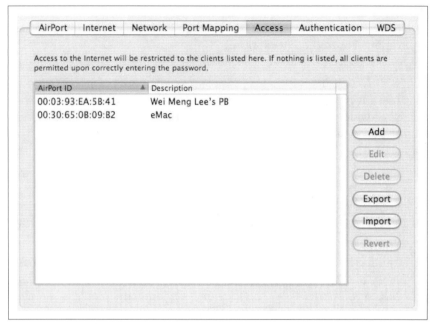

Figure 5-18. Specifying the access control list for wireless users

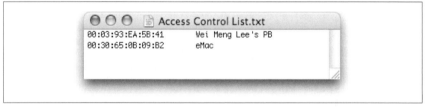

Figure 5-19. The access control list contained in a text file

 You can obtain the AirPort ID (also known as the MAC address) of your AirPort card by going to System Preferences → Network. Select AirPort under the Show pop-up menu (see Figure 5-20).

Disabling SSID broadcast. By default, an AirPort base station will broadcast its wireless network name to all computers that are wireless-capable. However, there are times where you do not want everyone to be aware of the existence of your network. In such cases, you can turn off this broadcast so that people who want to join your network must specify the network name in full.

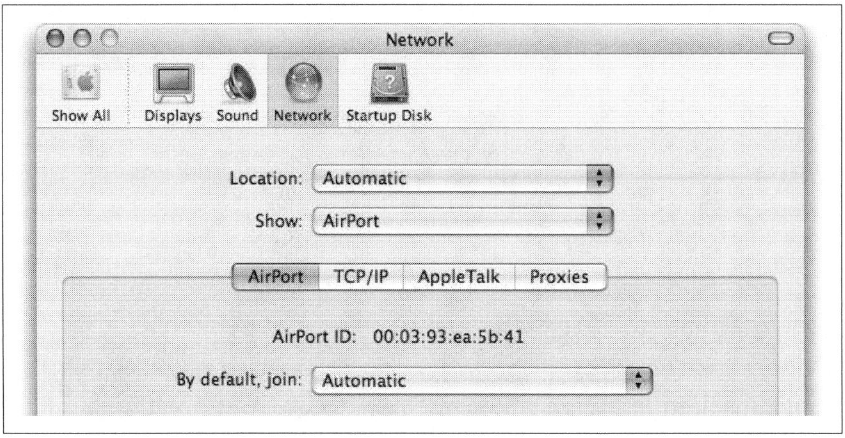

Figure 5-20. Obtaining the AirPort ID of an AirPort card

Disabling SSID broadcast prevents uninvited users from accessing the network. However, there are two fundamental flaws with this approach:

1. It is not difficult to guess the SSID of a network. Most users deploy wireless networks using the default SSID that comes with the access point. It is too easy to guess the SSID of a wireless network based on hints like the brand of the access point, or from clues like the thrown-away box of the access point.

2. When you disable SSID broadcast, the access point does not broadcast the SSID information. However, as soon as one user connects to the access point using the known SSID, it is possible to sniff the SSID that is transmitted in the network. Hence this method is secure only if there is no user on the network; as soon as one user is on the network, the SSID is no longer a secret.

   This is a useless measure most of the time, since anybody with a passive scanner such as KisMAC will still see your access point. It will probably keep your upstairs neighbor from siphoning off your bandwidth, but that's about it.

To turn off this broadcast, use the AirPort Admin Utility. Click on the Show All Settings button and select the Create a closed network checkbox (see Figure 5-21) under the AirPort Network group.

Using WEP. As we have discussed, WEP has some fundamental flaws that make it prone to hackers. For example, utilities such as KisMAC can recover the WEP key after collecting a sizeable number of packets from the wireless network.

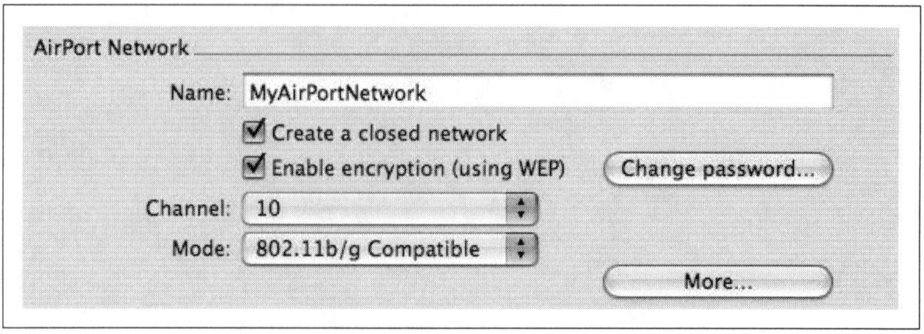

Figure 5-21. Disabling SSID broadcast

Even though WEP is not secure, it is still advisable to use it to make it somewhat difficult to breach your network, or at least to make it clear to honest users that you're not offering public access. Site surveys often show that the majority of wireless networks don't even use WEP! Using Snort or Ethereal, it's very easy to examine the data transmitted through the air. On a very busy network, we suggest using 802.1X, but this is non-trivial to set up. For networks that don't have lot of traffic, use WEP, but change your WEP keys from time to time (we recommend weekly, more frequently if you have a lot of network traffic).

CHAPTER SIX

Bluetooth

Wireless isn't just for Internet and computer-to-computer connectivity—it can also be used to move data between your Mac and your peripherals. This is where Bluetooth comes in. Bluetooth is a short-range, relatively low-speed wireless technology with an operating range of approximately 30 feet (10 meters) and a maximum transmission rate of only 1 Mbps.

If you think of Wi-Fi as Ethernet without wires, the comparable way to think of Bluetooth is USB without wires (though we're talking about the slower USB 1.0 standard used in most peripherals; USB 2.0 is quite zippy). For instance, hooking up a PDA used to require a USB-attached cradle, but you can now transfer data wirelessly between your Mac and Palm via Bluetooth.

A word of advice: the Bluetooth technology and its implementation on the Macintosh is a work in progress. Early press about Bluetooth raved about how it could be used to hook up printers, keyboards, and mice. Unfortunately, Apple's Bluetooth support is tweaky at best; we've found that Bluetooth tends to be flaky, and sometimes it just fails to work at all.

Why Bluetooth?

Bluetooth is a pretty weird name, if you think about it; unlike, say, Wi-Fi, Bluetooth doesn't have that high-tech ring. That's because the Bluetooth technology was named in honor of a real person, the Danish King Harald Blåtand, who ruled approximately from A.D. 960 to 985, and who is reported to have brought Christianity to Scandinavia and united Denmark and Norway. "Bluetooth" was a nickname that had nothing to do with blue teeth: it referred to the king's dark complexion, which was unusual for a Viking.

About Bluetooth

Like most widespread technologies, there is a standard and a standards body behind Bluetooth. In this case, it's the aptly named Bluetooth Special Interest Group (SIG). Ericsson invented Bluetooth and formed the Bluetooth SIG (*http://www.bluetooth.com/*) in February 2001. The Bluetooth SIG now boasts more than 2000 members, including Ericsson, Nokia, IBM, Microsoft, Intel, and, of course, Apple Computer.

Because the Bluetooth standard is designed for short-range, point-to-point data transfer between devices, no central hub (such as those used with, say, Ethernet, or a Wi-Fi access point) is needed. Like any wireless radio standard, you don't have to be within line of sight for two Bluetooth devices to communicate (though because the effective range is so short, you usually will be). Bluetooth shares the unlicensed-use 2.4 GHz band with Wi-Fi, and it is susceptible to the same sorts of household interference as Wi-Fi signals, such as microwave ovens and some cordless phones. In fact, running Bluetooth devices in the presence of Wi-Fi devices can result in some interference between the two, but it is usually not a big problem. Because Bluetooth can use a spread of many slightly different radio frequencies to transmit and receive data, it is fairly resistant to interference. If there is interference, the Bluetooth devices may simply need to resend a few data packets.

When two or more Bluetooth devices connect, they form an ad-hoc network called a *piconet*. A piconet can contain up to eight devices, and must contain one *master* (the device that initiates the connection) and one or more *slaves* (devices that were found by the master device). The important point here is that you can have no more than eight Bluetooth devices active and simultaneously connected. If one of those devices is your computer, and it uses Bluetooth to connect to its keyboard and mouse, you're already using three devices right there. You can quickly fill up the remaining slots with a Bluetooth-enabled cell phone, a PDA, and other devices, such as a digital camera.

Mac OS X allows you to use Bluetooth to transfer files between Bluetooth devices or synchronize information between devices. File transfers use the Bluetooth File Exchange application, found in */Applications/Utilities/* (see "Moving Data with Bluetooth" later in this chapter). For synchronization, Mac OS X relies on the iSync application (more about that later in this chapter, in "Using iSync").

Choosing and Installing a Bluetooth Adapter

Right now, most of Apple's shipping computers come with Bluetooth as a standard feature. For all others, you'll need a Bluetooth adapter. Thankfully, they're both inexpensive and easy to install.

Currently-shipping Macs fall into one of three categories:

Bluetooth Optional
> These Macs include a USB port, into which a separately purchased USB adapter may be plugged.

Bluetooth Ready
> When purchased, this Mac can be upgraded to include an internal Bluetooth card. Unlike AirPort cards, the internal Bluetooth cards cannot be purchased and installed later. If you're buying a Bluetooth Ready Mac and you have any interest in using Bluetooth devices at some later date, consider upgrading to Bluetooth Included at the time that you order the computer. Otherwise, your Mac is equivalent to Bluetooth Optional, and you'll have to purchase a USB Bluetooth adapter.

Bluetooth Included
> An internal Bluetooth card is factory-installed inside this Mac.

If you have a Bluetooth Optional or Bluetooth Ready Mac, you'll need a USB Bluetooth adapter. There are a number of companies that sell them, including Belkin, D-Link, MacWireless.com, and Keyspan. The price is usually in the $40 to $50 range. There are only small differences between them; several different manufacturers sell adapters so similar that they're probably the same product with different branding.

It costs about the same amount to upgrade a Bluetooth Ready Mac to Bluetooth Included as it does to buy an adapter and add it yourself, so you might wonder why it would be worthwhile to skip it at the time of purchase. In our experience (as mentioned above), Bluetooth's flaky behavior can result in a number of problems. In several cases, what fixed the problem was removing and reattaching the adapter, causing the Bluetooth driver to reload. This isn't an option if your Bluetooth card is internal.

Our personal favorite external Bluetooth adapter was the D-Link DWB-120M (shown in Figure 6-1), because it's reasonably priced, reasonably sized, and it's the one that Apple used to recommend. This endorsement was important because applications aren't guaranteed to work with all adapters—having an Apple-approved product helped minimize incompatibilities. Unfortunately, when Apple shipped their Bluetooth keyboard and mouse, they stopped recommending the D-Link adapter, and it's incompatible with both peripherals. Our current recommendation: figure out which devices you're likely to use with Bluetooth, then research what adapters work with each.

The only Bluetooth adapter we actively dislike is the Belkin F8T003; it's almost twice the size of the D-Link and its flashing blue light becomes annoying after only a short time (and even worse, turning Bluetooth connectivity off on the Mac doesn't stop the flashing).

Figure 6-1. The D-Link DWB-120M Bluetooth USB adapter

There are other Bluetooth adapters available that use different hardware interfaces than USB. There are PC Card adapters, which work in the slots on some PowerBooks; Compact Flash adapters, which need to be put into a PC Card adapter for use in a PowerBook; and a Secure Digital (SD) card adapter, which is designed to work with PDAs. Unless you enjoy mucking about with hardware and seeing what you can make work, you're better off sticking with either built-in Bluetooth (with newer Macs) or plugging in a USB adapter.

There's one other type of USB Bluetooth adapter, such as the Belkin F8T001, which is physically larger, more powerful, and has an antenna on it to allow longer-distance usage. Bluetooth normally reaches about 30 feet, and this higher-power unit allows a theoretical distance of up to 300 feet. We haven't found the extra distance to be worth the extra cost and the pain of the larger adapter; if you have a large office and need to sync your cell phone and your Mac from three offices away, you may find that it's worth it for you. However, your cell phone's Bluetooth range may not be great enough to even permit this!

Installing a USB Bluetooth adapter couldn't be easier. Find an open USB port on your Mac and plug it in. If you're using Mac OS X 10.2 or later, that should be the entire installation process. If you're running an older version of OS X, you'll need to upgrade. Bluetooth drivers are built into OS X 10.2, so you shouldn't have to install any other software.

All of your computer's USB ports full? If you're using a desktop Mac and an Apple keyboard, don't forget that there are two USB ports on the keyboard. Many displays have USB ports, too. You can also get an inexpensive (under $20) USB hub to give you more ports.

Connecting Cellular Phones

Once you've got Bluetooth on your Mac, it's time to do something with it. The most common use of Bluetooth is to simplify moving data between your computer and your cell phone. Instead of having to type in all of your contacts' names and phone numbers into both your Mac and your phone, Apple thinks that you should be able to synchronize the two devices. That makes sense to us, too.

We'll be using the Sony Ericsson T68i cell phone for the following examples. If you have a Sony Ericsson T68, T68c, or T68m, the following instructions should work as-is.

If you have a different Bluetooth-enabled phone (or are shopping for a Mac-friendly phone), check Apple's list of compatible cell phones (and other devices) at *http://www.apple.com/isync/devices.html*. In addition to the Sony Ericsson offerings, many Bluetooth phones from Nokia, Motorola, and Siemens can be configured to wirelessly sync with your Mac.

Pairing Your Phone and Mac

The first step is *pairing* your phone to your Mac via Bluetooth. Pairing is the process of telling your Mac to remember and trust your phone. As of Mac OS X 10.2.6, Apple has created several different ways of pairing phones to Macs, some of which are more dependable than others. This example gives the method that we've found works the most reliably.

In order for devices to find each other they must be made *discoverable*, which means that the device is broadcasting its availability for connection. To make your T68i cell phone discoverable, scroll to the Connect menu and choose option 3, Bluetooth. From the Bluetooth menu, choose option 1, Discoverable. The blue light on your phone will begin to blink, indicating that Bluetooth is active.

 Turning Bluetooth on will drain your cell phone's battery at an accelerated rate. It's a good idea to keep Bluetooth off when you don't need it for synchronization or for using a wireless headset.

On your Mac, choose the Bluetooth pane from System Preferences, as shown in Figure 6-2. Make sure that Bluetooth power is on, then click on the Devices tab, as shown in Figure 6-3. The first time you pair a device, the "Bluetooth Devices" list will be blank.

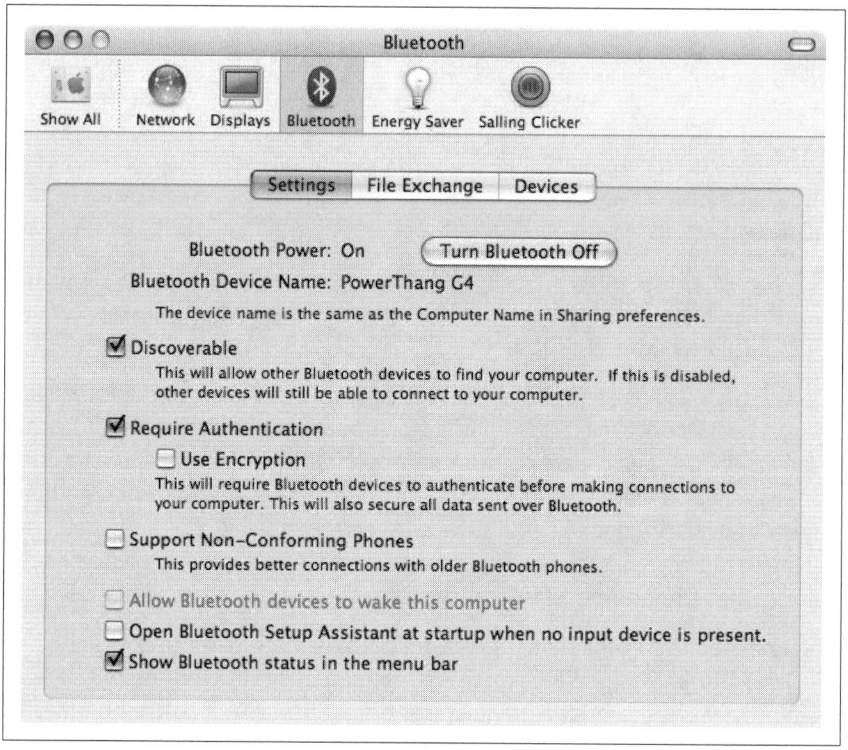

Figure 6-2. The System Preferences Bluetooth pane

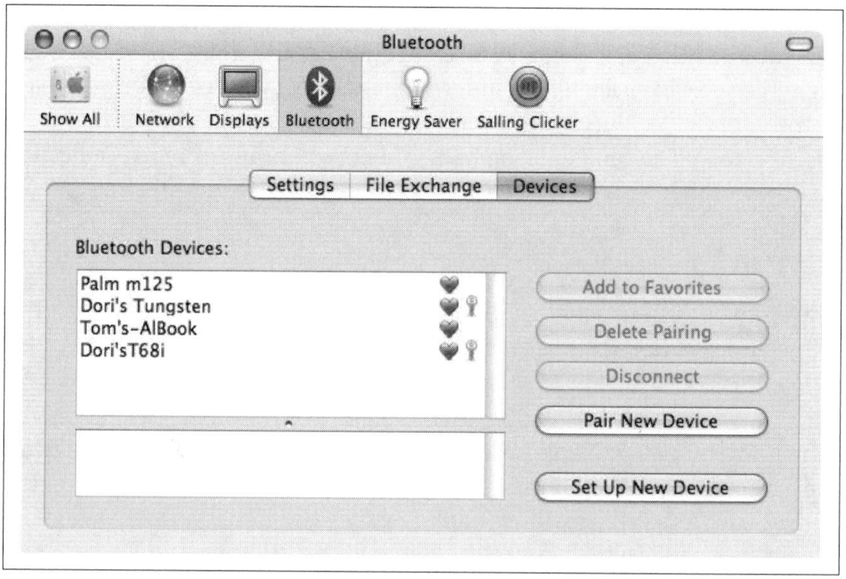

Figure 6-3. The Devices tab

Click "Set Up New Device." This will launch the Bluetooth Setup Assistant application. Select "Mobile Phone" as the type of device you want to set up, and click Continue. Step 1 (seen in Figure 6-4) of the pairing process is for the Mac to search for your mobile phone. When it's found, it will show up on the list. Click Continue to go to Step 2.

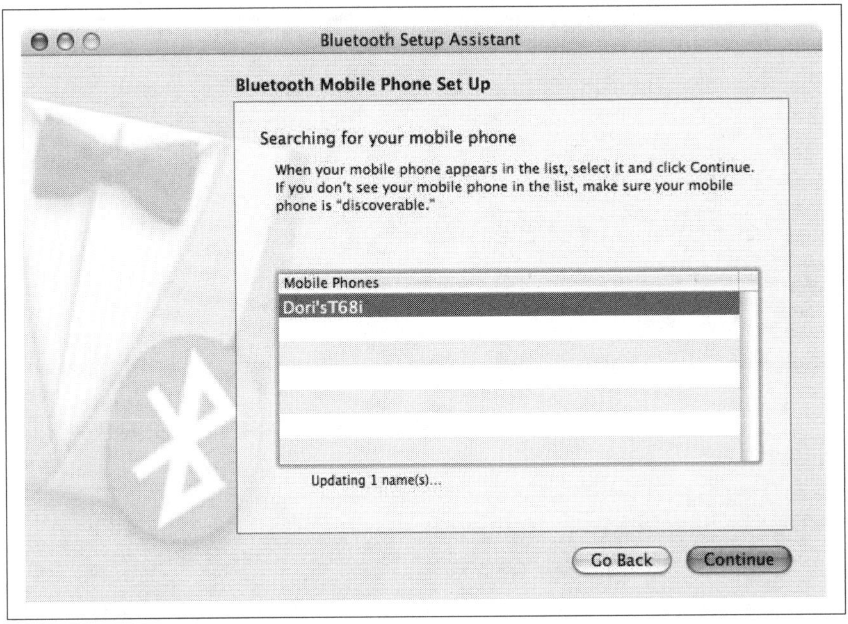

Figure 6-4. Bluetooth Setup Assistant, Step 1

In Step 2 (as shown in Figure 6-5), enter a *passkey*. This isn't a password: it's not bulleted out when it's entered, and you don't need to keep track of it for the future. It needs to be all numeric so that it can be entered on your phone.

In Step 3, your Mac will warn you that you need to pay attention to your phone, and display (in the clear) the passkey you entered on the previous window. If everything's working correctly, a window should pop up on your phone, where the title bar is the name of your computer, and the options are 1: Accept, 2: Add to paired, or 3: Decline. Choose option 2, Add to paired, enter the passkey, and then click the Yes button. At this point, your Mac and your phone are paired, but you're not quite done yet! Hit the Continue button, shown in Figure 6-6.

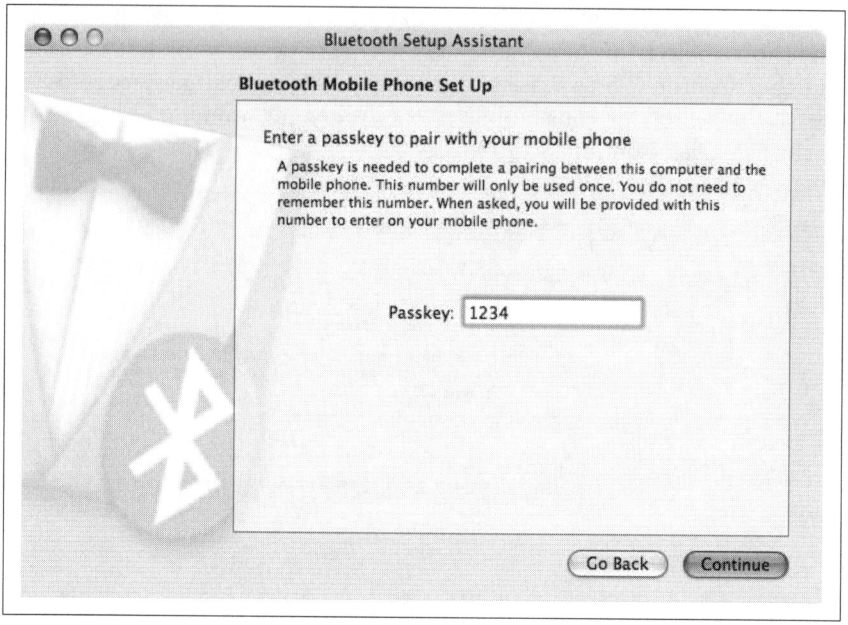

Figure 6-5. Bluetooth Setup Assistant, Step 2

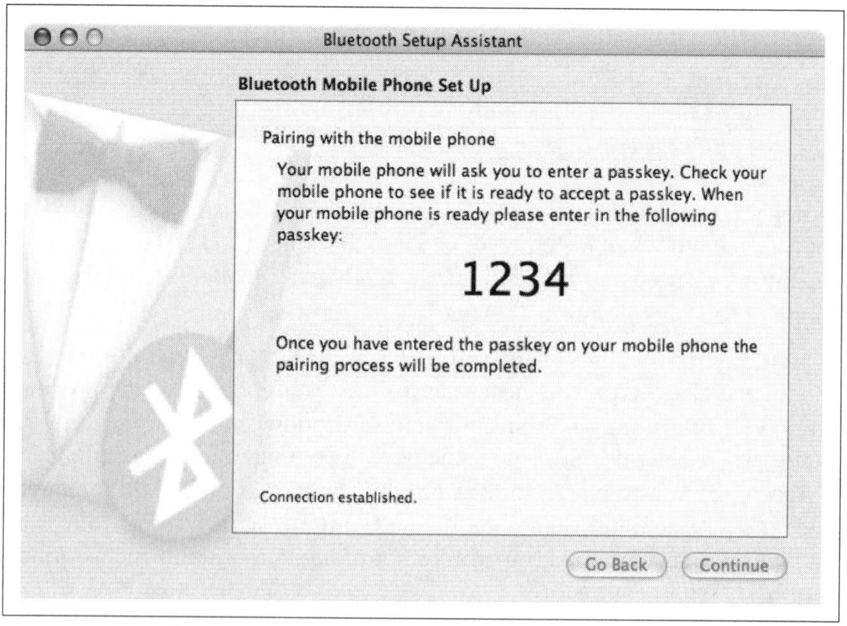

Figure 6-6. Bluetooth Setup Assistant, Step 3

Some phones, such as the Nokia 3650, do not automatically trust paired devices and will demand authorization each time you try to do something. To tell the phone it can trust your Mac, go to Menu → Connectivity → Bluetooth and press the right joystick button to bring up the list of paired devices. Next, select your Mac in the list and select Options → Set as authorized. Other phones may have a similar feature.

Your Mac now needs to figure out what services your phone can handle, and there may be a short pause while the two exchange information. Eventually, the Bluetooth Setup Assistant will switch to Step 4 (see Figure 6-7), where you can choose which of the available services you plan to use. You'll definitely want iSync and Address Book capabilities. If you plan on using your phone as a modem (covered in Chapter 7), choose the third option as well. Click Continue to go to the next step.

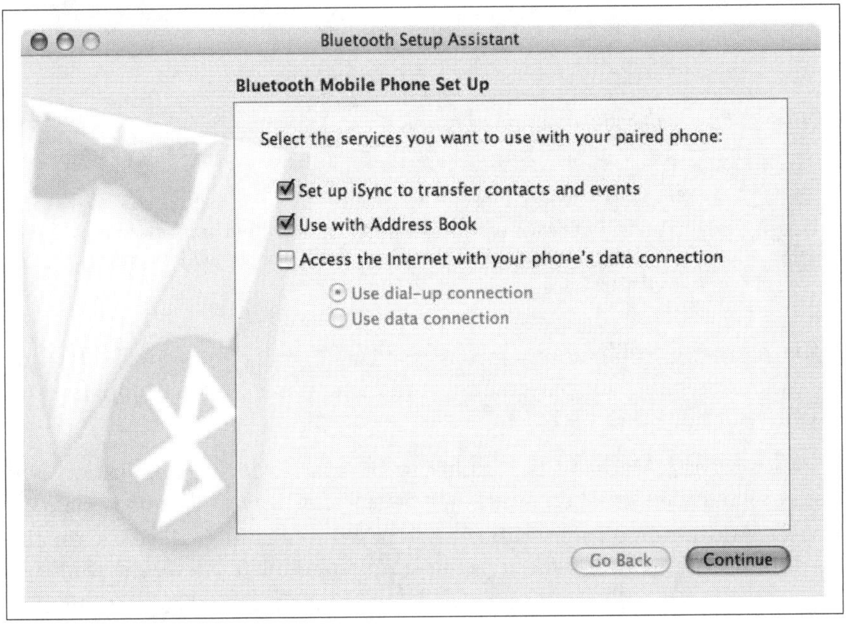

Figure 6-7. Bluetooth Setup Assistant, Step 4

The conclusion screen (see Figure 6-8) displays the features you've configured and tells you that you've completed the process. You can click Quit to leave the Setup Assistant and return to Bluetooth Preferences.

```
┌─────────────────────────────────────────────────────────────┐
│  ⊖ ○ ○              Bluetooth Setup Assistant                │
│                                                               │
│   Bluetooth Mobile Phone Set Up                               │
│   ┌─────────────────────────────────────────────────────┐   │
│   │  Congratulations! Your mobile phone is now set up to │   │
│   │  use your computer's Bluetooth features.             │   │
│   │                                                       │   │
│   │  Your computer and mobile phone were configured with │   │
│   │  the following services:                             │   │
│   │     • Use iSync to transfer contacts and events      │   │
│   │                                                       │   │
│   │     • Use with Address Book                          │   │
│   │                                                       │   │
│   │                                                       │   │
│   │                                                       │   │
│   │  Use this Setup Assistant again if you want to       │   │
│   │  change any of these settings.                       │   │
│   └─────────────────────────────────────────────────────┘   │
│   ( Set Up Another Device )        ( Go Back )  ( Quit )     │
└─────────────────────────────────────────────────────────────┘
```

Figure 6-8. Bluetooth Setup Assistant, conclusion

 If, in Step 4, you choose to use your cell phone to access the Internet, you'll see a fifth step asking for more information about your connection. The conclusion screen will be displayed afterwards.

Upon returning to Bluetooth Preferences (see Figure 6-9), you should now see your cell phone displayed under the list of both paired and favorite devices, but not connected.

In order for the Mac and the phone to be connected, an application will need to make the actual connection. The simplest way to do this is via Mac OS X's Address Book application. As shown in Figure 6-10, click on the black Bluetooth icon (it's the right-most one on the left side of the toolbar). Appropriately, the Bluetooth icon will turn blue, and also animate briefly. Your Mac and your phone are now both paired and connected, and Address Book can interact with your cell phone.

If you are trying to use iSync to synchronize your Address Book and your cell phone, but keep getting error messages from iSync, try enabling the Bluetooth button in Address Book. It's not always necessary to do this, but may help if you're having trouble.

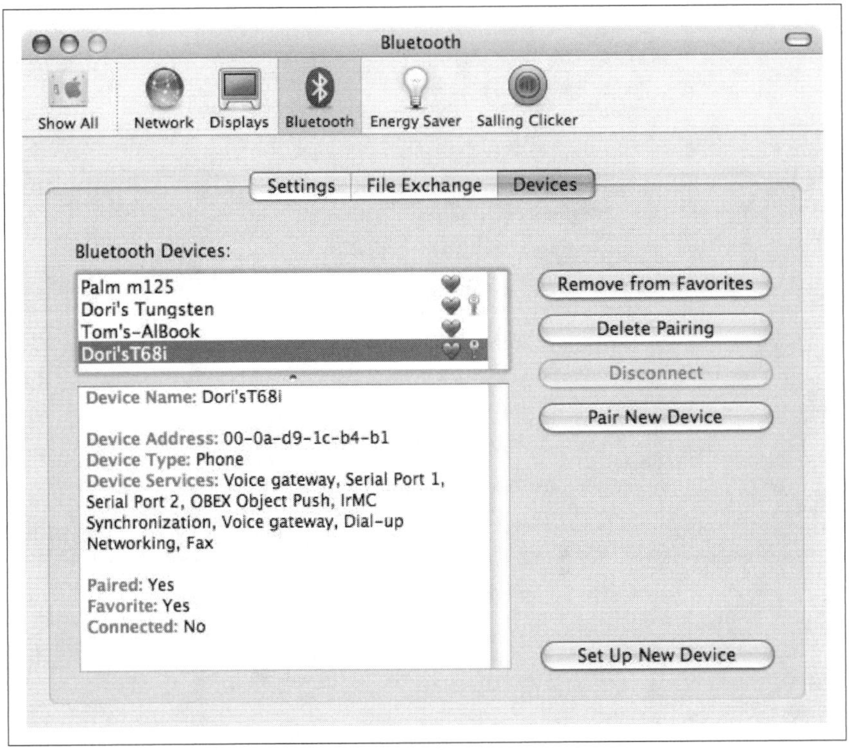

Bluetooth

Show All | Network | Displays | Bluetooth | Energy Saver | Salling Clicker

Settings | File Exchange | **Devices**

Bluetooth Devices:

Palm m125	♥
Dori's Tungsten	♥ ♀
Tom's–AIBook	♥
Dori'sT68i	♥ ♀

Device Name: Dori'sT68i

Device Address: 00-0a-d9-1c-b4-b1
Device Type: Phone
Device Services: Voice gateway, Serial Port 1,
Serial Port 2, OBEX Object Push, IrMC
Synchronization, Voice gateway, Dial-up
Networking, Fax

Paired: Yes
Favorite: Yes
Connected: No

Remove from Favorites
Delete Pairing
Disconnect
Pair New Device

Set Up New Device

Figure 6-9. Bluetooth Preferences after pairing; note that the selected phone is paired and a favorite, but not connected

Apple hasn't documented what they mean by "favorite" devices, and it doesn't appear to be meaningful as yet. All paired devices are added to the list by default; if you want one removed, just select it and click on "Remove from Favorites."

Another of the Bluetooth Preferences options (shown previously in Figure 6-2) is to show the Bluetooth status in the menu bar. This is very helpful, as it lets you see the current status at a glance. Figure 6-11 shows the various status symbols.

If you install a Bluetooth adapter, put the Bluetooth icon in the menu bar, but then remove the adapter, you'll find that you can no longer remove the icon from the menu bar because that option is now grayed out in the Preferences. If that's the case, hold down the Control key and drag the icon from the menu bar onto the desktop. It will vanish with a small puff of smoke.

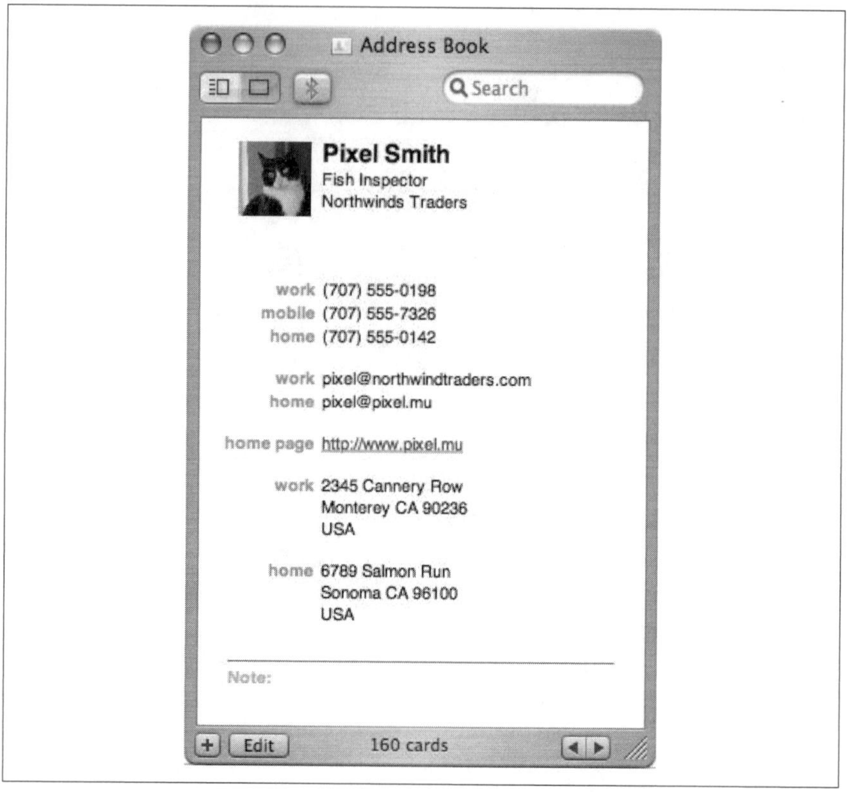

Figure 6-10. Turning Bluetooth on in Address Book

Figure 6-11. Bluetooth menu bar icons: disabled, enabled but off, enabled and on, and connected

Using Your Phone

At this point, your phone is paired and connected, so it's time to put it to work. Bluetooth phones work with your Mac in ways that you'll soon wonder how you lived without.

> If you can't get the following examples to work, make sure that you have Address Book running and the Address Book Bluetooth button is blue (i.e., on).

Announcing incoming calls. If someone calls your cell phone when you're within range of your Mac, a small window (see Figure 6-12) will pop up telling you that you have an incoming phone call. If the caller is in your address book, their name and the calling number will be displayed; otherwise, just the number will be shown.

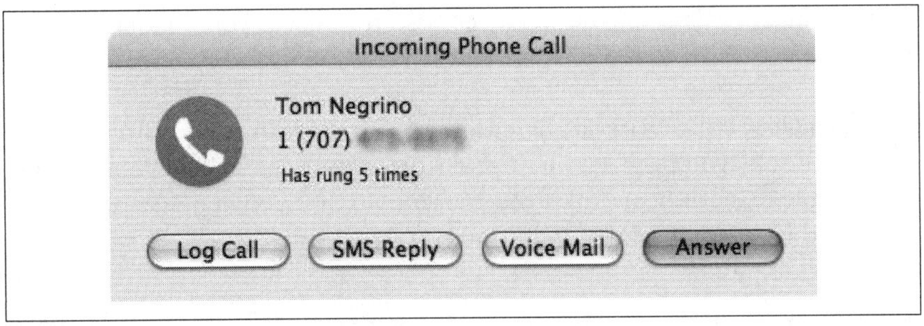

> ### Incoming Phone Call
>
> **Tom Negrino**
> 1 (707) ▓▓▓-▓▓▓▓
> Has rung 5 times
>
> (Log Call) (SMS Reply) (Voice Mail) (**Answer**)

Figure 6-12. Incoming phone call alert

This window gives you three choices:

SMS Reply
> A new sheet opens with a text box (Figure 6-13). You can use this form to enter an SMS message that will be sent (via your phone) to the caller. The caller will be automatically transferred to your voice mail.

> **Sending SMS message to: Tom Negrino**
> Messaging
>
> **Message:**
>
> | how r u? |
>
> 152 characters left.   (Cancel)   (Send)

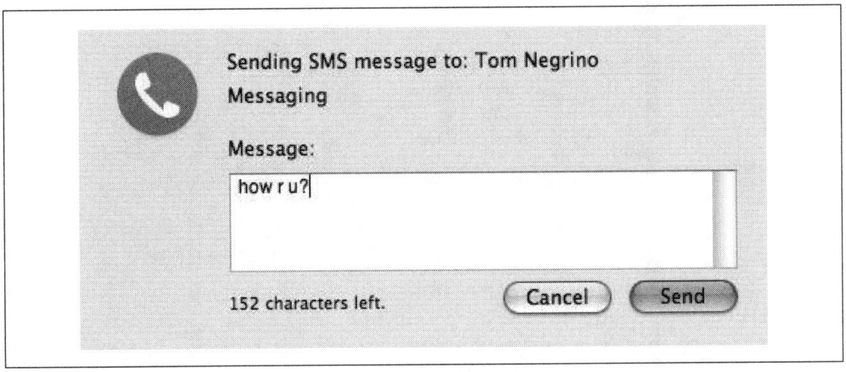

Figure 6-13. Outgoing SMS message box

This option will always be available, regardless of whether or not the recipient has the ability to receive SMS messages. If they don't, no error message is given.

Voice Mail

This is the same as refusing the call on your phone. If you choose this option, the caller is pushed to voice mail.

Answer

This option works the same way as just answering your phone.

If you don't pick any of these and choose to answer your phone instead, your Mac treats it as if you'd chosen "Answer."

Making outgoing calls. Without Bluetooth, if you click on a phone number in Address Book, you're given the option of displaying the number in large type. While this can be useful if you're trying to dial from a phone across the room, it'd be a lot simpler if your Mac could just tell your phone what number to dial. Bluetooth to the rescue!

If Bluetooth is active, there are two more options, as shown in Figure 6-14.

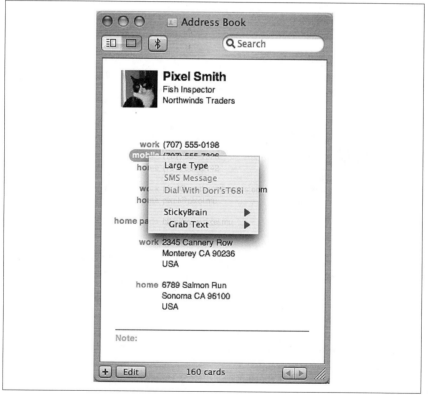

Figure 6-14. Outgoing call options in Address Book

SMS Message

A new sheet appears within the Address Book window, allowing you to enter your message into a text box (Figure 6-15).

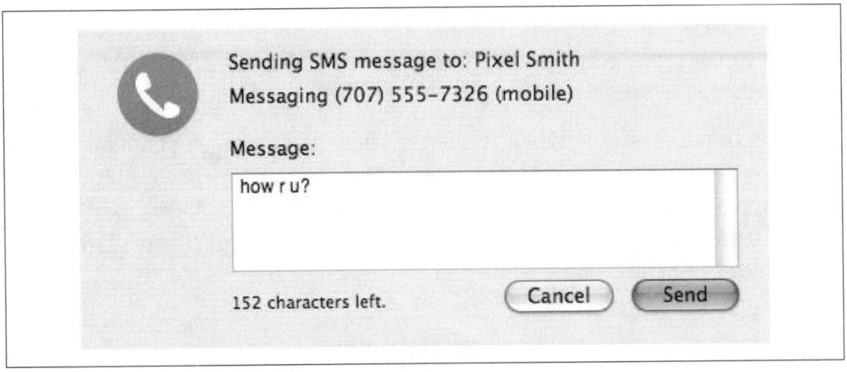

Sending SMS message to: Pixel Smith
Messaging (707) 555-7326 (mobile)

Message:

how r u?

152 characters left.   Cancel   Send

Figure 6-15. Sending an SMS message from Address Book

 Again, Address Book won't warn you if the number you're messaging can't receive SMS messages.

Dial

This works just about the way you'd imagine: pick this option, and your cell phone starts to immediately dial out.

Fun with Phones

Once Apple had Bluetooth connectivity handling the cell phone basics, third-party developers started having some fun. A couple of applications have been introduced that allow you to use your cell phone as a remote control for your Mac: Salling Clicker (formerly Sony Ericsson Clicker), shareware from Salling Software *http://clicker.salling.com/*, and Romeo, freeware from Arboreal Software *http://www.irowan.com/arboreal/*.

Salling Clicker. Salling Clicker hasn't been out long, but it's already impressive enough that an early version won Apple Design Awards for both "Best Mac OS X Product (Best of Show)" and "Most Innovative Mac OS X Product" at Apple's Worldwide Developer Conference in 2003. Clicker uses Bluetooth to tell your Mac to run AppleScripts that control your Mac and Mac applications. For instance, it's possible to control applications such as iTunes and DVD Player from across the room and, unlike previously available IR remotes, your Mac doesn't have to be in your line of sight.

In addition, Clicker has a proximity sensor, which can tell when your phone leaves or moves into range. This is useful for situations varying from the handy (pausing iTunes when you leave your desk and restarting when you come back) to the serious (starting up a password-protected screensaver when you move out of range). Clicker can also control both Microsoft PowerPoint and Apple Keynote, allowing you to give presentations without being tethered to your Mac.

Figure 6-16 shows Clicker's Preferences. There's just one gotcha here: it says that you can "access [Clicker's] menu from the Accessories menu," but many new Clicker users can't find the Accessories menu. Don't fret, on the T68i it's the last option under the "Connect" menu, and it's available only when your phone is paired to another Bluetooth device.

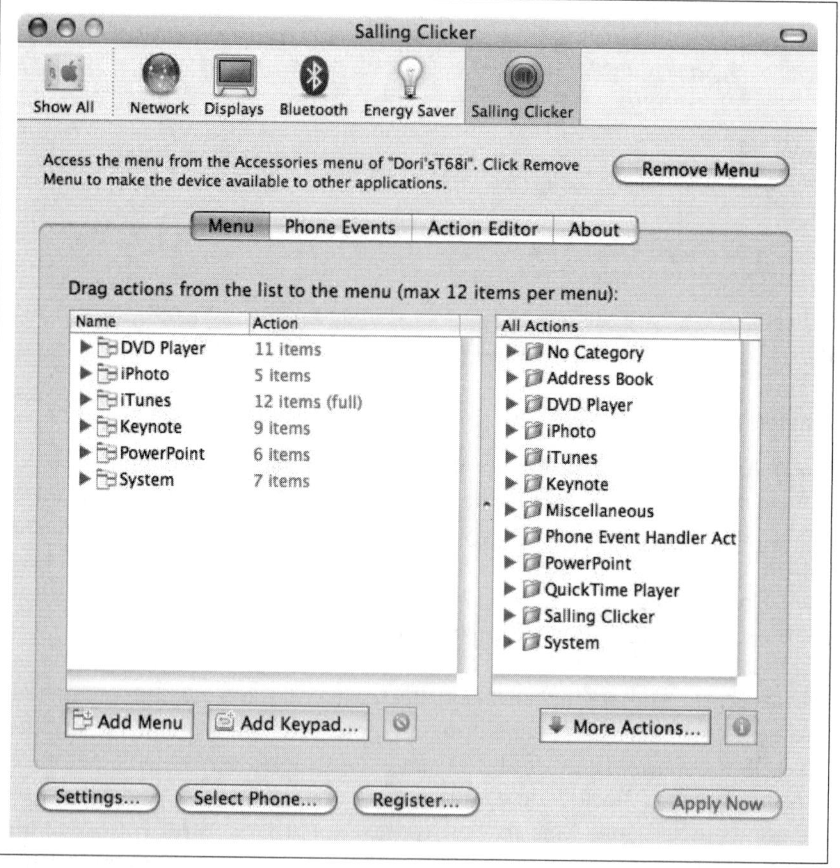

Figure 6-16. Salling Clicker 2.0's Preference pane

But wait, there's more! Clicker doesn't just let you use your cell phone as a remote, it also does the same for Bluetooth-enabled PDAs. Since Palm OS support was a little trickier, Clicker has two different price tags: $10 for phone usage versus $15 for Palm OS usage. If you want to use it with both your T68i *and* your Tungsten T, Clicker will set you back $25. But if you're the type who has to give frequent presentations, just being able to see slide notes on your Palm while controlling a PowerPoint presentation on your laptop makes Clicker a must-have.

Using Salling Clicker is beyond the scope of this book; refer to the program's documentation for more information.

Romeo. Like Salling Clicker, the open source (and free) Romeo lets you use a cellular phone as a remote, and also includes support for AppleScript. Although Romeo does not have Salling Clicker's Palm support built-in, you can use it with Palm devices, as well as the popular Nokia 3650 (and compatible Bluetooth-enabled Series 60 devices such as the Nokia 7650) using Veta Universal. Romeo supports several models of Sony Ericsson phones without requiring Veta Universal.

Veta Universal (*http://veta.irowan.com/*) is a shareware application that allows your Series 60 phone or Palm to emulate enough of the behavior of Sony Ericsson phones to work with Romeo. It does not support Salling Clicker, though. Romeo supports many of the same features as Salling Clicker, and both are well worth trying out. Figure 6-17 shows Romeo's options dialog, along with a window showing a connection to a Nokia 3650 phone.

Moving Data with Bluetooth

There are numerous ways to move data from your Mac to your phone: iSync (covered later in this chapter) and many third party utilities all let you shuttle bits wirelessly. Many of them, however, are just reinventing the wheel, since Mac OS X 10.2 includes Bluetooth File Exchange (found in your Utilities folder) to do just that.

Bluetooth File Exchange. Running Bluetooth File Exchange couldn't be simpler: just choose a file to send, pick a connected device to receive it, and off it goes! You can use this program to send homemade wallpaper to your phone. The T68i has a wallpaper resolution of 101×80 pixels at 256 colors and will happily accept GIFs. If you edit the GIF on your Mac, be sure to save it without a preview or resource fork, to keep its size down.

You can also use Bluetooth File Exchange to send installers (*.jar* or *.sis* files) for games and other applications to a smartphone such as the Nokia 3650 (the file will appear in your messaging inbox; when you open it, the installer will start running).

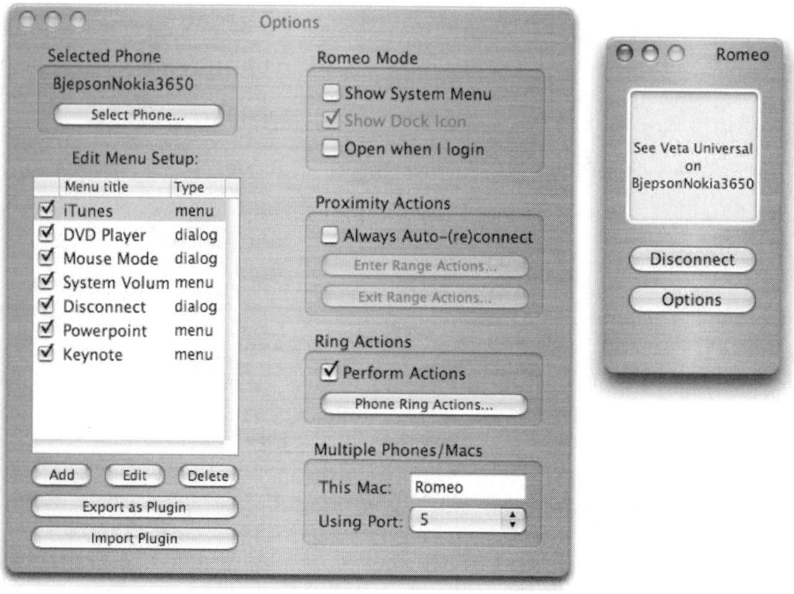

Figure 6-17. Using Romeo with a Nokia 3650

It's common for a warning to appear on your Mac saying that the target (receiving) device won't accept that type of file (Figure 6-18). It's been our experience that that's often not the case, and that the file arrives and works just fine—so if you get that message, try to send it anyway.

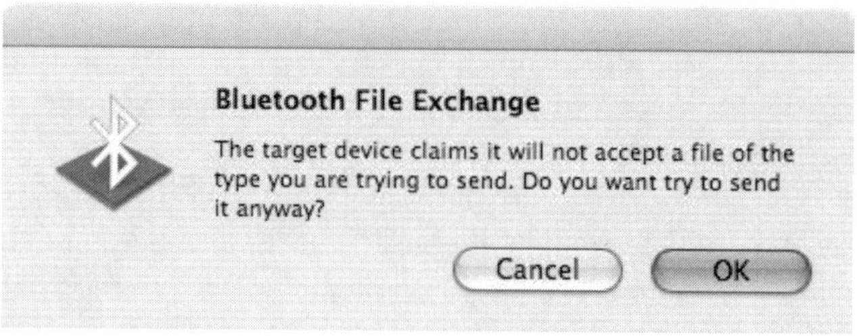

Figure 6-18. Bluetooth File Exchange's often-erroneous warning

Connecting a PDA

Phones aren't the only reason to use Bluetooth on your Mac. Some PDAs (such as the Palm Tungsten T) have built-in Bluetooth, while others (like the Palm m500 series) can add it on via a Bluetooth Secure Digital (SD) card.

Pairing Your PDA and Mac

If you've previously paired your Mac with a phone, most of this section should look pretty familiar. The primary difference is, unsurprisingly, setting up Bluetooth on your PDA. The following assumes that you have a Palm Tungsten T; other Palm devices should be fairly similar.

Pairing the Mac from the Palm. As with a phone, you can start pairing your PDA on either the Mac side or the Palm side. On the Palm, start by running the Prefs application, choosing Communication and then Bluetooth (see Figure 6-19).

```
┌─────────────────────────────────────────────────────┐
│                                                       │
│   ╔═══════════════╗                                   │
│   ║ Preferences   ║          Bluetooth                │
│   ╚═══════════════╝                                   │
│                                                       │
│          Bluetooth:  ▼ On                             │
│                                                       │
│        Device Name:  ┆Tom Tungsten┆                   │
│                                                       │
│       Discoverable:  ▼ Yes                            │
│                                                       │
│       Allow Wakeup:  ▼ No                             │
│                                                       │
│                                                       │
│                                                       │
│     ( Done ) ( Trusted Devices ) ( Help )             │
│                                                       │
└─────────────────────────────────────────────────────┘
```

Figure 6-19. Palm Bluetooth preferences

Turn Bluetooth on, give your PDA a meaningful device name, and set discoverable to "Yes." "Allow Wakeup" has three options: choosing "Yes" will enable your Mac to wake up your Palm when something's being exchanged. Choosing "Scheduled" is the same as "Yes," but only between the hours that you specify. Selecting "Yes" takes more battery power than "Scheduled," and "Scheduled" takes more battery power than "No."

> Just because you set your PDA to allow wakeup doesn't mean that any random Bluetooth device can wake it up. Only devices that are trusted and previously connected are allowed to do that.

Click the "Trusted Devices" button and a list will display of any previously paired devices (see Figure 6-20).

Figure 6-20. Trusted Devices window

Click on the "Add Device" button, and a "Bluetooth Discovery" window will appear, looking for a local, discoverable Bluetooth device. If found, a "Discovery Results" window will display, with a prompt showing the device. Select the device, and then click the "OK" button. A "Bluetooth Security" window will display requesting a passkey; when entered, a window will appear on your Mac (Figure 6-21) asking for the same passkey.

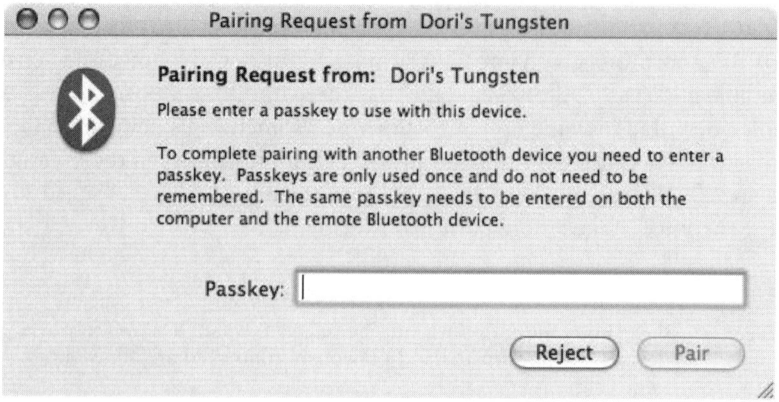

Figure 6-21. OS X's response to receiving a pairing request

At this point, it's been our experience that you will frequently receive an error on the Palm saying "Unable to add <*your Mac name*> to your trusted device list." It appears that this error message is itself in error, as the device has always been successfully added.

Pairing the Palm from the Mac. If you want to start the pairing procedure from the Mac, you'll still need to start off by setting the PDA to have Bluetooth on and be discoverable, as shown in the previous section. On the Mac, launch Bluetooth Setup Assistant and choose "Other Device" (as shown in Figure 6-22), and click "Continue."

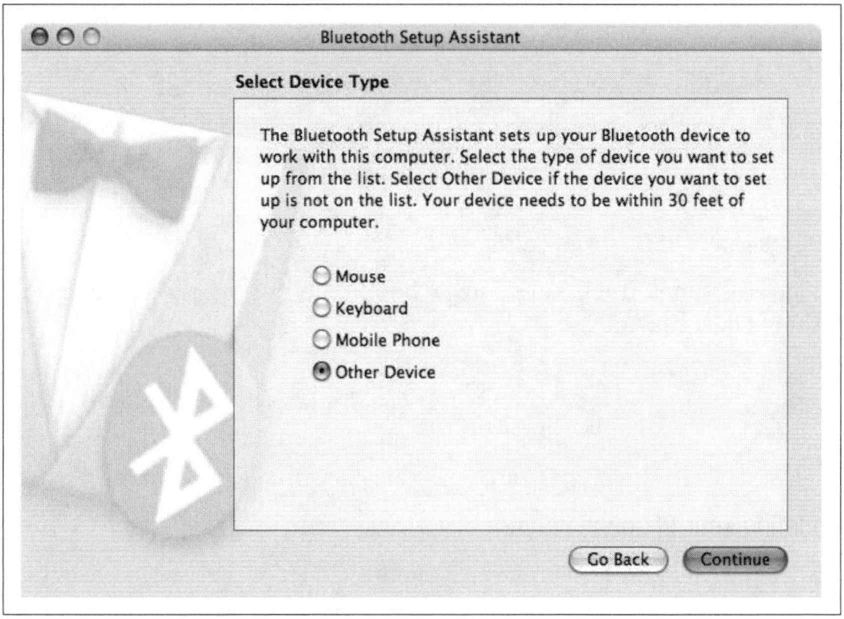

Figure 6-22. Bluetooth Setup Assistant for PDAs

A window similar to the one in Figure 6-23 will appear, showing your Palm device. Select it and click "Continue."

Once again, enter the same passkey on both the Mac and the Palm, and they're connected.

Using iSync

Apple's iSync application isn't a Wi-Fi–only application, but it works just fine over Bluetooth for both phones and Palm devices. While syncing a

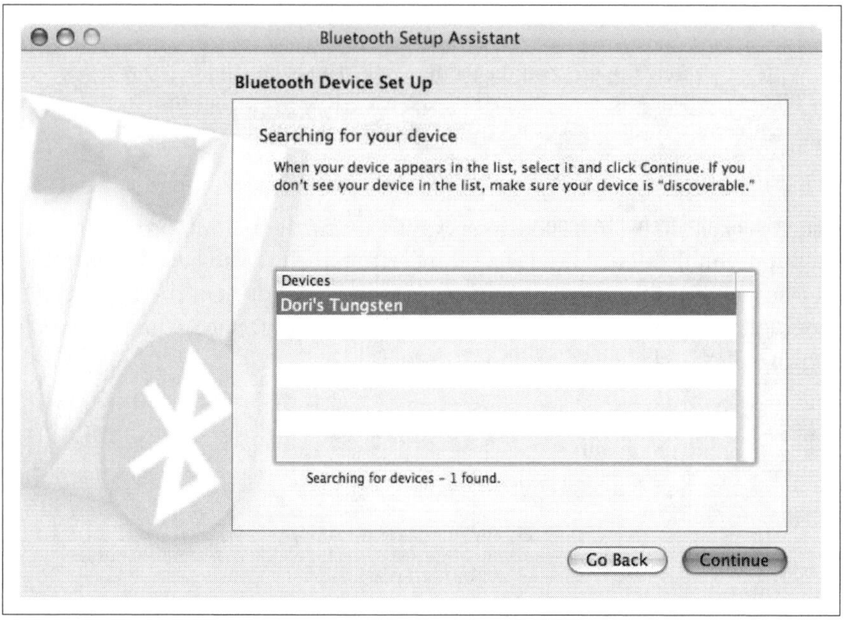

Figure 6-23. Bluetooth finding a PDA

phone is as simple as clicking a single button, it's not as easy or seamless as it should be for PDAs.

We used iSync 1.2 when writing this chapter; later versions should work in much the same way.

Updating Your Phone via iSync

To connect your phone with iSync, you must add it to the list of devices that iSync knows about. Launch iSync (which should be in your Applications folder) and choose "Add Device..." from the Devices menu. If you've paired your phone with your Mac in the past and your phone is discoverable, iSync should be able to find it. Double-click your phone to add it to the list of iSync-able devices.

Figure 6-24 shows iSync with two known devices (plus a .Mac account) and preferences that show the initial sync of a Sony Ericsson T68i phone. When first syncing, you're given the choice of merging the data on the computer and phone or clearing the data on the phone and then syncing. You can also choose whether to sync contacts and, if you do, to sync all contacts, or only those with phone numbers. Lastly, you can also sync your calendar, including a choice of some or all categories, and how many future calendar entries you want to transfer: 1, 2, 4, or 8 weeks.

When set up to your liking, simply click the "Sync Now" button, and voila! It's all done. If you've ever entered a few dozen names and numbers into a phone by hand or ransacked your desk looking for a connection cable, you'll wonder how you ever lived without iSync and Bluetooth.

Figure 6-24. Syncing the Mac and phone

One of us once had the brilliant idea of setting up a new Mac's Address Book by syncing all the contacts from an already-synced phone to the new Mac. Unfortunately, some phones (this was a T68i) don't distinguish between first and last names—they only have a single name field. This meant that all the names ended up in the Mac's Address Book with the entire name in the last name field and all the first name fields blank. While this plan originally seemed like a time-saver, it wasn't!

Updating Your PDA Via iSync

Updating your PDA via iSync isn't as simple, and requires several more steps to set up. Oddly enough, one of those steps is ignoring a message on your Mac saying that this process isn't even possible.

First, make sure that you have iSync 1.2 Palm Conduit (or later) installed. This program can be downloaded from Apple at *http://www.apple.com/isync/ download/*. Make sure that you're downloading the Conduit software, not the iSync software (available from the same page). Install it.

Next, launch Palm HotSync Manager (found in the Palm folder, which is inside your Applications folder) and choose the Connection Settings tab in the HotSync Software Setup window. If you've installed the iSync Palm Conduit software, you should find a "bluetooth-pda-sync-port" connection in the list. Click the on button to enable it, as shown in Figure 6-25.

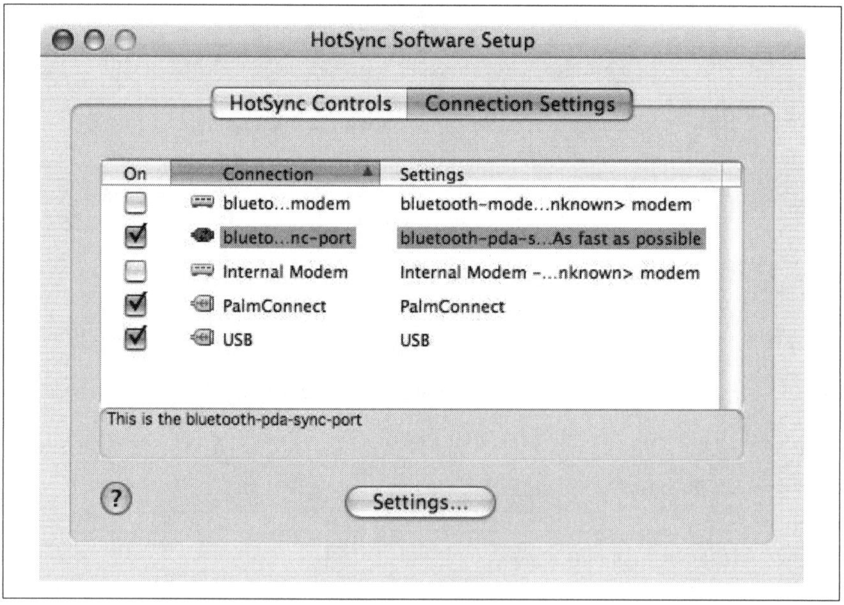

Figure 6-25. HotSync Manager's bluetooth-pda-sync-port

Under the HotSync menu, choose "Conduit Settings." Find the iSync Conduit (Figure 6-26) and double-click it. Choose to enable iSync for this Palm device, as shown in Figure 6-27.

When you next launch iSync, your Palm device should now display along with your other syncable devices (Figure 6-28). As with syncing a phone, you're given a choice of how you want to handle your first sync, as well as whether you want to sync contacts, calendars, or both.

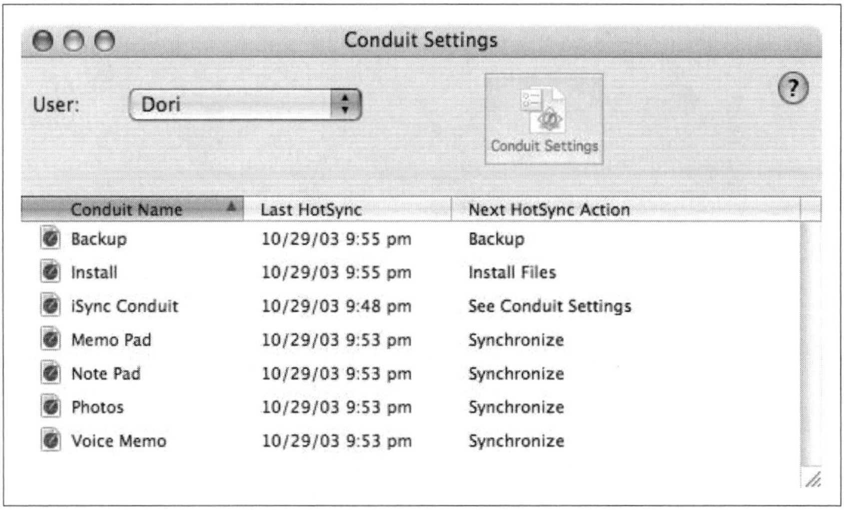

Figure 6-26. HotSync Manager's Conduit Settings

Figure 6-27. Conduit Setting's iSync Options

However, if you try to sync, you'll get the warning message shown in Figure 6-29, saying that you can only synchronize your PDA if it's sitting in its cradle. But that's not actually the case.

To sync using Bluetooth, you'll need to tell your PDA that it can handle the protocol. If you go into the Palm's Prefs → Communication → Connection, you'll see a list of connections that your Palm knows about. If Bluetooth isn't listed (which is how it ships), you can create it manually. Hit the

Figure 6-28. Syncing your PDA with your Mac

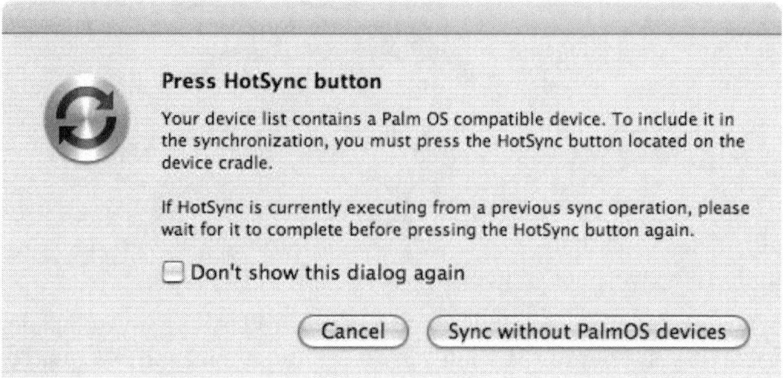

Figure 6-29. Syncing doesn't actually require cables and a cradle

"New…" button and change the name of the new connection to something meaningful, such as "BT Connect." Change the "Connect to:" option to "PC," the "Via:" to "Bluetooth," and tap the device box to find your Mac. When that's successful (see Figure 6-30), click OK, and you've created a new connection.

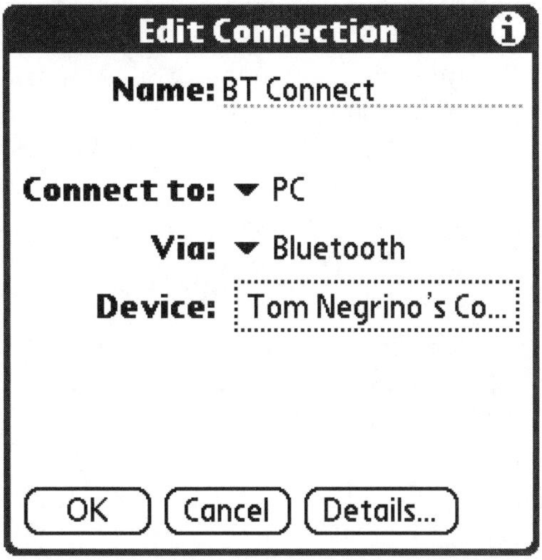

Edit Connection ℹ️

Name: BT Connect

Connect to: ▼ PC

Via: ▼ Bluetooth

Device: Tom Negrino's Co…

(OK) (Cancel) (Details…)

Figure 6-30. Setting up a Bluetooth connection method for syncing

Lastly, run the HotSync application on your Palm device. Choose "Local," and you'll see a list of the locally available connections. Pick "BT Connect" (or whatever you've named it) from the list, and start up your sync by tapping the HotSync button. No cradle or wires necessary!

Just because you can HotSync over Bluetooth, it doesn't mean that you always should. We found that synchronizing via Bluetooth was significantly slower than using the USB cradle if we had a lot of data to synchronize (when installing files on the Palm, for instance). If you just want to do a quick update of calendar and contacts, though, Bluetooth is speedy enough.

Bluetooth Security

In Chapter 5, you saw that wireless security is a big concern, and that Wi-Fi's WEP security system leaves much to be desired. If you're wondering about Bluetooth, it's not any more secure than Wi-Fi. There are authentication and encryption settings that you can enable in the Bluetooth panel of System Preferences, as shown in Figure 6-31.

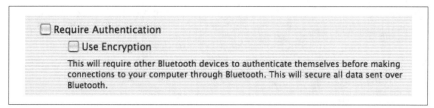

Figure 6-31. Enable Bluetooth security in the Bluetooth panel of System Preferences

The authentication setting will require the two devices attempting to connect to go through a process that checks that the PIN code is the same on both devices, after which a 128-bit link key is generated. The devices test the link key in a series of challenges, and if the authentication is successful, the devices make the connection. If the challenge fails, the Bluetooth device must wait for a while before it can attempt authentication again. This is a security measure designed to foil hackers who might be bombarding the device with a series of authentication requests.

The encryption setting will protect data transmitted between the two Bluetooth devices. The level of encryption is negotiated between the master and slave devices, and can use an encryption key of between 8 and 128 bits. Turning on encryption will make data transfers between devices somewhat slower.

As in any evaluation of security with a networking method, you have to decide how important the data being protected is, assess the likelihood that the data flowing between your devices will be intercepted, and make a judgment of how best to manage the potential risk. Because most Bluetooth networking occurs within 30-foot radius, it is easier for you to get a handle on the possible threat—you can often just look around.

You'll need to decide what you stand to lose if the data flowing between your computer and your cell phone or PDA is compromised. In our case, that data is mainly contact and scheduling information, which may be private, but since it's not secret we choose to keep encryption turned off.

Troubleshooting Bluetooth

Because it's new technology, Bluetooth can sometimes be extremely picky about pairing, connecting, and exchanging data. Here are some useful tips for getting Bluetooth to work:

- Turn Bluetooth off and back on again (for both the Mac and the Bluetooth device).

- Turn discoverability off and back on again (for both the Mac and the Bluetooth device).
- In Bluetooth Preferences, delete the paired device and set it up again.
- On the device, delete the paired Mac. With the T68i, this is done under Bluetooth → (2) Linked devices → choose the device → (2) Delete → Yes to delete. With the Palm, this is done under Prefs → Communications → Bluetooth → Trusted Devices → choose the device → Details... → Delete Device.
- Remove and reinstall the Bluetooth adapter, forcing the driver to reload. Obviously, you won't be able to do this if your Mac has a built-in Bluetooth module.
- If you normally pair devices from the Mac, try initiating the process from the device, and vice versa.
- Verify that the target device is discoverable and within 30 feet of your Mac.
- If all else fails, restart your Mac and start the process from the beginning.

CHAPTER SEVEN

Cellular Connectivity

In theory, cellular networking offers the ultimate unwired experience: network connectivity as long as you are in range of a cell tower. In practice, it's much less than its promise, but it's still getting better every day. Most unwired power users employ a combination of Wi-Fi hotspots and cellular networking to satisfy their lust for bandwidth.

Cellular Networking Price and Performance

Cellular networking offers the following downstream speeds (for activities such as receiving email, downloading files via FTP, and surfing the Web):

- 19.2 Kbps on first generation (1G) networks. Cellular Digital Packet Data (CDPD) is a once-popular 1G service that cellular providers are hoping to phase out.

- 30–70 Kbps on early third-generation (3G) networks (often referred to as 2.5G), sometimes peaking to 144 Kbps. General Packet Radio Services (GPRS) is the leading 2.5G service. AT&T Wireless uses GPRS for its mMode consumer-oriented data plans and its Mobile Internet business-oriented data plans. T-Mobile uses GPRS for its T-Mobile Internet data plans. Cingular also uses GPRS on their GSM network.

- 144 Kbps and higher on 3G networks. CDMA2000, Enhanced Data GSM Environment (EDGE), and UMTS are emerging 3G technologies. The first phase of CDMA2000 is 1x Radio Transmission Technology (1xRTT), which is used by Verizon's Express Network and Sprint's PCS Vision. At the time of this writing, EDGE is not widely available, but has reportedly been quietly deployed by AT&T Wireless and Cingular.

Upstream speeds (for activities such as sending email, using FTP to upload files, and uploading documents to web sites) are generally less than the downstream speeds, anywhere from 9.6 Kbps to about half the downstream speed.

One of the fundamental limits on cellular networking is the price of data. Typical packages offer a bucket of data with coverage charged per kilobyte over the limit. Table 7-1 shows some examples based on current U.S. pricing.

Table 7-1. 1G, 2.5G, and 3G pricing

Data quantity	1G	2.5G and 3G
Unlimited	$40-$60/month	$80 or more per month for 1xRTT or GPRS service. At the time of this writing, T-Mobile is the only GPRS provider offering cheap unlimited data plans ($20.00/month).
5 MB	n/a	$15–$20 per month
20 MB	n/a	$35–$55 per month

A busy user can easily blow through 20 MB in just a couple of hours of web surfing and email. Heavy users should opt for an unlimited pricing plan, or carefully plan out their usage to take advantage of (free, if possible) Wi-Fi hotspots and use the cellular service only when absolutely necessary (such as sending out an urgent email while sitting on a runway).

Even with a data allotment that you're comfortable with, service can be spotty, though coverage is most comprehensive in densely populated areas (especially Europe and Asia). However, in a densely populated area such as New York City, buildings can interfere with the signals, and many simultaneous users can limit the performance of the network in a given area.

As tempting as it is to chalk up performance problems to early adoption doldrums, the old maxim still stands: let the buyer beware. If you knowingly purchase poor service in the hopes that it will improve over time, keep in mind that there is no guarantee that it will. When in doubt, seek the opinions of others. Howard Forums (*http://www.howardforums.com*) is an excellent resource. Also, the Usenet hierarchy *alt.cellular* has many newsgroups devoted to specific carriers where you can read about peoples' experiences (you can read and post to these newsgroups through Google Groups at *http://groups.google.com/*). Be sure to get service from a provider who offers a complete refund, no questions asked, within a reasonable trial time (some providers offer 15 days, which is too little, so try pressuring the salesperson for a 30-day trial).

Before (and after) you buy a phone, check out the *maccellphone* Yahoo! Group (*http://groups.yahoo.com/group/ maccellphone/*), which includes helpful discussion for using cell phones with the Macintosh and modem scripts that you can download from the group's Files page. Spend some time perusing the *maccellphone* archives to find out which phones work best with the Macintosh.

GPRS

General Packet Radio Service (GPRS) is a data service that supplements other data services such as Circuit Switched Data (CSD, used for data and fax calls on GSM networks) and Short Message Service (SMS). The design of GPRS was informed by the fact that wireless data communications are bursty in nature. That is, the data is not sent in one long stream, but rather in short bursts. Traditional use of CSD, such as the Wireless Application Protocol (WAP) for data transfer, requires establishing connections between two communicating parties, which occupies bandwidth even when not transmitting data. With GPRS, data is sent as packets as and when required, so you can have always-on connectivity without having to pay for the time you're online; providers can bill customers based on usage instead.

In this section, we take a closer look at how GPRS works, and discuss some of the devices that you can use on the road.

GPRS and 3G

3G wireless (or Third-Generation wireless) is an initiative to provide enhanced voice, text, and data services. The main draw of 3G networks is the vastly increased data transfer rate of between 384 Kbps and 2 Mbps. With these speed improvements, applications that support real-time video and high-quality multimedia elements can be deployed.

However, deploying 3G networks is not an overnight affair. It requires heavy investment from wireless carriers, as well as from telephone and modem manufacturers. Another issue is the allocation of the wireless spectrum in the United States. The FCC has very strict rules on how much radio spectrum is available to each carrier in any given market, and 3G technology takes significantly more radio spectrum to implement. Rollouts of 3G services will be slowed due to this policy. In the midst of waiting for the next generation wireless networks, GPRS bridges the gap between the current 2G networks (such as GSM or TDMA) and the forthcoming 3G networks. As such a stopgap, GPRS is commonly known as 2.5G.

3G networks being built today use UMTS/WCDMA, which is backed by the largest vendors of telecommunications equipment and large players such as AT&T Wireless, NTT DoCoMo, and others.

In the United States today you can get wireless Internet access over UMTS from a handful of small wireless networks in parts of Montana, Hawaii, and other places. These networks do not support voice calling; they were built only for rapid deployment of wireless Internet access via UMTS.

GSM Networks and GPRS

GPRS is a packet-switched service built on the existing Global System for Mobile (GSM) communication voice network. GSM was designed primarily for voice services.

A GSM channel contains eight *timeslots* (portions of time allocated to transmit data), with each timeslot dedicated to each circuit-switched call. Traditionally, you can use a maximum of only one timeslot when using CSD. With GPRS, timeslots can be assigned dynamically, and you can use more than one timeslot. This results in increased throughput.

GSM networks have more worldwide coverage than any other cellular technologies, such as CDMA and PDC (Personal Digital Cellular, used in Japan). In Asia and Europe, the frequencies used for GSM are 900 and 1800 MHz. In North America, it is 1900 MHz. Phones that support all three frequencies are known as tri-band or "World" phones. Examples of tri-band phones are the Sony Ericsson T610 and the Nokia 3650. (see Figures 7-1 and 7-2).

Figure 7-1. The Sony Ericsson T68i

Figure 7-2. The Nokia 3650

How GPRS Works

GPRS uses multiple timeslots for sending data. In theory, GPRS can use up to eight timeslots, but physical constraints (such as the number of users currently on the network, as well as the coverage quality) have reduced the number to a maximum of five, with one or two timeslots reserved for upstream communications (leaving three or four for downloads). There are four coding schemes used in GPRS networks. Table 7-2 shows these, their data rate per timeslot, and the maximum data speed for eight timeslots.

Table 7-2. Coding schemes used in GPRS

Channel coding scheme	Data rate per timeslot	Top data speed with eight timeslots
CS-1	9.05 Kbps	72.4 Kbps
CS-2	13.4 Kbps	107.2 Kbps
CS-3	15.6 Kbps	124.8 Kbps
CS-4	21.4 Kbps	171.2 Kbps

The coding scheme is determined by the service provider and depends on factors such as the quality of the channel (the radio link between the phone and the base station). CS-1 has the highest reliability (but the lowest data rate), and CS-4 has the least reliability (but the highest data rate).

Each phone has a certain number of timeslots used for downloading and uploading. The manufacturer of the phone determines the number of timeslots. For example, the Sony Ericsson T68i has four timeslots allocated for downloads, and one for uploads, so it's called a 4+1 device. With the CS-1 coding scheme, the maximum download speed would be 36.2 Kbps (9.05 Kbps×4). The Nokia 3650 is a 3+2 device. With the CS-2 coding scheme, the maximum download speed would be 40.2 Kbps (13.4 Kbps×3).

What if a phone call comes in while you are connected to the Internet? Most phones will only let you do one thing at a time, and answering a phone call will put your GPRS connection on hold until you are done with the call.

GPRS Phones

You can use a GPRS-enabled phone (like the Sony Ericsson T610 and the Nokia 3650) to access WAP sites (a mostly text version of the Web) on your mobile phone. You can also view full web sites, if your phone's browser supports it; if not, you may be able to find a third-party web browser for your phone at *http://www.handango.com*. You can also connect your Macintosh to your mobile phone (through Bluetooth or infrared) and use it as a modem.

SIM cards. A SIM is a smart card placed inside a GSM phone that identifies the user account to the network. It handles tasks such as authentication and acts as data storage for user data such as phone numbers, SMS messages, and network information. Figure 7-3 shows a SIM card inserted into a mobile phone. A SIM card may also contain applications that run on the phone.

Configuring a Bluetooth-Enabled Mobile Phone for GPRS Access

If you have a Bluetooth-enabled mobile phone, such as the Sony Ericsson T68i or Nokia 3650, you can set it up as a Bluetooth modem. In this section, we will show you how to wirelessly connect your Mac to the Internet using GPRS. Before you begin, ensure that your Mac is Bluetooth-enabled. See Chapter 6 for more information about Bluetooth.

1. Go to the Bluetooth icon (on the menu bar) and select "Set up Bluetooth Device...," as shown in Figure 7-4.

2. The Bluetooth Setup Assistant window will appear. Select the device you want to set up (Mobile Phone) and click Continue.

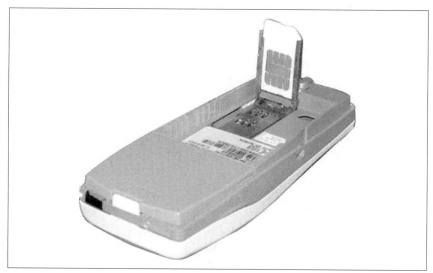

Figure 7-3. A SIM card inserted into a mobile phone

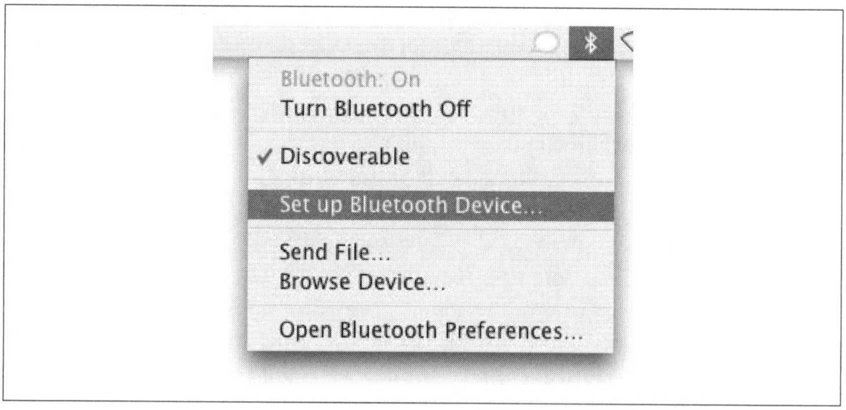

Figure 7-4. Setting up a Bluetooth device

3. Set your Bluetooth-enabled mobile phone to discovery mode.

4. When your mobile phone is found, Bluetooth Setup Assistant will show the name of your mobile phone. Select the phone and click Continue.

5. You will be asked to supply a passkey to pair up your Mac with the mobile phone. Ensure that you enter the same passkey on your phone.

6. You will also be asked to select the services that you want to use with your mobile phone. Select "Use data connection" to access the Internet (see Figure 7-5). Click Continue.

7. You also need to supply the credentials for dialing up to your ISP (see Figure 7-6). You should consult your ISP for such information. Click Continue to complete the setup.

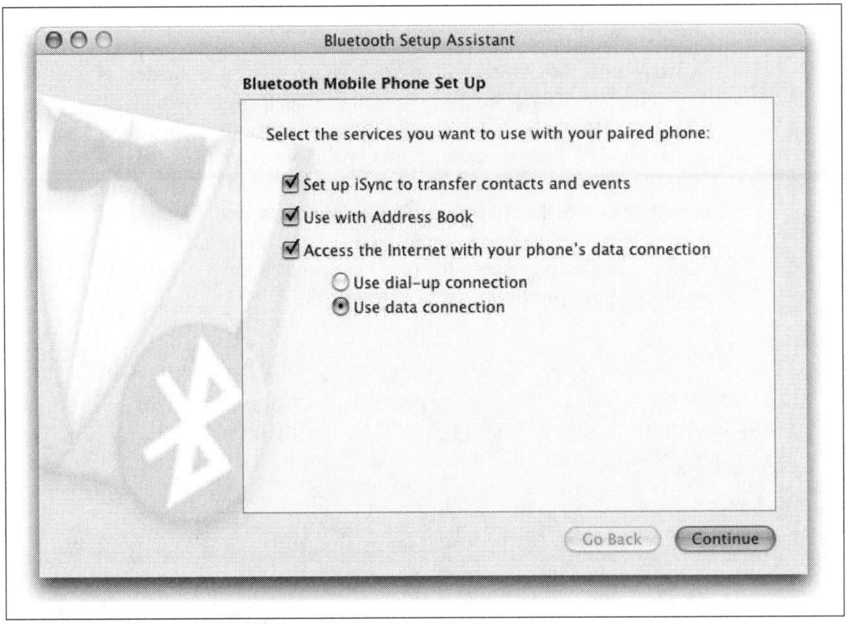

Figure 7-5. Configuring a mobile phone for data access

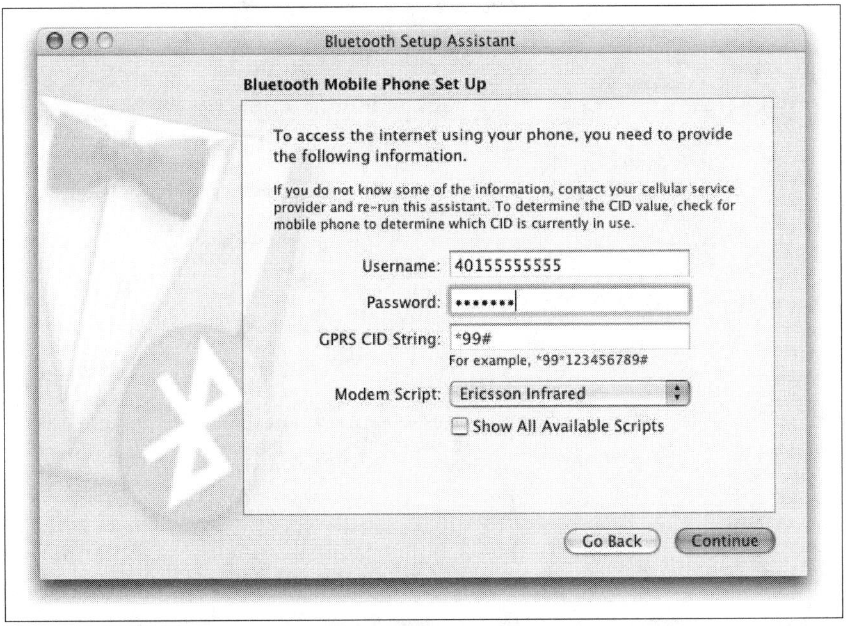

Figure 7-6. Entering credentials for dialing up to your ISP

Some cellular providers do not require a username or password—they only need the GPRS dialing sequence, which is typically *99*CID#, where CID is your connection ID (usually 1, as in *99*1#). This uses one of the connections defined on your phone. The modem scripts available from Ross Barkman's page (*http://www.taniwha.org.uk/gprs.html*) let you specify your cellular provider's GPRS access point as a telephone number (and you won't need to specify the CID string). That page also includes a list of access point names (APNs) for major cellular providers across the world.

8. You can dial the connection by going to System Preferences and selecting Network. Under the Show pop-up menu, select USB Bluetooth Modem Adapter. Click on "Dial Now..." to dial the connection (see Figure 7-7).

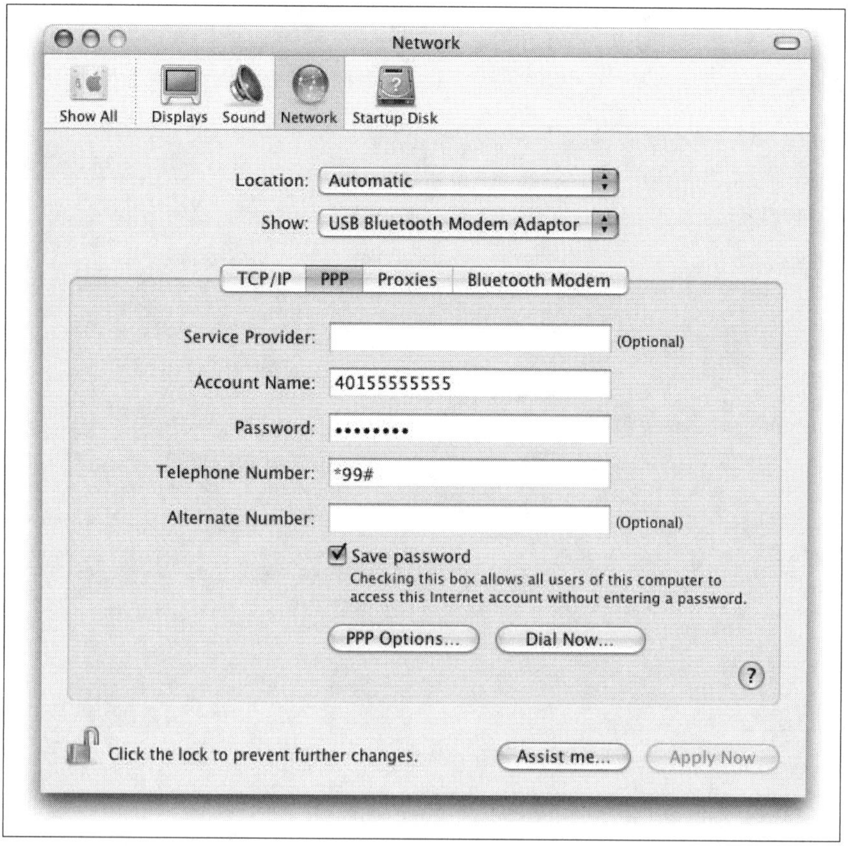

Figure 7-7. Dialing the Bluetooth data connection

9. You can also dial the connection by going directly to Internet Connect (located in the Applications folder) and clicking Connect (see Figure 7-8).

Figure 7-8. Using Internet Connect to dial the Bluetooth data connection

10. Once established, you should see the status of the connection (see Figure 7-9).

11. Launch your Web browser and see if you can connect to the Internet!

You can also connect your cell phone to the Internet via your Mac's Bluetooth connection. If you don't have a data plan (or have a limited data plan and want to save on usage charges), use C.K. Sample III's Share2Blue2th AppleScripts, available from *http://3650anda12inch.blogspot.com/*, to set up your computer as a GPRS access point over Bluetooth. This option allows you to use web browsers and services such as AvantGo (which downloads content optimized for your phone) without a data plan—you can simply sync when within Bluetooth range of your computer. Installation and configuration of the scripts is beyond the scope of this book, but we recommend giving them a try if you want to share an existing broadband Internet connection with your Bluetooth phone.

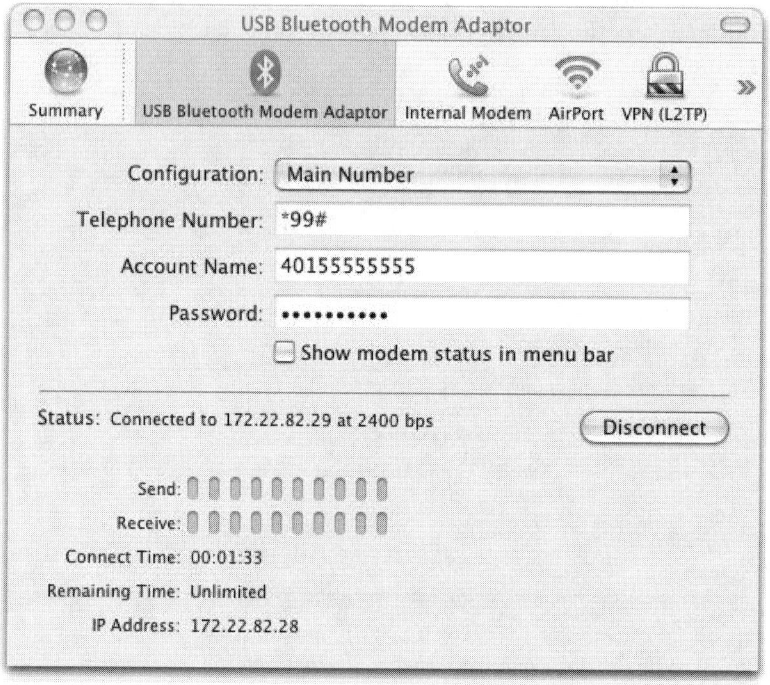

Figure 7-9. Viewing the status of the Bluetooth connection

Dialing an ISP with a Bluetooth-Enabled Mobile Phone

Circuit Switched Data (CSD) is a plain-vanilla way to transfer data using a circuit switching technique. It is like making a voice call between two parties—you have to establish a connection first. Once you are connected, you can start talking. With CSD, you're charged by the minute. CSD allows a data rate of 9.6 Kbps to 14.4 Kbps.

High Speed Circuit Switched Data (HSCSD) is the same as CSD except that its data rate is much higher—up to 43.2 Kbps is possible.

Compared to CSD, GPRS charges are usually billed based on the data actually transferred, not by connection time. However, some providers offer very limited GPRS service. For example, it would not be unusual to get 500 to 1000 voice minutes per month for $40 but to get only 20 MB of data for another $40. So, when you run out of megabytes at GPRS speeds (around 40 Kbps), you can switch over to dialing into a dial-up ISP or your workplace at CSD speeds, at which point you start using up your voice minutes (and whatever fees your ISP charges). Note that some U.S. providers do not permit CSD calls. For example, as of this writing, it is impossible to initiate a CSD call with AT&T Wireless's GSM service.

SMS Messaging

SMS messaging is very popular in Asia and is growing in popularity in the U.S. Teenagers can often input text faster (using numeric keypads on the phones) than some adults can type on a computer keyboard!

If you haven't tried sending an SMS message from your phone, the following description may put you off the idea entirely (but read on for a way to use your Macintosh to send and receive those messages).

Each numeric key on your phone is assigned three to four letters, shown in Table 7-3.

Table 7-3. Mapping numeric keys to letters

Key	Letters
2	a, b, c
3	d, e, f
4	g, h, i
5	j, k, l
6	m, n, o
7	p, q, r, s
8	t, u, v
9	w, x, y, z

To form a word, you must press the corresponding digits that make up the letters of that word. For example, to form the word "is," you would press "4" three times ("i" is the third letter on this key), then press "7" four times. This input method is commonly known as the *multitap* method.

Most mobile phones sold today support the T9 input method. T9 stands for "Text on 9 keys." Here is how T9 works. Look for the letters that you want and press the assigned digit once. Using the same example, to form the word "is," press "4," followed by "7." A phone utilizing the T9 technology has a compressed database of all the commonly used words. In this case, the database returns "is" as a likely word.

There are many cases when a particular key sequence may generate multiple words, such as the sequence "4663." Two possible words are "good" and "home." In this case, you just need to select the word you want from a menu on your phone. If a desired word cannot be found in the database, you can add it in. For more information on T9 input, go to *http://www.t9.com/*.

Even with T9 turned on, it's much easier to use your computer keyboard to type messages. Chapter 6 shows how to use Mac OS X to easily send SMS messages.

CDMA

In the U.S., Code Division Multiple Access (CDMA) is a popular cellular technology that's an alternative to GSM. CDMA uses Spread Spectrum Technology (SST), which allows a unique code to be attached to each conversation and to spread conversations across wide segments of the cellular broadcast spectrum. Each receiver decodes on the same frequency segment as the sender. Because multiple signals can be transmitted over the same spectrum, CDMA allows many more possible conversations when compared to other cellular technologies. Sprint PCS and Verizon Wireless use CDMA.

Connecting via Express Network

The Motorola v120e (Figure 7-10) is a data-capable phone that can connect to a CDMA2000 1xRTT network. Although it doesn't have Bluetooth (at the time of this writing, few Bluetooth-enabled CDMA phones were available), you can connect it to your Mac using a USB cable and get online at speeds faster than those currently available with a GPRS phone.

Figure 7-10. Plugging a Motorola v120e into a Macintosh PowerBook

To use this phone as a modem:

1. Obtain a data cable. Your best bet is to get one that is made by the manufacturer of your phone. We used the Motorola SKN6311B USB Data Cable with the v120e.

2. Download the *VZW_Generic_1X_ON_230400* script from the Modem Scripts section of the *maccellphone* Yahoo! group Files page (*http:// groups.yahoo.com/group/maccellphone/files*) and copy it into */Library/ Modem Scripts*. If you have trouble obtaining this script, you can skip this step and use the Sprint PCS Vision modem configuration, described later.

3. Make sure the System Preferences application is closed. Plug the phone into your Macintosh and be sure that both the phone and the Mac are turned on. You should hear a sound (two beeps) from the phone.

4. Open System Preferences and select Network. The New Port Detected dialog will appear, as shown in Figure 7-11. Click OK.

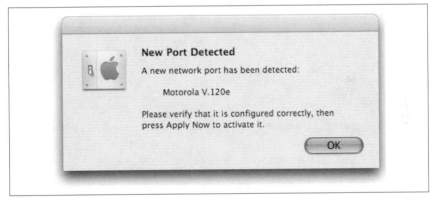

Figure 7-11. Mac OS X detecting the newly-connected cell phone

5. From the Show menu, select Motorola V.120e. Click the PPP tab and enter your information. Your Account Name should be your phone number followed by @vzw3g.com, your password should be vzw, and the phone number should be #777, as shown in Figure 7-12.

6. Select the Modem tab, and set your Modem to *1_VZW_Generic_1X_ ON_230400*, as shown in Figure 7-13. (If you can't locate that script, or if it gives you trouble, you can use the Sprint PCS Vision Modem configuration, which is included with Mac OS X.) Click Apply Now to apply the configuration.

7. Return to the PPP tab and click Dial Now. The Internet Connect window will appear, as shown in Figure 7-14. Click Connect to dial.

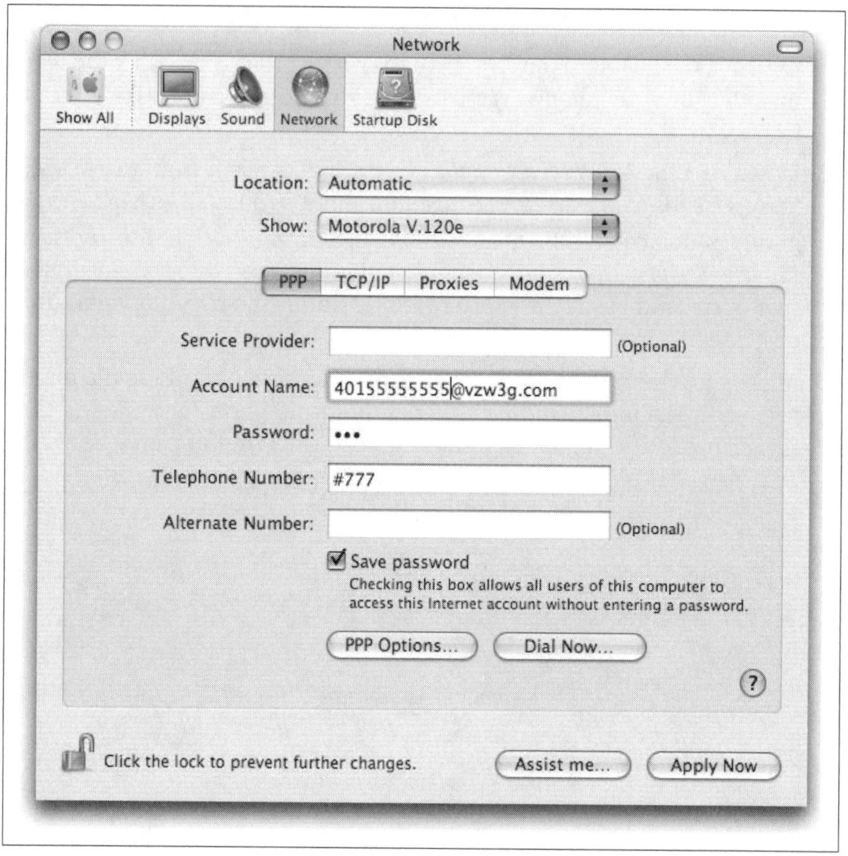

Figure 7-12. Setting up an Express Network connection

The steps will be similar for other phones, as well as for Sprint's PCS Vision network, which also uses CDMA2000 1xRTT. Contact your cellular provider for such details as username, password, and the phone number to dial.

Acceleration

Although GPRS and CDMA can reach speeds close to or faster than a regular dial-up Internet connection, they can't compete with a good solid Wi-Fi connection. But they can get slightly closer by putting a little intelligence between your notebook and the Internet. Cellular providers accomplish this in two ways: *client-server compressing proxies* require you to run a small client program on your desktop to communicate with a server responsible for compressing content you load from the Internet; *transparent accelerators* silently intercept and modify web content so that it loads faster on your computer.

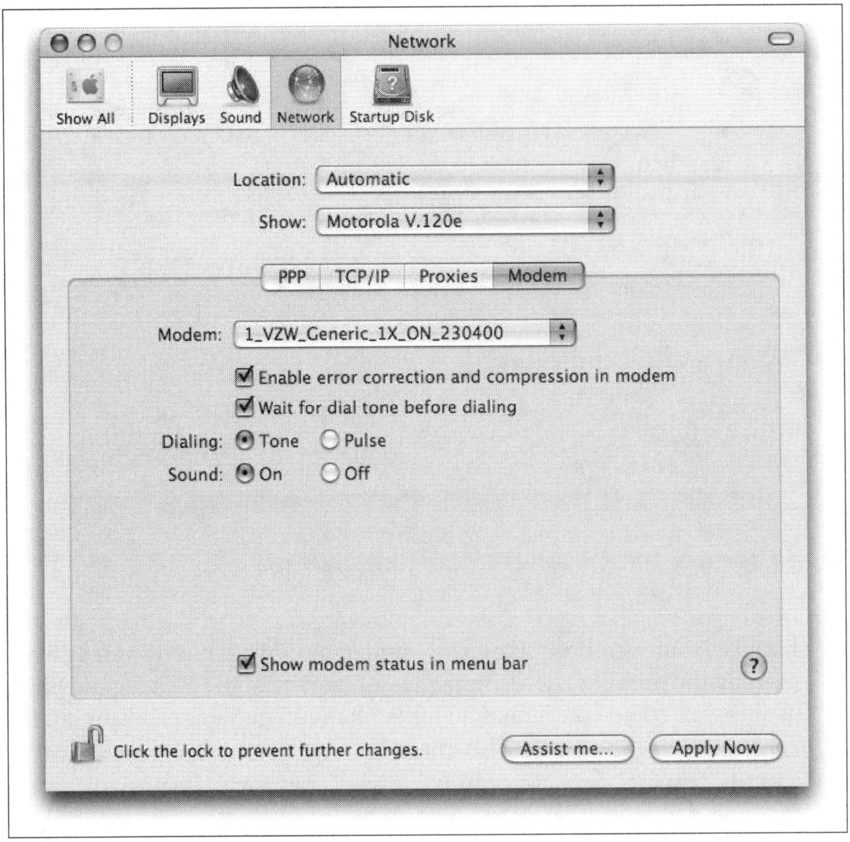

Figure 7-13. Selecting the modem type for the Express Network connection

Your mileage may vary using either type of acceleration: sometimes it speeds things up, but you can also end up waiting so long for the accelerator to do its processing that it's better to not use it. You should try acceleration and see how it works; your cellular provider should be able to tell you how to turn this feature on or off.

Client-Server Compressing Proxies

Verizon Wireless and AT&T Wireless support this kind of accelerator. The process involves two pieces of middleware that sit between your web browser and the Internet, a client and a server.

The compressing proxy server

This is a proxy server that sits in your cellular carrier's "cloud" (some-where on their network). When a request comes for an HTML file, graphic, or text file, this proxy server downloads the content, com-presses it, and sends it back to whoever requested it (you).

Figure 7-14. Using Internet Connect to dial the Express Network

The client

> Because your web browser doesn't understand the compression scheme used by the proxy server up in the cloud, you need to run a second piece of software on your computer. This is often referred to as a client, and is generally invisible to you. This client is actually a mini proxy server that accepts requests from your web browser, forwards them to the compressing server in the cloud, and decompresses the responses before sending them back to your browser.

At the time of this writing, no Mac OS X client is available for either of these compressing proxy servers. However, if you are an AT&T Wireless or Verizon Wireless customer, be sure to contact them and ask, in case this has changed (or at least to let them know the demand exists!).

Transparent Accelerators

Sprint and T-Mobile have transparent acceleration on their network. Unlike the previously described solutions, this is completely clientless; it transparently intercepts and compresses network traffic so that the images and documents received by your web browser are as small as possible. To do this, it reduces the quality of images and compresses HTML files before sending them on to your browser.

Figures 7-15 and 7-16 show detail from an image that was compressed on T-Mobile's network using no compression and maximum compression. This 799×599 pixel image was originally 96k; after compression, it is only 48k.

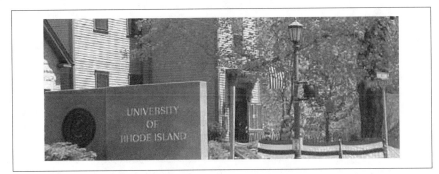

Figure 7-15. Photograph with no compression

Figure 7-16. Photograph with maximum compression

In Figure 7-16, some artifacts are visible; even though the file size is roughly 50 percent of the uncompressed version, it is hard to tell the difference between the two. Figure 7-17 shows the T-Mobile Internet Accelerator configuration page (*http://getmorespeed.t-mobile.com*).

Tips for Road Warriors

Use a Wi-Fi network whenever one is around. When you are in transit, such as on a train, you can manually switch to GPRS access. The downside is that GPRS access is slower and much more costly than Wi-Fi access. The theoretical speed of 40.2 Kbps is not achievable in the real world—expect performance of closer to 30 Kbps for activities such as web browsing.

Since GPRS is much slower and costs more, turn off image loading in your web browser when surfing the Web. This causes the web pages to load faster and saves you money.

If your cellular provider supports a compressing proxy (See "Acceleration," previously in this chapter), give it a try. Such a proxy server can increase speed and reduce your bandwidth consumption.

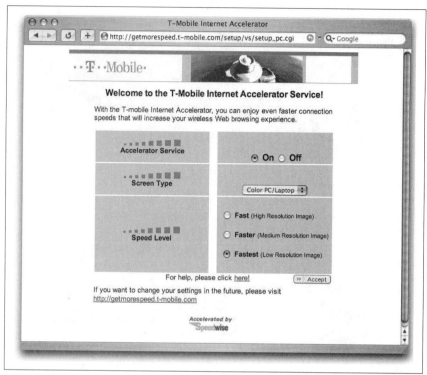

Figure 7-17. Configuring the T-Mobile Internet Accelerator

GPRS speed is acceptable for checking email, but it is advisable to configure your email client to download message headers only: if someone sends you a multi-megabyte attachment or even a long message, it could take a long time to download and use up your bandwidth allotment. Use an IMAP mail server and client if possible, as IMAP is particularly well-suited for high-latency networks. You can then decide on a message-by-message basis whether you want to view the message body and/or download attachments. You should also install a spam filter in your email application to avoid downloading huge junk emails. Many email clients include some spam-blocking features, and typically analyze the email headers (rather than the body of the message) to determine whether a message is spam.

Lastly, make full use of the SMS feature. Sending SMS messages may be cheaper than making a voice call. You can type them with the keyboard on your notebook and they will be delivered quickly. SMS is also more discreet than talking on the phone!

CHAPTER EIGHT

Rendezvous

Ever wished that your computers and devices were all truly plug-and-play? After all, computers were designed to make your life easier, so why should you waste your time configuring your computers and devices so that they can communicate with each other on the network? In an ideal world, the computers and devices on your network should all be able to talk to each other without any intervention on your part from the moment you connect them.

In Mac OS X, Apple has built in a revolutionary technology called Rendezvous, which is designed to make your computers and devices truly plug-and-play. Using Rendezvous, you can create an instant network, thereby allowing communication with other devices on the network without having to hire your own system administrator or go through a complicated setup.

What Is Rendezvous?

The first step towards understanding how Rendezvous works is to realize that every device (such as your Mac, or a printer) participating in a network (be it a wired or wireless one) must have an IP address. This IP address can be allocated from a DHCP server, or it can simply be self-assigned. When a device participates in a network without an IP address (due to absence of DHCP or because it has no self-assigned IP address), Rendezvous will automatically assign an IP address using *link-local addressing* (self-assigned IP addresses in the 169.254.0.0 subnet). Basically, it randomly chooses an IP address from a predetermined range of addresses (set aside for local-link addressing by the Internet Assigned Numbers Authority, or IANA) and assigns it to the device.

The device then broadcasts a message to all the other devices on the network to see if its IP address is already in use. If it is, Rendezvous reassigns the IP address and repeats the same procedure. If not, the IP address is assigned and the device is ready to communicate with the other devices on the network.

Rendezvous and Zeroconf

Rendezvous is Apple's name for their implementation of Zeroconf, a technology managed by a working group of the same name in the Internet Engineering Task Force (IETF). The charter of Zeroconf is to enable "zero configuration for IP networking." Put simply, with Zeroconf technology, if you put two notebooks together (either through wired or wireless networking), they should be able to start communicating with each other without manual configuration of IP addresses. This greatly simplifies the process of ad-hoc network communications.

A device running Rendezvous "advertises" its service by sending Multicast DNS-Service Discovery (mDNS-SD) notifications. These notifications include the following information:

- Type of service
- Name of service
- IP and port numbers

Besides advertising its own service, a device joining a network also needs to know what other services are available. To do that, it sends a query to all devices on the network asking them to enumerate their services. The impact on network performance is negligible: when a device needs to make use of a particular service, such as a file service, it sends out a query asking for devices that support that service. Unlike AppleTalk and NetBEUI (a Windows networking protocol), Rendezvous does not constantly broadcast messages to discover other devices; it does so only when required.

Rendezvous will work only on your local (home or office) subnetwork; it can't cross routers to work over more than one subnetwork.

Rendezvous Applications

A number of Mac OS X applications make use of Rendezvous. They include:

iChat AV

iChat AV is an instant messaging application that supports audio and video conferencing. iChat uses Rendezvous to discover other iChat users on the network.

File sharing

In Mac OS X, you can share files easily using the Go → Connect to Server option in the Finder. The Personal File Sharing feature uses Rendezvous to tell other users on the network that shared files are available.

Safari

The popular Safari web browser uses Rendezvous to detect web addresses of devices on the network. This allows you to easily configure devices that support web interfaces for configuration and to share web documents in ad-hoc networks.

iTunes

iTunes uses Rendezvous to inform other users on the network that you have music collections available for sharing. Using iTunes and Rendezvous, users can now view and play music collections from other computers.

Besides the bundled Mac OS X applications, some third-party applications use Rendezvous technology. Some of these products are:

Camino (http://www.mozilla.org/projects/camino/)

Like Safari, Camino uses Rendezvous to detect devices with web addresses.

SubEthaEdit (http://www.codingmonkeys.de/subethaedit/)

SubEthaEdit (formerly known as Hydra) is a collaborative text editor that allows multiple users to simultaneously edit a document.

Some other types of products that use Rendezvous technology are:

Printers

New printers are incorporating Rendezvous technology so that they are truly plug-and-play when first connected to a network. Brother's HL-5070N was the one of the first printers to support Rendezvous.

Webcams

EvoCam is a webcam application with a built-in web server that can be discovered from any Rendezvous-capable browser such as Safari, thus enabling users to easily view its content.

Home theater components

The SLIMP3 (http://www.slimp3.com), from Slim Devices, is a networked MP3 music player that accepts an Ethernet connection, and has stereo outputs for your home theater system. It has a web-based interface and uses Rendezvous for discovery on the network. The SLIMP3 reads your iTunes music library and playlists, too. We own two of them.

Games

Games such as the NASCAR Racing 2002 Season use Rendezvous to make it easy for players to find and join games on the network.

Setting Up Peer-to-Peer Networking

If you don't have a network available, you can set up a wireless peer-to-peer network to allow multiple computers to share services via Rendezvous. Use this method when you need to wirelessly collaborate but there is no available network to which you can connect.

Here is how you do it:

1. First, ensure that the AirPort in your Mac is configured to "create networks." You can verify this in the Network (AirPort section) section in System Preferences.

2. Create a peer-to-peer network by clicking on the AirPort menu at the top of the screen and selecting Create Network...

3. Give your new network a name and click OK (see Figure 8-1).

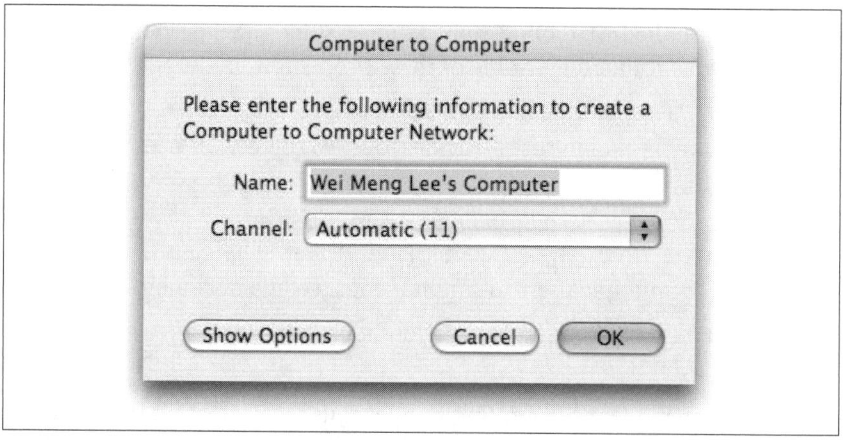

Computer to Computer	
Please enter the following information to create a Computer to Computer Network:	
Name:	Wei Meng Lee's Computer
Channel:	Automatic (11)
Show Options	Cancel OK

Figure 8-1. Creating a peer-to-peer network

4. Note that your AirPort icon has changed, as shown in Figure 8-2 (left).

Figure 8-2. The icon of the AirPort in peer-to-peer (left) and infrastructure mode (right)

5. Other Mac users within range can see your network name by selecting the AirPort menu item (see Figure 8-3).

You don't need to use peer-to-peer networking in order to use Rendezvous messaging; it will still work when you are connected to a wireless network such as an AirPort Extreme base station. However, these instructions may come in handy if you find yourself in situations where you want to work with other users, but don't have an access point nearby.

Figure 8-3. Selecting the peer-to-peer network

Using Rendezvous with iChat AV

Imagine you're in the midst of a session at a conference and want to find someone to chat with in the room (but you don't know them yet). Using iChat AV and Rendezvous, you can instantly locate each other and start chatting immediately.

Invoking iChat AV

Once peer-to-peer networking is established, invoke iChat AV. Make sure that Rendezvous messaging is enabled in the iChat Accounts screen (see Figure 8-4).

You should now be able to see your newfound friends in Rendezvous!

Using Rendezvous with Safari

Another Mac OS X application that makes good use of Rendezvous (but not obviously so, since it is not shown by default) is Safari. Safari uses Rendezvous to browse Rendezvous-enabled web sites and hardware devices on a local network. This feature can be great fun at conferences: check out any web sites that appear in Safari's Rendezvous menu, since a fellow attendee may have set up a personalized site running on her Mac. Also, devices that support Rendezvous may support web interfaces for configuration, which makes it easy for you to configure them.

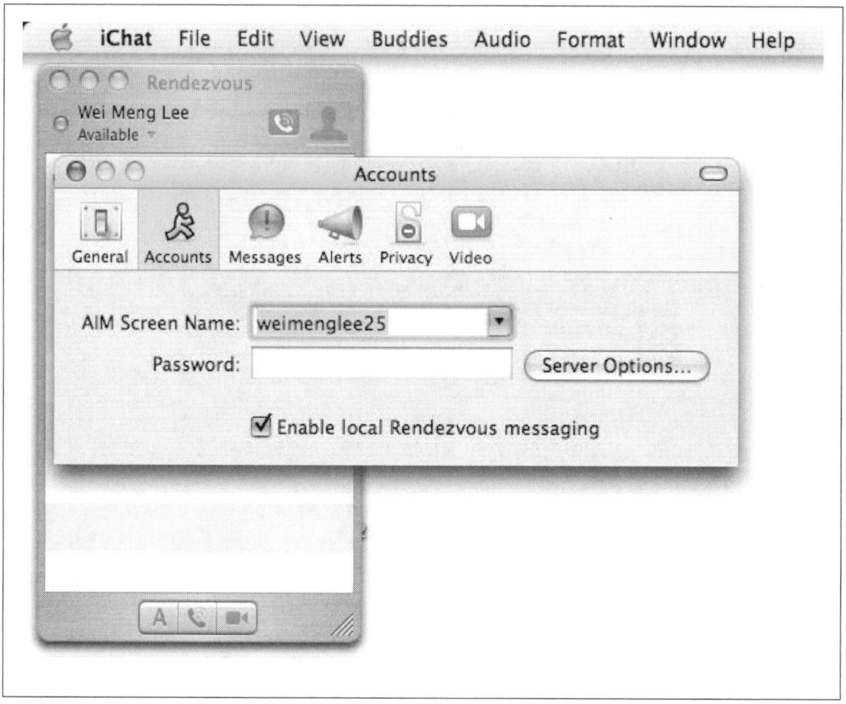

Figure 8-4. Enabling Rendezvous messaging

1. To show Rendezvous in the Bookmarks bar in Safari, launch Safari and choose Safari → Preferences.

2. Select the Bookmarks tab and check the Include Rendezvous checkbox in the Bookmarks bar (see Figure 8-5).

3. When you click on the Rendezvous menu item at the Bookmarks bar, you should see the web addresses of other devices in the network that support Rendezvous. In Figure 8-6, you can see the web addresses of three other users.

As of Mac OS X 10.3 Panther, Personal Web Sharing does not automatically advertise the web site in your home directory, nor does it advertise your computer's main home page (contained in */Library/WebServer/Documents*). Personal Web Sharing will advertise your web site only if you have modified the default *index.html* file contained in the *Sites* subdirectory of your home directory. You will need to restart Personal Web Sharing (System Preferences → Sharing) after you modify your web page for the first time, in order for Mac OS X to notice it has changed.

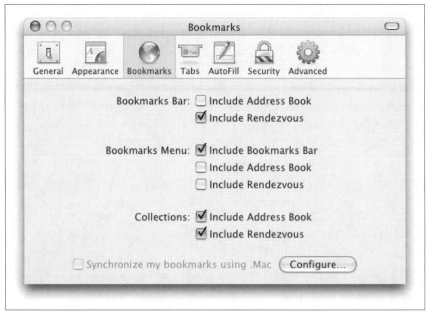

Figure 8-5. Displaying Rendezvous in Safari's Bookmarks bar

Figure 8-6. Viewing a web address using Rendezvous in Safari

Using Rendezvous with Camino

Camino is an alternative web browser for Mac OS X. At the time of writing, Camino is still in the beta development stage. You can download a copy of Camino at *http://www.mozilla.org/projects/camino/*.

Like Safari, Camino uses Rendezvous to display all the web addresses of nearby computers and FTP servers. Support for Rendezvous in Camino is turned off by default (at least in Version 0.7, which is what we're using), so you need to do some work to turn it on.

Here is how to enable Rendezvous in Camino:

1. When you install Camino, the following folders will be created under your home directory: *Library/Application Support/Chimera/Profiles/default/71p3qxph.slt* (see Figure 8-7). The folder *71p3xph.slt* is arbitrary; you are likely to have a different name on your machine.

Figure 8-7. Creating a user.js file in the Profiles folder

2. In the *71p3qxph.slt* folder (or whatever it is named on your machine), create a plain text file and name it *user.js* containing the following line:

```
user_pref("chimera.enable_rendezvous", true);
```

 If you use TextEdit to create the *user.js* file, select Format → Make Plain Text before saving to keep TextEdit from saving it as rich text. If TextEdit asks whether you want to append the extension ".txt," click the Don't Append button.

3. Restart Camino. A Local Network Services item should appear under the Go menu (see Figure 8-8). In this example, the browser detected web addresses (*http*) from three other users and an FTP server (*eMac*).

Figure 8-8. Viewing web and FTP addresses using Rendezvous in Camino

Sharing Files Using Rendezvous

Modern Macs do not come with a floppy drive for easy file exchange. This is because Apple believes that you should be able to exchange files using the network, and because many files these days are too big for floppies, anyway. Sharing files in Mac OS X is a breeze, as Rendezvous automatically detects which computers are on the network.

Sharing Files

To enable file sharing, go to System Preferences and select the Sharing icon. Under the Services button, check the Personal File Sharing checkbox to turn on file sharing (see Figure 8-9).

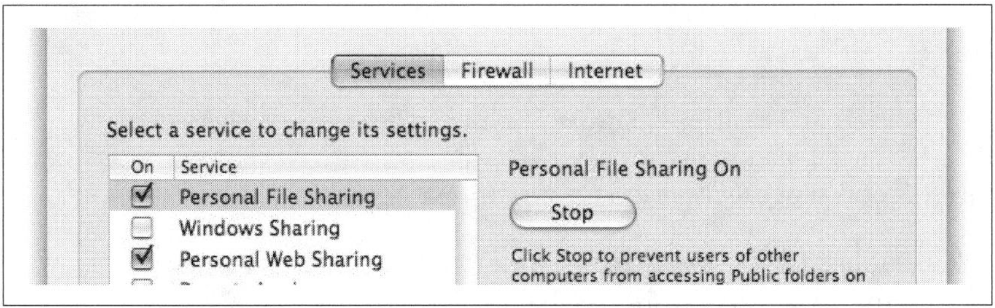

Figure 8-9. Enabling Personal File Sharing

Connecting to a File Server

To use the files shared by another user:

1. Go to the Finder, click on the Go menu, and select Connect to Server...

2. The Connect to Server window will appear (see Figure 8-10). Click the Browse button.

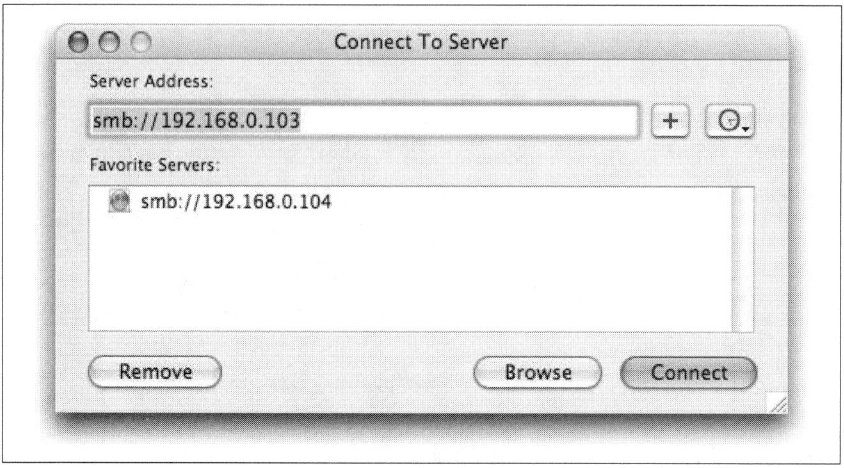

![Connect To Server dialog showing Server Address smb://192.168.0.103, Favorite Servers smb://192.168.0.104, with Remove, Browse, and Connect buttons](connect-to-server)

Figure 8-10. Browsing for computers on the network

3. The Network window will appear to display the computers on the network. In Figure 8-11, *eMac* is a remote machine on the network.

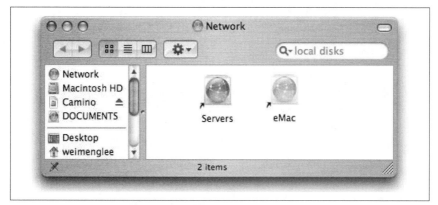

Figure 8-11. Viewing the computers on the network

4. Double-click on the machine you want to connect to, then enter your username and password (see Figure 8-12).

Figure 8-12. Connecting to the remote computer as a registered user

Remote Login

You can also use Rendezvous to connect to SSH, FTP, and Telnet servers that are Rendezvous-enabled. To browse a list of servers on your local network, open the Terminal application (located in */Applications/Utilities*), and select File → Connect to Server. The Connect to Server dialog appears, as shown in Figure 8-13. Select the server you want to connect to, set the username (or leave blank to use the account name you logged into your Mac under), choose the proper SSH protocol (if connecting to a Secure Shell or Secure File Transfer server), and click Connect. A new Terminal window will appear, and you'll be prompted for your password (see Figure 8-14).

Collaborative Editing with SubEthaEdit

One of the challenges in working in a group is maintaining version control on shared documents. SubEthaEdit (created by a group of three computer science students known as "The Coding Monkeys") redefined the meaning of collaborative working. Using SubEthaEdit, multiple users can edit a single document at the same time. SubEthaEdit uses Rendezvous to discover other users who can join in and collaborate.

You can download SubEthaEdit from *http://www.codingmonkeys.de/ subethaedit/*.

Figure 8-13. Selecting a remote server

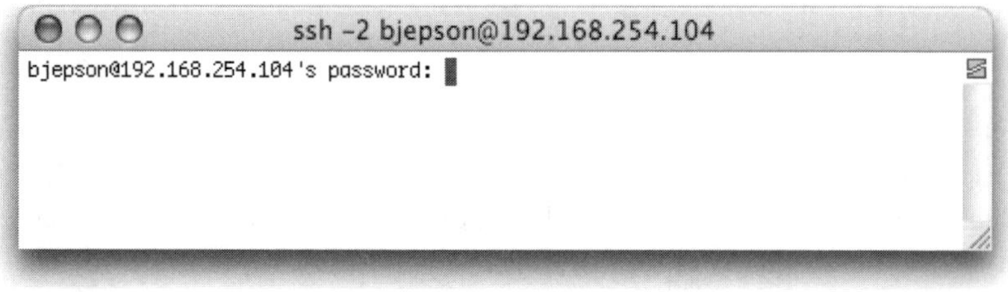

Figure 8-14. Logging into a remote server

1. Launch SubEthaEdit.

2. You can start editing or writing your document in the text editing area Click on the Share button (see Figure 8-15) to share your document with other Rendezvous users.

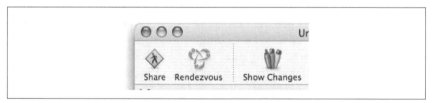

Figure 8-15. Sharing a document

3. SubEthaEdit will reveal the access control list, showing the people who are currently editing the document (see Figure 8-16).

Figure 8-16. Viewing the access control list

4. Other users who want to join in need to run SubEthaEdit as well. To see a list of shared documents, click on the Rendezvous button (see Figure 8-17). Here, you can see that Wei Meng Lee is editing a document entitled *Untitled.txt*.

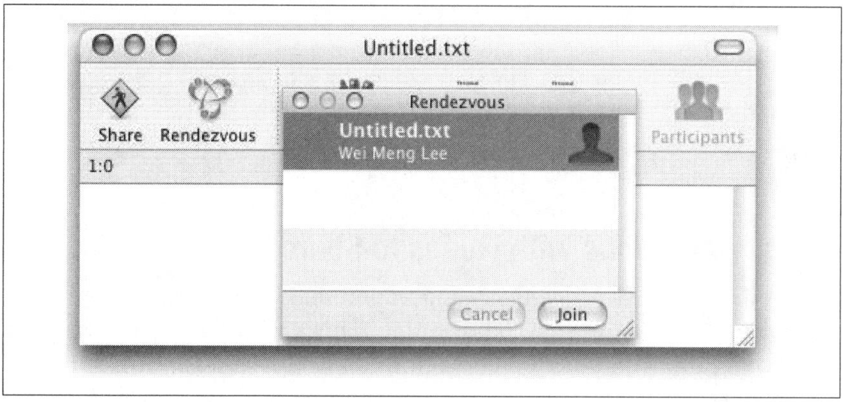

Figure 8-17. Viewing the list of users via Rendezvous

5. Double-click on the document that you want to edit, and your name will appear in the access control list of the document master (see Figure 8-18). The document owner can then simply select your username and click on the check (to allow access) or cross icon (to deny access).

6. By default, text that every user types is highlighted with a pink background. To choose your own color, go to SubEthaEdit → Preferences. You can now distinguish who typed what using the different background colors (see Figure 8-19).

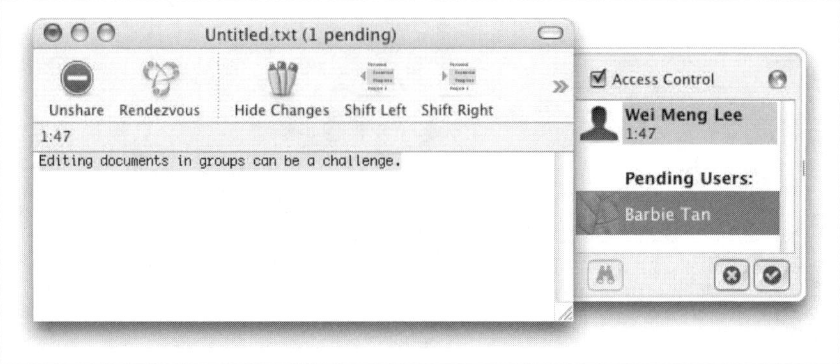

Figure 8-18. Granting (or denying) permissions to a user using the access control list

Figure 8-19. Multiple users editing a document

Using Rendezvous with iTunes to Share Music

Besides iChat, another Mac OS X application that incorporates Rendezvous technology is iTunes. Using Rendezvous, iTunes allows you to share your music collection with other Macs that are on the network. Here's how:

1. Launch iTunes, then choose iTunes → Preferences.

2. Click the Sharing icon in the Preferences window and check the "Share my music" checkbox (see Figure 8-20). You can either share the entire library or selectively choose the playlists to share.

3. You can optionally specify a password so that users who want to view your music collections must enter a password. Click OK.

4. iTunes will display a message, reminding you that sharing is for personal use only (see Figure 8-21).

5. Other Macs on the network will now be able to see the music collection that you've shared (see Figure 8-22).

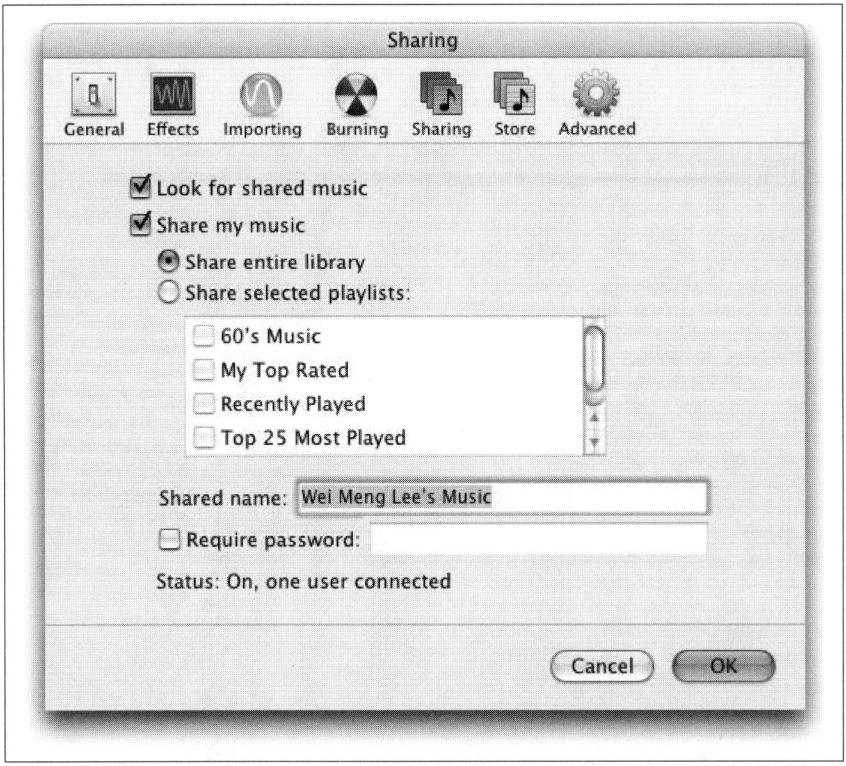

Figure 8-20. Sharing music collections in iTunes

Figure 8-21. Apple's reminder that sharing is for personal use

Figure 8-22. Viewing the shared music collection

RF and Infrared

Radio frequency (RF) and infrared (IR) are two of the older ways that Apple computers have been able to wirelessly communicate with each other and with peripherals. At this point, they're both on their way out, which is why they only rate an appendix in this book. But, because some of of what this book covers is not-quite-here-yet technology, IR and RF may still have a place on your Mac.

Radio Frequency (RF)

Until very recently, if you wanted a wireless keyboard, mouse, or trackball, you needed to use RF technology. Bluetooth devices have just started shipping, so the majority of wireless peripherals around for the near future are likely to be RF.

RF devices have one big plus to go along with their multiple negatives. The big plus is that they don't (unlike IR) require line-of-sight. The bad news:

- Each RF device requires its own receiver, unless you purchase devices (such as Logitech's keyboards and mice) that are particularly engineered to work together.

- RF devices don't play well together, so it's recommended that you have only one attached at a time. Receivers and peripherals from different manufacturers may not—and probably will not—work together.

- Manufacturers of RF devices recommend that their devices (with a few exceptions) be placed within three feet of their receivers. The receivers themselves need to be at least a foot away from your computer and monitor, and far from AM/FM radios (the further the better).

- RF devices often require proprietary drivers, so they aren't just the standard Mac plug-and-play.

- Unlike their wired counterparts, RF peripherals need batteries. The receivers are USB powered, but the keyboards and mice are not. Consequently, keep an eye out for the ones with rechargeable batteries—they may cost more to purchase, but not having to frequently replace batteries will pay for itself over time. However, check to make sure that you can replace the rechargeable batteries cheaply, since they will not last forever.

Keyboards and Mice

Unlike the limited number of manufacturers of Bluetooth input devices, most of the usual third-party Mac hardware companies make keyboards, mice, and trackballs that work wirelessly via RF. Companies such as Logitech, MacAlly, and Kensington all make wireless variants of their wired devices, generally for just a few dollars more. Figure A-1 shows the Logitech Cordless MX Duo, which allows you to unwire both your keyboard and mouse with a single receiver.

Figure A-1. The Logitech Cordless MX Duo includes a cordless keyboard, a cordless rechargeable mouse, and a USB receiver

Installation of these peripherals varies from maker to maker, but for the most part they consist of three steps: plug in the receiver to one of your Mac's USB ports (or to a port on an external USB hub), install the accompanying software, and verify that the device can communicate with the receiver. Some manufacturers include multiple channels on their devices so that you can change them if you run into interference: if that's the case, make sure both the device and the receiver are on the same channel.

To get the best results, carefully read any accompanying documentation that may ship with your devices. Common recommendations include not using mice on glass or metal surfaces: use wood or plastic instead.

Other Peripherals

Keyspan ships their Keyspan Presentation Remote (shown in Figure A-2), which (unlike their Digital Media Remote, mentioned below) works with a small RF receiver to allow you to control your Mac. The KPR is a handy device if you frequently make presentations, and it even includes a laser pointer.

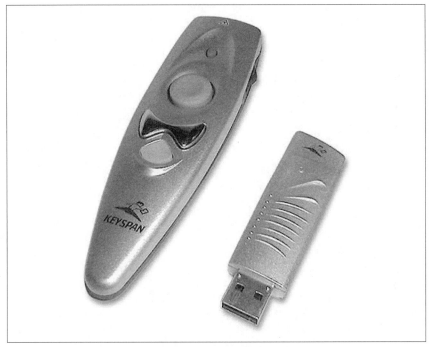

Figure A-2. The Keyspan Presentation Remote and receiver

We've had mostly good results with the KPR, but have a one major recommendation if you want to use it: make a small copy of the instructions and put them inside the carrying case. In order to keep the device from getting turned on accidentally and using up the battery, Keyspan made the on/off instructions so convoluted that you'll forget how to turn the remote on if you don't use it regularly. And, speaking from experience, it's unpleasant to be setting up for a presentation session and find that you can't recall how to work your remote.

Infrared (IR)

IR is another technology that's seen better days, but once again, its replacements are still struggling to standardize. Consequently, you may find it worth your time and effort to make IR work on your Mac.

As mentioned in Chapter 1, IR is also referred to as IrDA, short for Infrared Data Association. IrDA is the name for both the body that creates IR standards as well as the protocol they've created.

IR is quite possibly the most popular form of wireless technology on earth, simply because it's used in so many places other than computers: it's the technology that's used by most remote controls, so it's included in almost everything in your home theater setup. A short time ago, we replaced an air conditioner in our office, and the new unit came with an IR remote control. And, as you already know from having to point your remote at your TV set in order to change the station, IrDA involves short-range line-of-sight connections between two devices.

However, Apple's made it pretty darn clear that IR is the past, and Bluetooth is the future. If you're considering buying a phone or Palm device with IR support, we strongly recommend that you consider one with Bluetooth instead (or in addition). IR in Mac OS X has considerably fewer capabilities than it did under OS 9 (such as file transfers), and it's not likely that Apple will offer much in the way of future support. After all, they haven't introduced an IrDA-equipped Mac in almost two years.

If you have a Mac that was introduced after January 2002, you don't currently have IrDA. If you have an older Mac, the "Apple and IR: a Brief History" sidebar and Table A-1 will tell you if your Mac currently has an IR port. You can also tell by looking for an IR port; Figure A-3 shows its location on a PowerBook G4.

Table A-1. Which Macs support IRTalk and which support IrDA

Macintosh model	IRTalk	IrDA
PB 190	Yes	No
PB 5300	Yes	No
PB 1400	Yes	No
PB 3400	Yes	Yes
PB 2400	Yes	Yes
PB G3 (early)	Yes	Yes
PB G3 (later)	No	Yes
PB G4 (through Gigabit Ethernet)	No	Yes
iMac (Rev. A and B only)	No	Yes

Figure A-3. The IR port (circled) on a PowerBook G4 (Gigabit Ethernet)

Apple and IR: A Brief History

Apple has shipped a variety of Macs with number of different infrared receivers, starting with the Mac TV in 1993. Unfortunately, this machine (along with a few others) only used IR for input, so the included remote control could send commands to the Mac's internal TV tuner.

Starting with the PowerBook 190, Apple started to include IR on its laptops as an early way to share files if you didn't happen to have network cables on hand. These machines (which also included the PowerBook 5300 and Power-Book 1400) were not IrDA-compliant—instead, they used an Apple-proprietary technology called IRTalk, which was used to transport AppleTalk via IR. These were the first Macs with bi-directional IR, although IRTalk has data throughput speed of only 230 Kbps. In effect, IRTalk was a wireless replacement for an AppleTalk or serial cable between machines.

In 1997, with the PowerBook 3400, Apple made the decision to support both IRTalk and IrDA, as the latter can handle AppleTalk and TCP/IP as well as connecting to external devices at up to 4 Mbps. Consequently, the 3400, 2400, and early G3 models are the only laptops that can use IR to communicate with both early and later IR-equipped machines.

In 1998, Apple shipped their only IrDA-compatible desktop machine and their first IR-capable machine to not support IRTalk: the Revision A and B Bondi Blue iMacs. IR on the desktop was discontinued in 1999 with the fruit-colored (revision C) iMacs.

The PowerBook G3 Series (Bronze Keyboard) shipped in 1999, and was the first IR-equipped PowerBook to not support IRTalk. All PowerBooks from this one up until the PowerBook G4 (Gigabit Ethernet) in 2001 came with IrDA-only capability. No iBook has come with IR.

The PowerBook G4 (Gigabit Ethernet) was the last Mac to include IR, and Macintoshes introduced in 2002 and later do not ship with IR. Table A-1 shows which Macs support which protocol.

Don't have IrDA on your Mac? If you find that you need it, don't give up yet—as long as you have USB, you can use MadsonLine's (*http://www. madsonline.com/*) $58 USB-IrDA Adapter (seen in Figure A-4). Just plug it in, and you've got an IR-equipped Mac. In fact, because IR is so picky about line-of-sight and distance issues, it can be easier to use the MadsonLine adapter, because it attaches to your Mac via a USB cable—so you can point it in any direction you want.

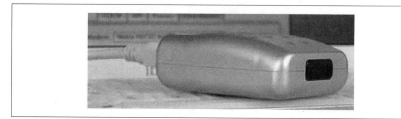

Figure A-4. MadsonLine's USB-IrDA Adapter

 If you're using a PowerBook that's plugged into a BookEndz dock, you have two choices if you want to use IR: use the MadsonLine adapter, or detach your laptop from the dock every time you need to use IR. Photo Control (the makers of the BookEndz dock) claim that "the angled IrDA port allows easy side access to infrared transmission," but we've never been able to get that to work.

Hooking the adapter up is as easy as plugging in a USB cable. Once you do that, go into your Network Control panel, and you'll see a message like the one in Figure A-5.

Configuring IrDA

Whether your Mac came with IR installed, or whether you added it via an adapter, it needs to be set up to use it. Start off by going into the Network Control Panel. To modify the IrDA Modem Port preferences, show the Network Port Configurations Pane and click the "On" button next to "IrDA Modem Port," as shown in Figure A-6.

Figure A-7 shows the IrDA Modem Port Pane and the IrDA Modem tab. IrDA devices can be used as a modem in a similar fashion to the way Bluetooth devices can be used as a modem, as described in Chapter 7.

If you click the "Show IrDA status in menu bar" check box, the current status of the IR port will be displayed. Depending on the current status, different icons are shown, as in Figure A-8.

The first icon is "Discovering" and the second is "Idle." So long as IrDA is on and no IrDA-compatible devices are found within range, your Mac will constantly cycle between these two icons. If IrDA is turned off, the third icon will display. The fourth icon, "Connected," will display when an IrDA

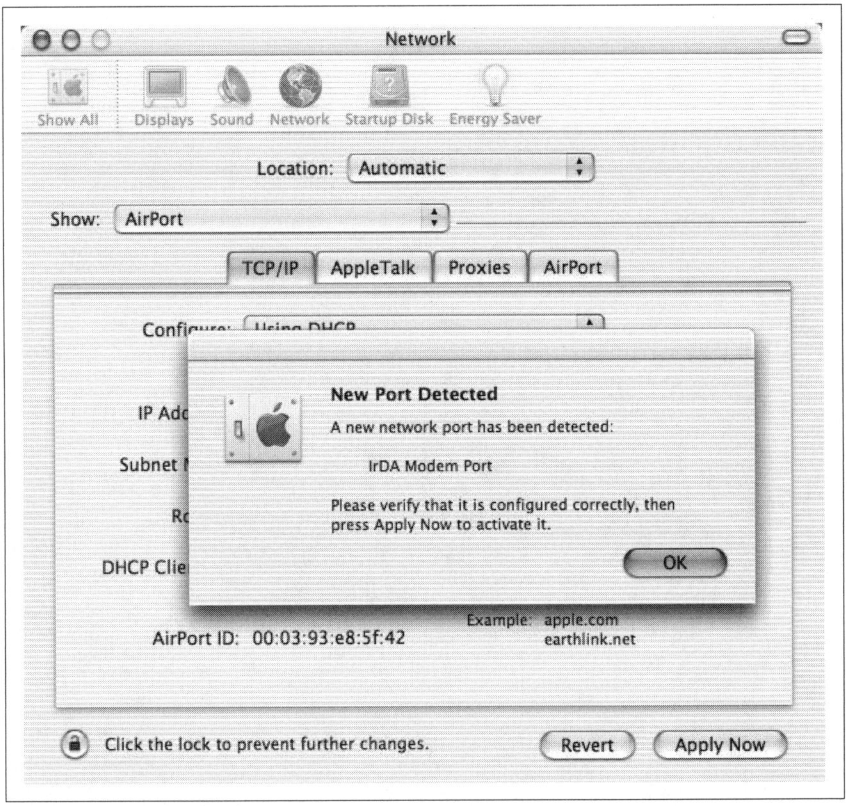

Figure A-5. Mac OS X has recognized a new device; in this case, the IrDA adapter

device is found. The last icon, "Broken Beam," will display if you've been connected, but the connection has been interrupted.

If you take a look at the IrDA pull down menu while you're connected, you'll see a menu like the one in Figure A-9. The first line tells you information about your connection, the second allows you to turn IrDA off, and the third lets you control whether or not you want sounds to be played when a device is found.

IR and Palm Devices

Before Bluetooth was added to Palm devices, there was IR, and Palm still sells many devices that don't have Bluetooth. No, you don't always have to lug around cables and docks—you can use IrDA to sync the two. Syncing your Palm using the IR port on your Mac is almost identical to that of using Bluetooth, as described in Chapter 6. Consequently, we'll only cover the differences here.

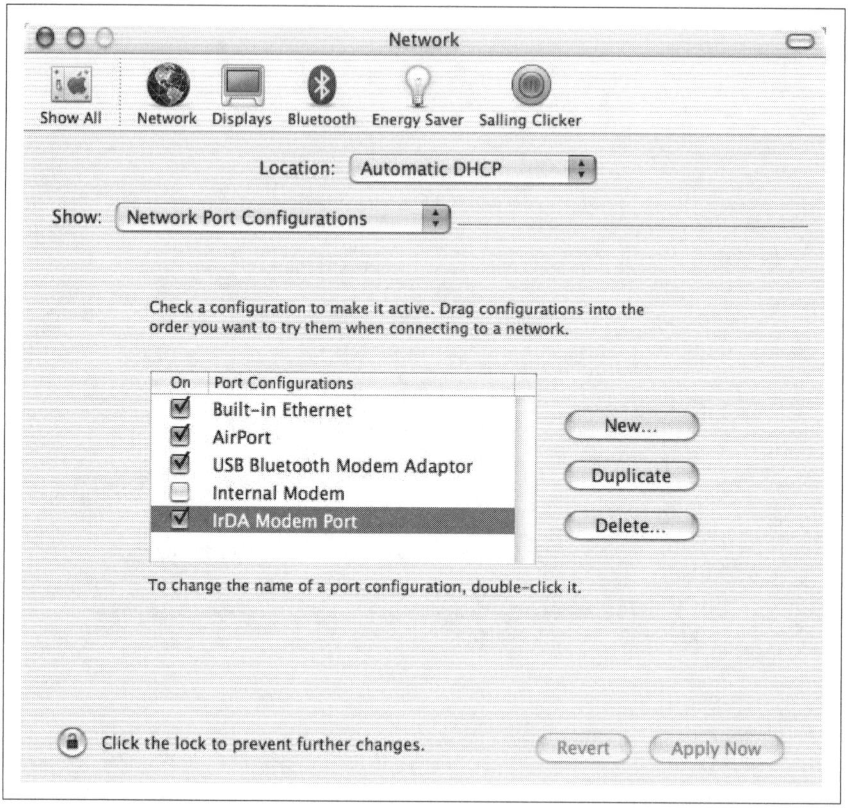

Figure A-6. The IrDA Modem Port needs to be turned on in order to configure it

1. Turn off the IrDA Modem Port off, as shown back in Figure A-6. The IR port can only be used for one purpose at a time.

2. Make sure that the IR port is turned on in HotSync Software Setup → Conduit Settings, as shown in Figure A-10.

3. On the Palm, change the connection type to "IR to a PC/Handheld," and make sure you've chosen a "Local" connection.

4. Make sure that the IR port on the Palm and the IR port on the Mac are facing each other, and are less than three feet away.

5. Tap the HotSync button on the Palm, and syncing should begin.

6. Have patience, as syncing via IR can be very slow.

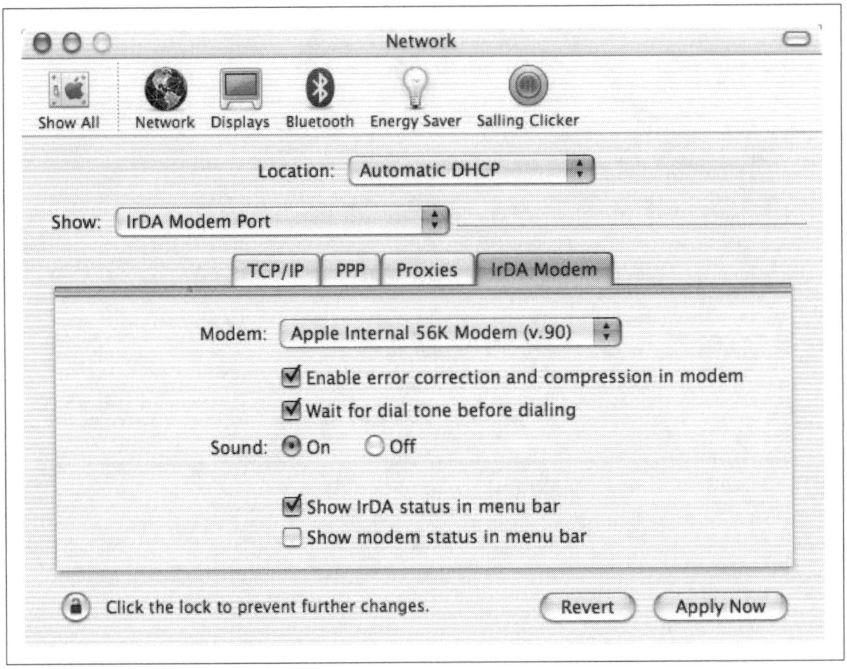

Figure A-7. The IrDA Modem Port pane

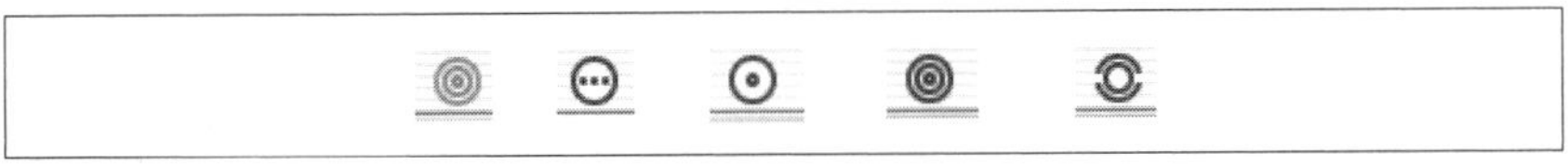

Figure A-8. The five faces of IrDA: discovering, idle, off, connected, and broken beam

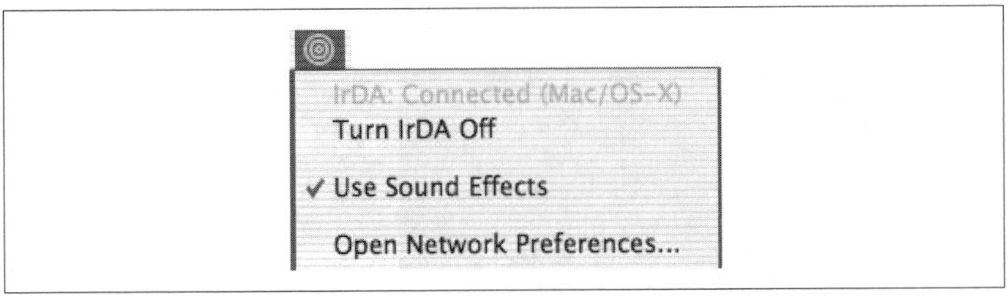

Figure A-9. A successful IrDA connection

Other IR Devices

There are a number of other IR devices of varying usefulness, but overall, they're becoming less common as Mac OS X becomes more popular. The accessories don't make the transition—for instance, when was the last time you used a Newton? IR-enabled printers, for example, are being phased out as Wi-Fi and Bluetooth-capable printers are being introduced.

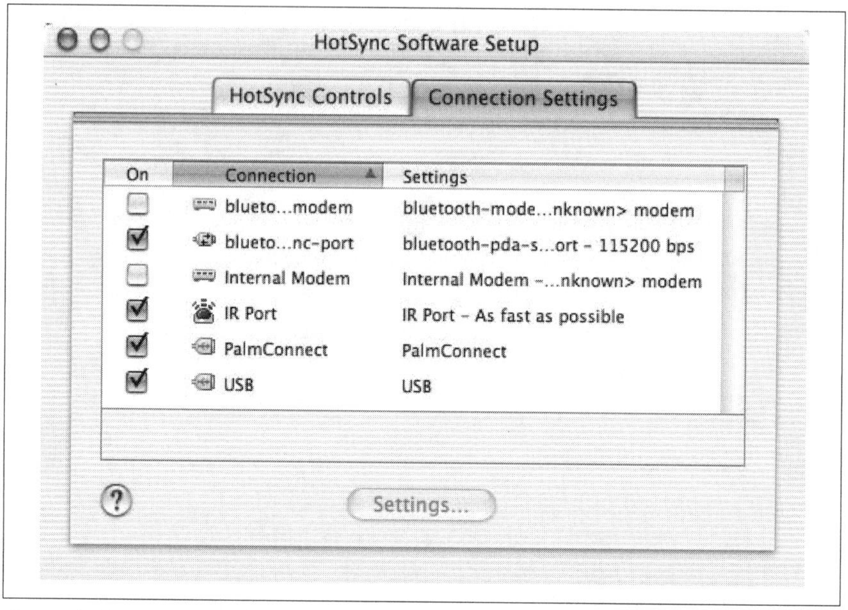

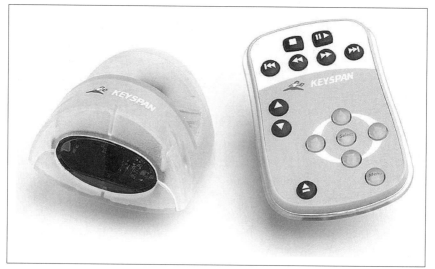

Figure A-10. Turning on the IR port

One handy device we've found, though, is the Keyspan Digital Media Remote, (Figure A-11) particularly if you don't have the capability to run Salling Clicker, which uses Bluetooth.

Figure A-11. The Keyspan Digital Media Remote and receiver

This device comes with its own IR receiver, which works (or so Keyspan claims) up to 35 feet away from the remote. You do have to be in line-of-sight, but from our experience, it's fairly forgiving. It can control everything from PowerPoint to Keynote to iTunes to DVD Player. Installation is simple; just plug it in and install drivers.

The Keyspan Presentation Remote (mentioned earlier) clearly came out after the Keyspan DMR, because the former went overboard in fixing a problem of the latter: it's too easy to press the buttons on the DMR, causing it to run out of battery life just because the remote got wedged tightly in your briefcase. We've found two good solutions:

1. Put a piece of paper or light cardboard in between the battery and the case, so that the remote can't be turned on without it being removed.

2. The remote is just slightly smaller than the size of a typical metal container of mints. Clean the tin out thoroughly, put the remote in the tin, put the tin in your briefcase, and it'll never get wedged again.

Infrared is likely to be the last technology you'll have to deal with that will require both devices to be within line-of-sight of each other. Thankfully, its short distance and location requirements have combined to make it trailing-edge technology.

Glossary

1xRTT
See CDMA2000.

3G
Third generation cellular service; expected to handle voice communication as well as broadband data access and live video. Slowly being rolled out.

802.11a
IEEE networking standard providing 54 Mbps speed in the 5 GHz band. Not supported by Apple.

802.11b
IEEE networking standard providing 11 Mbps speed in the 2.4 GHz band. Apple refers to this as "AirPort." 802.11g, also known as "AirPort Extreme," has superseded it.

802.11g
IEEE networking standard providing 54 Mbps speed in the 2.4 GHz band. Apple refers to this as "AirPort Extreme." Backward compatible with 802.11b.

802.11i
A draft IEEE standard to address security concerns in wireless networks. It uses a combination of 802.1X, TKIP, and AES to secure wireless networks.

802.1X
A port-based authentication mechanism for wired and wireless networks.

Access Point
A hardware device that connects wireless users to a wired local network; also referred to as an AP or base station.

Ad-hoc network
A wireless network consisting of two or more devices communicating with each other without an access point. Also known as computer-to-computer networks.

Advanced Encryption Standard
See AES.

AES
Advanced Encryption Standard is the U.S. government's next-generation cryptography algorithm that will be used in future versions of 802.11i and replace DES and 3DES.

Aggregator
A provider who allows access to hotspots run by multiple providers with a single membership.

AirPort
See 802.11b.

AirPort Extreme

See 802.11g.

AP

See Access Point.

Authenticating server

In a WLAN using 802.1X and EAP, a supplicant requests access to an authenticator, which requests the supplicant's identity, which is then passed to an authenticating server. This server (which may use RADIUS) follows its set algorithm to decide whether to accept or reject the supplicant.

Authenticator

In a WLAN using 802.1X and EAP, a supplicant requests access to an AP, which is known as the authenticator. The AP requests the supplicant's identity, which is then passed to an authenticating server, which then either accepts or rejects the supplicant.

Base station

See Access Point.

Bluetooth

A short-range wireless protocol used for connecting peripherals to a computer and to each other. Typically used in cell phones, keyboards, mice, and PDA's.

Bridge

A device that connects one LAN to another LAN, either of which may be a WLAN.

Captive Portal

A web page that offers you the opportunity to sign in to a secured public Wi-Fi network. At a for-pay Wi-Fi provider, this is where you make your payment arrangements.

CDMA

Code Division Multiple Access, a protocol used by a family of cellular technologies, some of which are 2G and some of which are nearly 3G in performance. Used today in the USA, South America, and Korea. There are CDMA networks being built in various countries.

CDMA2000

A 3G flavor of CDMA; the data side is known as 1xRTT.

CDPD

Cellular Digital Packet Data, a popular 1G cellular telephone specification supporting wireless Internet access via packet switching on an AMPS800 network. Supports up to 19.2 Kbps, but is being phased out in favor of 2.5G and 3G.

Cellular Digital Packet Data

See CDPD.

Centrino

A package from Intel that puts wireless networking and a Pentium processor on a single chip.

Circuit Switched Data

See CSD.

Class A

A network with almost 17 million possible IP addresses.

Class B

A network with almost 66,000 IP possible IP addresses.

Class C

A network with up to 254 possible IP addresses.

Code Division Multiple Access

See CDMA.

Community Network

A WISP, set up by a local community for the benefit of that community.

Computer to computer network

See Ad-hoc network.

CSD

Circuit Switched Data is a service used for data and fax calls on GSM networks, with a rate of 9.6 Kbps to 14.4 Kbps.

DHCP

Dynamic Host Configuration Protocol, a method for automatically assigning unique IP addresses.

Discoverable

Two Bluetooth devices that are within each other's range can be paired when they are both discoverable by the other.

DMZ host

A computer on a wireless network that is purposefully exposed to the Internet.

Dotted quad

The four parts of a numeric IP address, combined together.

Dynamic Host Configuration Protocol

See DHCP.

Dynamic IP addresses

An IP address assigned by an ISP. Costs less than a static IP address, but is subject to change at the ISP's whim.

EAP

Extensible Authentication Protocols, a standard protocol for handling security on a network.

Enhanced Data GSM Environment

See EDGE.

EDGE

Enhanced Data GSM Environment, a faster version of GSM wireless service. Delivers rates up to 384 Kbps using existing frequencies. Requires equipment that can access EDGE and base station upgrades for providers.

Extensible Authentication Protocols

See EAP.

Firewall

A firewall is used to intercept packets coming in from the Internet before they reach computers inside the network.

Firmware

The software run by hardware chips; it can be updated via firmware upgrades.

General Packet Radio Service

See GPRS.

Global System for Mobile

See GSM.

GPRS

General Packet Radio Service, a data service that supplements other data services such as CSD and SMS.

GSM

Global System for Mobile communications, the most widely used of the three digital wireless telephone technologies (the others are TDMA and CDMA).

High speed CSD

See HSCSD.

Host

A computer on a TCP/IP network.

Host number

The last number in a dotted quad, which identifies the particular machine on a network.

Hotspot

Any location that offers wireless Internet access.

HSCSD

A high-speed version of CSD, with a data rate of up to 43.2 Kbps.

Hub

A device that connects multiple computers together, generally via Ethernet.

IEEE

The Institute of Electrical and Electronics Engineers is the organization that creates standards such as the 802.11 family. Pronounced eye-triple-E.

IETF

The Internet Engineering Task Force is a working group that manages standards such as Zeroconf.

Infrared

See IR.

Initialization vector

A component of WEP, used to increase the unpredictability of the encryption scheme.

Internet sharing

The ability of one computer to act as a base station via software, providing wireless network access for other local computers. Formerly referred to as a software base station.

IP

Internet Protocol is how data is sent between computers on the Internet.

IP address

A computer's address on the Internet. A machine name (such as *www. example.com*) is converted into an IP address, which is then used to find that machine.

IPv4

32-bit scheme used to currently identify up to 4.3 billion hosts on the Internet.

IPv6

128-bit scheme that is slowly superseding IPv4.

IR

Infrared, a line-of-sight technology using light (vs. radio waves), once supported on the Mac and most commonly used for television remote controls.

IrDA

This term is used for both the Infrared Data Association and the infrared standard that it created.

Kbps

Kilobits per second, or 1,024 bits per second—a way to measure bandwidth.

ISP

An Internet Service Provider, who provides access to the Internet.

L2TP

Layer 2 Tunneling Protocol, a communication protocol similar to that of PPTP, except that it does not include encryption. Mac OS X Panther supports L2TP over IPSec for encrypted links to remote networks.

LAN

A Local Area Network, also described as a group of computers in one common location connected together. See also WAN.

Layer 2 Tunneling Protocol

See L2TP.

Local Area Network

See LAN.

Link-local addressing

The method by which Rendezvous automatically assigns IP addresses.

MAC Address

A computer's Ethernet hardware address.

MacStumbler

One of several OS X applications that can be run to find any locally available wireless access points.

Main base station

A component of a WDS that is connected to the Internet and shares its Internet connection with remote and relay base stations.

Master

The hub of a Bluetooth piconet.

Mbps

Megabits per second, or 1,048,576 bits per second—a way to measure bandwidth.

mDNS-SD

Multicast DNS-Service Discovery notifications are how Rendezvous devices broadcast what services they offer.

Multicast DNS-Service Discovery

See mDNS-SD.

Multitap

A lengthy and time-consuming way to enter letters into an SMS message. Use T9 instead if it's available.

NAT

Network Address Translation allows a network behind a router to appear to use a single IP address.

Network Address Translation

See NAT.

Network number

The first three parts of a dotted quad, which identify the network a computer is connected to.

NoCatAuth

Linux-based software for handling community networks.

Pairing

The process of telling two Bluetooth-enabled devices that the other is to be remembered and trusted.

PDC

Personal Digital Cellular, an alternative cellular technology used in Japan.

Personal Digital Cellular

See PDC.

Piconet

An ad-hoc Bluetooth network, which can contain up to eight devices.

Point-to-Point Tunneling Protocol

See PPTP.

Port

See TCP/IP port.

PPP Over Ethernet

See PPPOE.

PPPOE

PPP Over Ethernet, an alternative method of connecting a cable or DSL modem that requires extra security information to be passed.

PPTP

A communication protocol designed by Microsoft (and other companies) to create a secure tunnel between two computers. PPTP provides authentication and encryption services, and encapsulates PPP packets within IP packets.

RADIUS

Remote Authentication Dial-In User Service, used by some authenticating servers to identify valid PPP connections, commonly for dial-up users. RADIUS can be used to authenticate many services, including wireless network users.

Relay base station

A component of a WDS that shares the main base station's Internet connection and passes on the connection to other remote or relay base stations.

Remote Authentication Dial-In User Service

See RADIUS.

Remote base station

A component of a WDS that shares the main base station's Internet connection.

Rendezvous

Apple's name for the technology known as Zeroconf, a set of protocols which allow devices on a network (wired or wireless) to self-identify what services they can handle, thereby eliminating setup.

RF

Radio Frequency, a method (on its way out) for connecting devices such as keyboards and mice wirelessly to a computer.

Roaming

The ability to get cellular access while outside of your provider's service area.

Roaming network

A single wireless network consisting of multiple base stations with the same SSID hooked up to an Ethernet network.

Router

A device on a network that handles figuring out where on the network packets should be sent.

scp

A secure way to transfer files, replacing rcp.

Secure Shell

See SSH.

Service Set Identifier

See SSID.

sftp

A secure way to transfer files, replacing FTP.

Short Message Service

See SMS.

SIM card

A smart card placed inside a GSM phone that identifies the user account to the network.

Slave

A device on a Bluetooth piconet, paired to a single master device.

SMS

Short Message Service, a way to send text messages between GSM cell phones.

Software base station

See Internet sharing.

Spread Spectrum Technology

See SST.

SSH

Secure Shell. Lets users initiate a shell session (similar to Telnet) or exchange files with a remote server, with the information exchanges encrypted.

SSID

Service Set Identifier, a name that uniquely defines a wireless local network.

SST

Spread Spectrum Technology, which spreads conversations across wide segments of the cellular broadcast spectrum.

Static IP address

An IP address that is assigned by an ISP, which (in return for a higher payment) is set to not change. See Dynamic IP address.

Subnet Mask

A sequence of bits that specifies the network that an IP address is part of.

Supplicant

In a WLAN using 802.1X, a user (called the supplicant) requests access to the authenticator. The authenticator then requests the supplicant's identity, which is then passed to an authenticating server, which then either accepts or rejects the supplicant.

Switch

A hub with additional features that allow it to do a better job of routing packets.

T9

An input method for writing SMS messages with a cell phone keypad; faster than multitap.

TCP/IP

Transmission Control Protocol/Internet Protocol, the networking standard used by the Internet.

TCP/IP port

A 16-bit number (between 1 and 65535) used by the TCP/IP protocol to address services that run on a computer, such as an FTP server or a Web server.

TDMA

Time Division Multiple Access was the predecessor of GSM. TDMA operates similarly to network packet switching—it divides the signal into multiple segments, thereby allowing multiple calls to take place.

Temporal Key Integrity Protocol

See TKIP.

Time Division Multiple Access

See TDMA.

Timeslot

In a cellular network, a portion of time allocated to transmit data.

TKIP

Temporal Key Integrity Protocol, a short-term solution for solving WEP's problems by using 128-bit dynamic keys that are utilized by different clients. Because of the changing keys, intruders would not have time to collect enough packets to compromise the security scheme.

Tunneling

The transmission of private data securely through a public network.

UMTS

Universal Mobile Telephone Service is a 3G broadband standard. It provides a packet-based standard for cellular telephones which is planned to allow data transmissions of up to 2 Mbps.

Universal Mobile Telephone Service

See UMTS.

Virtual Private Network

See VPN.

VPN

A Virtual Private Network is a method of allowing remote users to securely work as though they are connected to a local network.

WAN

A Wide Area Network is a computer network that is spread out over multiple physical locations. See also LAN.

WAP

Wireless Application Protocol, standards to enable wireless devices to access the Internet.

Warchalking

Symbols (usually written in chalk) on the outside of buildings, denoting the existence of a wireless network.

Wardriving

Driving in a car while searching for wireless networks.

WCDMA

Wideband CDMA is a 3G version of CDMA.

WDS

Wireless Distribution System, a scheme that allows multiple base stations to act as a single wireless network.

WEP

Wired Equivalent Privacy, an early security protocol that had the goal of making wireless networks as secure as wired networks but has since proven insecure.

Wide Area Network

See WAN.

Wideband CDMA

See WCDMA.

Wi-Fi

Short for Wireless Fidelity, Wi-Fi is the shorthand term for wireless technologies such as 802.11b and 802.11g.

Wi-Fi Protected Access

See WPA.

Wireless Application Protocol

See WAP.

Wireless Distribution System

See WDS.

Wireless ISP

See WISP.

Wireless Fidelity

See Wi-Fi.

Wireless LAN

See WLAN.

Wireless Network Name

See SSID.

Wireless router

A device that fulfills both the functions of a router and an Access Point.

Wired Equivalent Privacy

See WEP.

WISP

An ISP that provides wireless access.

WLAN

A Wireless Local Access Network (LAN), a network to which a computer can be wirelessly connected.

WPA

Wi-Fi Protected Access, an interim wireless security protocol designed to improve on WEP, before the 802.11i specification is eventually ratified.

Zeroconf

See Rendezvous.

Index

We'd like to hear your suggestions for improving our indexes. Send email to *index@oreilly.com*.

About the Authors

Tom Negrino is a book author and contributing editor for *Macworld* magazine. He began his writing career in 1985 with *MacGuide* magazine, joining the *Macworld* ranks in 1987. Tom's articles have appeared in several other magazines, and this is his twenty-second book since 1994. With Dori Smith, he is coauthor of the best-selling *JavaScript for the World Wide Web: Visual QuickStart Guide, 5th Edition*. A frequent speaker at Macworld Expo and other computer trade shows, Tom teaches seminars on Mac and Windows software.

Dori Smith is co-author of *JavaScript for the World Wide Web: Visual QuickStart Guide, 5th Edition*, the author of *Java 2 for the World Wide Web: Visual QuickStart Guide*, and a contributor to numerous online and print computer industry magazines. She's a frequent speaker at industry conferences, belongs to the Steering Committee for the Web Standards Project, and serves as the publisher and ListMom for the Wise-Women's Web organization.

Colophon

Our look is the result of reader comments, our own experimentation, and feedback from distribution channels. Distinctive covers complement our distinctive approach to technical topics, breathing personality and life into potentially dry subjects.

The item on the cover of *Mac OS X Unwired* is a dog collar. Collars have been worn by dogs to identify both the pets and their owners since humans domesticated the animals.

The collar pictured on the cover of this book belonged to Morgaine, a black labrador mix who was adopted in 1991 from Angell Memorial Animal Shelter in Boston at the age of 2. When the Taylor-Lovis family first saw her, Morgaine was laying quietly with a stuffed animal in the back of her cage. After they took her outside, however, she came alive with energy. In the many happy years following her adoption, she would always run as if there were no tomorrow when let her off her leash. Indoors, she continued to be a quiet, extremely well-mannered lady. She lived for her meals and a little loving, and died at age 14 of natural causes. She's remembered by her family as "more than a dog...the best friend we could ever ask for."

Philip Dangler was the production editor and copyeditor for *Mac OS X Unwired*. Sada Preisch was the proofreader. Genevieve d'Entremont and Claire Cloutier provided quality control. John Bickelhaupt wrote the index.

Edie Freedman designed the cover of this book. The cover image is an original photograph by Edie Freedman. Emma Colby produced the cover layout with QuarkXPress 4.1 using Adobe's Helvetica Neue and ITC Garamond fonts.

David Futato designed the interior layout. This book was converted by Julie Hawks to FrameMaker 5.5.6 with a format conversion tool created by Erik Ray, Jason McIntosh, Neil Walls, and Mike Sierra that uses Perl and XML technologies. The text font is Linotype Birka; the heading font is Adobe Helvetica Neue Condensed; and the code font is LucasFont's TheSans Mono Condensed. The illustrations that appear in the book were produced by Robert Romano and Jessamyn Read using Macromedia FreeHand 9 and Adobe Photoshop 6. This colophon was written by Philip Dangler and Tracy Taylor.